MEDIA/11

POLITICS OF THE GIFT

Crosscurrents

Exploring the development of European thought through engagements with the arts, humanities, social sciences and sciences

Series Editor
Christopher Watkin, University of Cambridge

Editorial Advisory Board

Andrew Benjamin
Martin Crowley
Simon Critchley
Frederiek Depoortere
Oliver Feltham
Patrick ffrench
Christopher Fynsk
Kevin Hart
Emma Wilson

Titles available in the series

Difficult Atheism: Post-Theological Thinking in Alain Badiou, Jean-Luc Nancy and Quentin Meillassoux by Christopher Watkin

Politics of the Gift: Exchanges in Poststructuralism by Gerald Moore

Visit the Crosscurrents website at www.euppublishing.com/series/cross

POLITICS OF THE GIFT

Exchanges in Poststructuralism

Gerald Moore

EDINBURGH UNIVERSITY PRESS

Edinburgh University Press Ltd
22 George Square, Edinburgh

www.euppublishing.com

Typeset in 10.5/13 pt Sabon
by Servis Filmsetting Ltd, Stockport, Cheshire, and
printed and bound in Great Britain by
CPI Antony Rowe, Chippenham and Eastbourne

A CIP record for this book is available from the British Library

ISBN 978 0 7486 4202 1 (hardback)

Contents

Acknowledgements

Sections from the Introduction, 'Spectres of Mauss', and Chapter 2, 'The Eternal Return of the Gift', were presented initially as papers to the Annual Conference of the Society for French Studies, University of Leeds, July 2005; the Cambridge University, Department of French, Modern French Research Seminar, October 2006; and more recently, in June 2010, at the London School of Economics (LSE). A section from Chapter 2, on Nietzsche and Pierre Klossowski, was presented to the Nietzsche Society of Great Britain and Ireland, Peterhouse College, Cambridge, September 2006. A small amount from the section, 'Wiederkehr des Gleiches', in Chapter 3, appears in *The Oxford Literary Review*, under the title 'Corpus diei' (2007). An earlier draft of Chapter 4 was presented to the Possible Politics Research Seminar, King's College, London, March 2006; other sections were delivered at conferences on Derrida's Legacies (LSE, March 2008), and Politics and Ontology (Queen Mary's, University of London, June 2008). Subsequent drafts have therefore benefited from the comments of audience members, participants and editors.

The genesis of this work lies further back, however, drawing its initial impetus from a highly unconventional course on ethics taught by Miguel de Beistegui, at the University of Warwick in 1999. The abortive undergraduate dissertation to which this gave rise was subsequently and more successfully reprised on multiple occasions, at graduate level and beyond, and its various incarnations have benefited from the critical purview of numerous supervisors, friends and colleagues. In Cambridge, Sarah Kay, briefly, and Ian James and Martin Crowley, repeatedly and with excessive generosity, added a wealth of ideas and encouragement. So too, at various stages, did Shahidha Bari, Ferzina Bernaji, Andrew Counter, Stuart Elden, John Forrester, Patrick ffrench, Kristy Guneratne, Jean Khalfa, Mike Lewis, Dora Osborne and Chris Watkin. The transition from thesis to book was facilitated by Colin Davis, Sophie Fuggle, Simon Glendinning, Marcel Hénaff and, in particular, Christina Howells and Alan Schrift. My editor at Edinburgh, Carol Madonald, has also been invaluable, not least in her efforts to find a decent subtitle.

Needless to say, any mistakes are my own.

The writing of the book was made possible by funding from the Arts and Humanities Research Council, formerly Board, and a number of expenses furnished by Downing College, Cambridge. A debt of recognition is also owed to my former colleagues in the Department of English at the UFR de Science, Université Paris-Est Créteil, and to the fellowship, students and staff of Wadham College, Oxford.

G.M., August 2010, Oxford

Abbreviations

The following lists a key of frequently cited works and, in some cases, texts more commonly identified as part of a complete works. The most readily available published English translations are given first wherever possible, with the original language reference given after the backslash (/). Where translations have been modified, they are marked [TM] in the text. Where only the English version, or more usually only the French or German version, of a text exists, this is denoted by the abbreviation followed by either 'e', 'f', or 'g'. The abridgement of Alexandre Kojève's translated *Introduction to the Reading of Hegel*, for example, will mean that some of the French references have not been translated, hence (IRHf, xx). Where no English reference is given, all translations have been done by the author.

In cases where an additional pagination is given to concord with a work's first edition, this is given in the text in square brackets, next to the page numbers of the complete works; so too, where deemed useful, is the section (§) number.

AŒ   Gilles Deleuze and Félix Guattari, *Anti-Oedipus: Capitalism and Schizophrenia*, trans. Robert Hurley, Mark Seem and Helen R. Lane (London: Continuum, 2004); *L'Anti-Œdipe: Capitalisme et schizophrénie, I* (Paris: Minuit, 1972).

AS   Georges Bataille, *The Accursed Share: An Essay on General Economy, vol.* 1: *Consumption*, trans. Robert Hurley (New York: Zone, 1989); *Œuvres complètes, tome VII: La Part maudite, Théorie de la religion* (Paris: Gallimard, 1976).

BSP   Jean-Luc Nancy, *Being Singular Plural*, trans. Robert D. Richardson and Anne E. O'Byrne (Stanford, CA: Stanford University Press, 2000); *Être singulier pluriel* (Paris: Galilée, 1996).

BT   Martin Heidegger, *Being and Time*, trans. John Macquarie and

Edward Robinson (Oxford: Blackwell, 1962); *Gesamtausgabe, band 2: Sein und Zeit* (Frankfurt am Main: Vittorio Klostermann, 1977).

C   Jean-Luc Nancy, *Corpus*, trans. Richard A. Rand (New York: Fordham University Press, 2008); *Corpus* (Paris: A. M. Métaillé, 1992).

CI   Gilles Deleuze, *Cinema I: The Movement–Image*, trans. Hugh Tomlinson and Barbara Habberjam (Minneapolis, MN: University of Minnesota Press, 1986); *Cinéma I: L'Image-mouvement* (Paris: Minuit, 1983).

CWG   Jean-Luc Nancy, *The Creation of the World, or Globalization*, trans. François Raffoul and David Pettigrew (Albany, NY: SUNY Press, 2007); *La Création du monde ou la mondialisation* (Paris: Galilée, 2002).

D   Gilles Deleuze and Claire Parnet, *Dialogues II*, trans. Barbara Habberjam and Hugh Tomlinson (New York: Columbia University Press, 2007); *Dialogues* (Paris: Flammarion, 1977/1999).

DR   Gilles Deleuze, *Difference and Repetition*, trans. Paul Patton (London: Continuum, 2004); *Différence et répétition* (Paris: Presses Universitaires de France, 1968).

E   Jacques Lacan, *écrits: The First Complete Edition in English*, trans. Bruce Fink, Héloïse Fink and Russell Grigg (New York: W. W. Norton, 2006); *Écrits*, ed. Jacques-Alain Miller (Paris: Seuil, 1966).

EF   Jean-Luc Nancy, *The Experience of Freedom*, trans. Bridget McDonald (Stanford, CA: Stanford University Press, 1993); *L'Expérience de la liberté* (Paris: Galilée, 1988).

EPR   G. W. F. Hegel, *Elements of the Philosophy of Right*, ed. Allen W. Wood, trans. H. B. Nisbet (Cambridge: Cambridge University Press, 1991); *Werke 7: Grundlinien der Philosophie des Rechts* (Frankfurt: Suhrkamp, 1970).

F   Gilles Deleuze, *Foucault*, trans. and ed. Seán Hand (London: Athlone, 1999); *Foucault* (Paris: Minuit, 1986).

FK   Jacques Derrida, 'Faith and Knowledge: the Two Sources of "Religion" at the Limits of Reason Alone', trans. Samuel Weber, in *Religion*, ed. Jacques Derrida and Gianni Vattimo (Stanford, CA: Stanford University Press, 1998); *Foi et savoir*, suivi de 'Le Siècle et le pardon' (Paris: Seuil, 2000).

FT   Jean-Luc Nancy, *A Finite Thinking*, ed. Simon Sparks (Stanford, CA: Stanford University Press, 2003); *Une Pensée finie* (Paris: Gallimard, 1991).

G Marcel Mauss, *The Gift: The Form and Reason for Exchange in Archaic Societies*, trans. W. D. Halls (London: Routledge, 1990); *Sociologie et anthropologie* (Paris: Presses Universitaires de France/Quadrige, 2004).

GD Jacques Derrida, *The Gift of Death*, trans. David Wills (Chicago, IL: University of Chicago Press, 1995); *Donner la mort* (Paris: Galilée, 1999).

GM Friedrich Nietzsche, *On the Genealogy of Morality*, ed. Keith Ansell-Pearson, trans. Carol Diethe (Cambridge: Cambridge University Press, 1994); *Zur Genealogie der Moral*, in *Nietzsche Werke Kritische Gesamtausgabe*, vol. VI, tome 2, ed. Giorgio Colli and Mazzino Montinari (Berlin: Walter de Gruyter, 1968).

GS Friedrich Nietzsche, *The Gay Science*, trans. Walter Kauffman (New York: Vintage, 1974); *Die Fröhliche Wissenschaft*, in *Nietzsche Werke Kritisch Gesamtausgabe*, vol. V, tome 2, ed. Giorgio Colli and Mazzino Montinari (Berlin: Walter de Gruyter, 1973).

GT Jacques Derrida, *Given Time: Counterfeit Money*, trans. Peggy Kamuf (Chicago, IL: University of Chicago Press, 1992); *Donner le temps: la fausse monnaie* (Paris: Galilée, 1991).

HES Georges Bataille, *The Accursed Share: An Essay on General Economy, vols 2 and 3: The History of Eroticism and Sovereignty*, trans. Robert Hurley (New York: Zone, 1991); *Œuvres complètes, tome VIII: L'Histoire de l'érotisme, La Souveraineté* (Paris: Gallimard, 1976).

HHG Martin Heidegger, *Gesamtausgabe, band 39: Hölderlins Hymnen 'Germanien' und 'Der Rhein'* (Frankfurt: Vittorio Klostermann, 1980).

HHI Martin Heidegger, *Hölderlin's Hymn 'The Ister'*, trans. Will McNeill and Julia Davis (Bloomington, IN: Indiana University Press, 1996); *Gesamtausgabe, band 53: Hölderlins Hymne 'Der Ister'* (Frankfurt: Vittorio Klostermann, 1984).

IC Jean-Luc Nancy, *The Inoperative Community*, ed. Peter Connor, trans. Peter Connor, Lisa Garbus, Michael Holland and Simona Sawhney (Minneapolis, MN: Minnesota University Press, 1991); *La Communauté désœuvrée* (Paris: Christian Bourgeois, 1986).

IE Georges Bataille, *Inner Experience*, trans. Leslie Anne Boldt (Albany, NY: SUNY Press, 1988); *Œuvres complètes, tome V: La Somme athéologique, I* (Paris: Gallimard, 1973).

IM Martin Heidegger, *Introduction to Metaphysics*, trans. Gregory

Fried and Richard Polt (New Haven, CT: Yale University Press, 2000); *Gesamtausgabe, band 40: Einführung in die Metaphysik* (Frankfurt: Suhrkamp, 1983).

IMM　Claude Lévi-Strauss, *Introduction to the Work of Marcel Mauss*, trans. Felicity Baker (London: Routledge & Kegan Paul, 1987); 'Introduction à l'œuvre de Marcel Mauss', in Marcel Mauss, *Sociologie et anthropologie* (Paris: Presses Universitaires de France/Quadrige, 2004).

IRH　Alexandre Kojève, *Introduction to the Reading of Hegel*, ed. Allan Bloom, trans. James H. Nichols, Jr (New York: Basic, 1969); *Introduction à la lecture de Hegel* (Paris: Gallimard, 1947).

LH　Martin Heidegger, 'Letter on Humanism', in *Basic Writings*, revised and expanded edn, ed. David Farrell Krell (London: Routledge, 1993); 'Brief über den Humanismus', in *Gesamtausgabe, band 9: Wegmarken* (Frankfurt: Vittorio Klostermann, 1976).

LO　Jacques Derrida, 'Living On', trans. James Hulbert, in Harold Bloom *et al.*, *Deconstruction and Criticism* (London: Continuum, 1979); 'Survivre', in *Parages* (Paris: Galilée, 1986).

LPH　G. W. F. Hegel, *Lectures on the Philosophy of World History: Introduction*, trans. H. B. Nisbet (Cambridge: Cambridge University Press, 1975); *Werke 12: Vorlesungen über die Philosophie der Geschichte* (Frankfurt: Suhrkamp, 1970).

LS　Gilles Deleuze, *The Logic of Sense*, ed. Constantin V. Boundas, trans. Mark Lester and Charles Stivale (London: Continuum, 1990); *Logique du sens* (Paris: Minuit, 1969).

M　Jacques Derrida, *Margins of Philosophy*, trans. Alan Bass (Chicago, IL: Chicago University Press, 1982); *Marges – de la philosophie* (Paris: Minuit, 1972).

N　Martin Heidegger, *Nietzsche, vols III and IV: The Will to Power as Metaphysics and as Freedom, Nihilism*, ed. David Farrell Krell, trans. David Farrell Krell, Joan Stambaugh and Frank A. Capuzzi (San Francisco, CA: HarperCollins); *Gesamtausgabe, band 6.2: Nietzsche* (Frankfurt: Vittorio Klostermann, 1977).

NE　Georges Bataille, 'The Notion of Expenditure', in *Visions of Excess: Selected Writings 1927–1939*, ed. Alan Stoekl, trans. Alan Stoekl, Carl R. Lovitt and Donald M. Leslie, Jr (Minneapolis, MN: University of Minnesota, 1985); 'La Notion de dépense', in *Œuvres complètes, tome I: Premiers écrits, 1922–40* (Paris: Gallimard, 1970).

OM　Martin Heidegger, 'Overcoming Metaphysics', trans. Joan

Stambaugh, in Richard Wolin, ed., *The Heidegger Controversy: A Critical Reader* (Cambridge, MA: MIT Press); 'Überwindung der Metaphysik', in *Vorträge und Aufsätze* (Pfullingen: Neske, 1954).

OT   Michel Foucault, *The Order of Things: An Archaeology of the Human Sciences*, trans. Alan Sheridan (New York: Pantheon, 1970); *Les Mots et les choses* (Paris: Gallimard, 1966).

OWA   Martin Heidegger, 'The Origin of the Work of Art', in *Basic Writings*, revised and expanded edn, ed. David Farrell Krell (London: Routledge, 1993); 'Der Ursprung des Kunstwerkes', in *Gesamtausgabe, band 5: Holzwege* (Frankfurt: Vittorio Klostermann, 1977).

PC   Jacques Derrida, *The Post-Card: From Socrates to Freud and Beyond*, trans. Alan Bass (Chicago, IL: University of Chicago Press, 1987); *La Carte postale: de Socrate à Freud et au-delà* (Paris: Flammarion, 1980).

PF   Jacques Derrida, *Politics of Friendship*, trans. George Collins (London: Verso, 1997); *Politiques de l'amitié*, suivi de 'L'Oreille de Heidegger' (Paris: Galilée, 1994).

PS   G. W. F. Hegel, *The Phenomenology of Spirit*, trans. A. V. Miller (Oxford: Oxford University Press, 1977); *Werke 3: Phänomenologie des Geistes* (Frankfurt: Suhrkamp, 1970).

PWM   Martin Heidegger, 'Postscript to *What is Metaphysics?*', in *Pathmarks*, trans. and ed. William McNeill (Cambridge: Cambridge University Press, 1998); 'Nachwort zu *Was ist Metaphysik?*', in *Gesamtausgabe, band 9: Wegmarken* (Frankfurt: Vittorio Klostermann, 1976).

QT   Martin Heidegger, 'The Question Concerning Technology', in *Basic Writings*, revised and expanded edn, ed. David Farrell Krell (London: Routledge, 1993); 'Die Frage nach der Technik', in *Vorträge und Aufsätze* (Pfullingen: Neske, 1954).

R   Jacques Derrida, *Rogues: Two Essays on Reason*, trans. Pascale-Anne Brault and Michael Naas (Stanford, CA: Stanford University Press, 2005); *Voyous* (Paris: Galilée, 2003).

RJ   Philippe Lacoue-Labarthe and Jean-Luc Nancy, eds, *Rejouer le politique* (Paris: Galilée, 1981).

RP   Philippe Lacoue-Labarthe and Jean-Luc Nancy, *Retreating the Political*, ed. Simon Sparks (London: Routledge, 1997).

RT   Philippe Lacoue-Labarthe and Jean-Luc Nancy, eds, *Le Retrait du politique* (Paris: Galilée, 1983).

SA   Marcel Mauss, *Sociologie et anthropologie*, preceded by Claude Lévi-Strauss, 'Introduction à l'œuvre de Marcel Mauss', ed.

Georges Gurvitch (Paris: Presses Universitaires de France/ Quadrige, 2004).

SIII Jacques Lacan, *The Seminar of Jacques Lacan, book III: The Psychoses*, trans. Russell Grigg (New York: W. W. Norton, 1997); *Le Séminaire, livre III: Les Psychoses (1955–6)*, ed. Jacques-Alain Miller (Paris: Seuil, 1981).

SIV Jacques Lacan, *Le Séminaire, livre IV: La Relation d'objet (1956–7)*, ed. Jacques-Alain Miller (Paris: Seuil, 1994).

SVII Jacques Lacan, *The Seminar of Jacques Lacan, book VII: The Ethics of Psychoanalysis 1959–1960*, trans. Dennis Porter (New York: W. W. Norton, 1997); *Le Séminaire, livre VII: L'Éthique de la psychanalyse (1959–60)*, ed. Jacques-Alain Miller (Paris: Seuil, 1986).

SVIII Jacques Lacan, *Le Séminaire, livre VIII: Le Transfert (1960–1)*, ed. Jacques-Alain Miller (Paris: Seuil, 2001).

SX Jacques Lacan, *Le Séminaire, livre X: L'Angoisse (1962–3)*, ed. Jacques-Alain Miller (Paris: Seuil, 2004).

SXI Jacques Lacan, *The Four Fundamental Concepts of Psychoanalysis*, trans. Alan Sheridan (London: Karnac, 1977); *Le Séminaire, livre XI: Les Quatre Concepts fondamentaux de la psychanalyse (1963–4)*, ed. Jacques-Alain Miller (Paris: Seuil, 1990).

SXVII Jacques Lacan, *The Seminar of Jacques Lacan, book XVII: The Other Side of Psychoanalysis*, trans. Russell Grigg (New York: W. W. Norton, 2007); *Le Séminaire, livre XVII: L'Envers de la psychanalyse (1969–70)*, ed. Jacques-Alain Miller (Paris: Seuil, 1991).

SXX Jacques Lacan, *The Seminar of Jacques Lacan, book XX: On Feminine Sexuality, the Limits of Love and Knowledge*, trans. Bruce Fink (New York: W. W. Norton, 2000); *Le Séminaire, livre XX: Encore! (1972–3)*, ed. Jacques-Alain Miller (Paris: Seuil, 1999).

SM Jacques Derrida, *Specters of Marx: The State of Debt, the Work of Mourning and the New International*, trans. Peggy Kamuf (London: Routledge, 1994); *Spectres de Marx* (Paris: Galilée, 1993).

SW Jean-Luc Nancy, *The Sense of the World*, trans. Jeffrey Librett (Minneapolis, MN: Minnesota University Press); *Le Sens du monde* (Paris: Galilée, 1993).

T Jacques Derrida, *On Touching – Jean-Luc Nancy*, trans. Christine Irizarry (Stanford, CA: Stanford University Press); *Le Toucher, Jean-Luc Nancy* (Paris: Galilée, 2000).

TB   Martin Heidegger, *On Time and Being*, trans. Joan Stambaugh
        (Chicago, IL: Chicago University Press, 2002). *Zur Sache des
        Denkens* (Tübingen: Max Niemeyer, 1969).

TD   Jean-Luc Nancy, *The Truth of Democracy*, trans. Pascale-Anne
        Brault and Michael Naas (New York: Fordham University
        Press, 2010); *La Vérité de la démocratie* (Paris: Galilée, 2008).

TI   Emmanuel Levinas, *Totality and Infinity: An Essay on
        Exteriority*, trans. Alphonso Lingis (The Hague: Kluwer
        Academic, 1991); *Totalité et infini: Essai sur l'extériorité* (The
        Hague: Kluwer Academic, 1971).

TP   Gilles Deleuze and Félix Guattari, *A Thousand Plateaus:
        Capitalism and Schizophrenia*, trans. Brian Massumi (London:
        Athlone, 1988); *Mille plateaux: Capitalisme et schizophrénie II*
        (Paris: Minuit, 1980).

TR   Georges Bataille, *Theory of Religion*, trans. Robert Hurley
        (New York: Zone, 1989); *Œuvres complètes, tome VII: La Part
        maudite, Théorie de la religion* (Paris: Gallimard, 1976).

TRM   Gilles Deleuze, *Two Regimes of Madness: Texts and Interviews
        (1975–95)*, rev. edn, trans. Ames Hodges and Mike Taormina
        (New York: Semiotext(e)/Foreign Agents, 2007); *Deux régimes
        de fous et autres textes (1975–95)*, ed. David Lapoujade (Paris:
        Minuit, 2007).

WCT   Martin Heidegger, *What is Called Thinking*, trans. Fred D.
        Wieck and J. Glenn Gray (New York: Harper & Row, 1968);
        Gesamtausgabe, band 8: Was heisst Denken? (Frankfurt:
        Vittorio Klostermann, 2002).

WD   Jacques Derrida, *Writing and Difference*, trans. Alan Bass
        (London: Routledge, 1978); *L'écriture et la différence* (Paris:
        Seuil, 1967).

WIP   Gilles Deleuze and Félix Guattari, *What is Philosophy?*, trans.
        Graham Burchell and Hugh Tomlinson (London: Verso, 1993);
        Qu'est-ce que la philosophie? (Paris: Minuit, 1991).

Z   Friedrich Nietzsche, *Thus Spoke Zarathustra*, trans. R. J.
        Hollingdale (London: Penguin, 1969); *Also Sprach Zarathustra,
        Nietzsche Werke Kritische Gesamtausgabe*, vol. VI, tome 1,
        ed. Giorgio Colli and Mazzino Montinari (Berlin: Walter de
        Gruyter, 1968).

Series Editor's Preface

Two or more currents flowing into or through each other create a turbulent crosscurrent, more powerful than its contributory flows and irreducible to them. Time and again, modern European thought creates and exploits crosscurrents in thinking, remaking itself as it flows through, across and against discourses as diverse as mathematics and film, sociology and biology, theology, literature and politics. The work of Gilles Deleuze, Jacques Derrida, Slavoj Žižek, Alain Badiou, Bernard Stiegler and Jean-Luc Nancy, among others, participates in this fundamental remaking. In each case disciplines and discursive formations are engaged, not with the aim of performing a pre-determined mode of analysis yielding a 'philosophy of x', but through encounters in which thought itself can be transformed. Furthermore, these fundamental transformations do not merely seek to account for singular events in different sites of discursive or artistic production but rather to engage human existence and society as such, and as a whole. The cross-disciplinarity of this thought is therefore neither a fashion nor a prosthesis; it is simply part of what 'thought' means in this tradition.

Crosscurrents begins from the twin convictions that this re-making is integral to the legacy and potency of European thought, and that the future of thought in this tradition must defend and develop this legacy in the teeth of an academy that separates and controls the currents that flow within and through it. With this in view, the series provides an exceptional site for bold, original and opinion-changing monographs that actively engage European thought in this fundamentally cross-disciplinary manner, riding existing crosscurrents and creating new ones. Each book in the series explores the different ways in which European thought develops through its engagement with disciplines across the arts, humanities, social sciences and sciences, recognising that the community of scholars working with this thought is itself spread across diverse faculties. The object of the series is therefore nothing less than to examine and carry forward the unique legacy of European thought as an inherently and irreducibly cross-disciplinary enterprise.

Christopher Watkin
Cambridge

Introduction: Spectres of Mauss

> If the people of Dogville have a problem with acceptance, what they really need is something for them to accept. Something tangible, like a gift.

Lars von Trier's *Dogville* (2003) opens with the self-appointed philosopher-in-residence of a tiny mountain hamlet speculating over a solution to the moral shortcomings of his neighbours. Thomas Edison, Jr (Paul Bettany) hazards that what is needed to awaken the townsfolk of Dogville from their dogmatic slumbers is something new, something different, something suggestive of a future. 'Something tangible, like a gift.' The gift duly arrives in the form of a beautiful young runaway (Nicole Kidman), who stumbles accidentally upon the town after taking flight from an unspecified figure of authority. Appropriately, she is called Grace – a name connoting God's gift of unmerited and spontaneous, unconditional salvation. As the film's narrator observes, Grace 'hadn't chosen Dogville from a map, or sought out the town for a visit. She had elected to give herself up to him at random, as – yes – a gift. Generous, very generous, thought Tom.'

After a difficult start, the people of Dogville warm to Grace, who, under Tom's guiding influence, distinguishes herself by giving them precisely what they do not need, doing the jobs that no one knew needed doing prior to her arrival. This early phase of warmth does not last, however. The more Grace gives, the more the recipients of her gifts become resentful of her; the more the gift is perceived as a burden that threatens to undermine the integrity, the identity of its recipients; the more Grace is seen to be taking hold, or possession, of the town. In a reversal of roles, Grace herself becomes the obliging host to whom the rest feel indebted. We soon see an attempt to reinstate the previous hierarchy. Emphasising the risks they run in harbouring a wanted fugitive, the people of Dogville assert their right to a greater countergift in return for their own gift of hospitality. Grace alone is no longer enough. Before long, her alleged debt to them is so great that she is reduced to a slave, performing all manner of menial duties for the women and all manner of sexual favours for the men and children. In the last instance, Grace is reduced to an object that stands outside the symbolic order of the community. Her status as an irredeemable outsider is confirmed when she is presented as a sacrificial offering to the forces of the law from which she fled.

The sacrifice fails, revealing in so doing the complicity between the gift and the law, the *nomos*, that stands as its inverse face. The dreaded force of law turns out to be a gangster, Grace's father, who merely sought to incorporate her into the family business. Having been rescued from captivity, Grace returns to the town and, in the film's final scene, proceeds to rain down death on every last one of Dogville's (human) inhabitants. No longer recognisable as such, the gift is released from the fatal economy that negated it. No longer 'tangible', or recognisable as a gift, it finally achieves what it always threatened to achieve with the unbearable intensity of its imperative: not just the undermining, but also the destruction, of the identity of its recipients in the very moment of its receipt.

In the second instalment of von Trier's anticipated *America* trilogy, *Manderlay* (2005), we see Grace stumble across an Alabaman slave plantation and, with all the generosity her name suggests, respond once again to the call to bestow her gift on a people apparently grateful to receive it. Wresting power from its white colonial mistress, Grace (this time played by Bryce Dallas Howard) turns Manderlay into a democratic cooperative, presenting each of its black workers with a 'deed of gift' that entitles them to communal ownership and a share in the profits of cotton production. Not everyone is happy, however, and when the collapse of the traditional order leads to the late sowing of crops and an ensuing shortage of food, the fears of one older ex-slave, Wilhelm (Danny Glover), prove justified. The emancipated slaves are simply not ready for freedom and the ungrounding collapse of identity it brings with it. They cannot bear the greatest weight of the gift they have received. As in *Dogville*, we are presented with a politics that, though beginning with hospitality and an openness toward the gift, veers toward its sacrifice and suppression. *Dogville* concludes with the traumatic discovery that the gift is not just Grace – not just unqualified redemption – but also poison. *Manderlay* ends with a similar inversion of hospitality, a similarly futile attempt to confine the gift. The freed slaves ochlocratically vote to imprison Grace, to force her to fill the role of the old colonial mistress and administer a return to the 'old ways' of slavery. Her gift of freedom is once again met with a countergift that negates it, even if the negation is once again destined to fall short of what it takes to contain her. As the credits roll for the second time, Grace breaks free and takes flight, repeating the inappropriability, the ability to exceed containment and confinement to the present that characterised her escape from Dogville.

GIFTS AND LEGACIES

There is a temptation to interpret both films, *Dogville* and *Manderlay*, as illustrations of what the anthropologist Marcel Mauss called the economy of the gift, the threefold obligation to give, to receive and to reciprocate. Mauss famously argues that this threefold obligation constitutes the *élan vital* of archaic society, the force of life that binds communities together through a network of gift exchange designed to prevent the accretion of destabilising concentrations of power and wealth. At the very least, one could see *Dogville* as an attempt to trace the life of the gift under conditions of capitalism, after the breakdown of the archaic gift economy, coinciding with the birth of *homo economicus*, the atomised individual for whom obligation without contract no longer represents a profitable investment and an efficient use of scarce resources. To do so, however, would be to risk missing an entire history of post-Maussian thought contained within the films, a history in which the logic of the gift is pushed to the extreme, leaving it unrecognisable. *Dogville* may begin with a Maussian notion of gifts inscribed within an economy, but it soon becomes an affirmation of the claim made by Derrida and supported by Bataille, Klossowski, Lacan, Deleuze and Nancy: namely, that there is a gift that exceeds any economy, and which is accordingly impossible, except where it occurs in the absence, or in excess, of subjectivity. The sequel illustrates all the more starkly how this gift relates to politics; how the impossibility of receiving the gift corresponds to what Deleuze and Guattari call 'the fundamental problem of political philosophy' (AŒ, 31/36), why we desire our own repression, or – to recast it – why it is easier to refuse a gift than to accept it.

Over the course of this book, it will hopefully become apparent that the impossible gift is not the sacrificial offering as such, but that which returns to haunt in the failure of its offering, a moment of excess that escapes any and every confinement, which moreover transforms or even obliterates that which attempts to receive it. The people of Dogville and Manderlay are haunted by the spectre of Grace, by the figure of a gift that, surviving its own sacrifice, returns, takes flight and refuses to die. In the same way, might we say that twentieth-century thought in general is haunted by the spectre of *The Gift*, the spectre, or rather spectres of Marcel Mauss's *Essai sur le don*?

This somewhat tentative claim is borne out in the legacy of Mauss's masterwork, the essay that first identified the economy of the gift as 'one of the rocks on which our societies are built' (G, 4/148 [TM]). Mauss's revolutionary argument consists in contesting the idea that, prior to the advent of capitalism and advanced monetary systems, the germ of the market economy is recognisable in a system of barter where the market place serves as the site of rational, utilitarian exchange. Analysing fieldwork undertaken amongst the indigenous tribes of Melanesia, the South Pacific and the American Northwest, Mauss argues that these societies exhibit 'nothing that might resemble what is called a "natural" economy' (G, 5/150 [TM]). In place of the methodological individualism of later economists (Hayek 1944: 44; Hayek 1949: 6–11; Joseph 1975: 37), he elaborates a theory of group behaviour and the 'total social fact' first developed by his uncle, Émile Durkheim. He thus rejects the idea that society is an aggregate of self-seeking, utility-maximising individuals, organised around distinct public and private spheres, the market (*agora*) and the home (*oikos*). Underlying this rejection is the claim that economic man is a relatively recent phenomenon. It makes its debut, Mauss suggests, in the early eighteenth century, at around the time of Mandeville's *Fable of the Bees* (G, 76/271). Mandeville's poem (1714) and subsequent commentaries thereon (1732) portray man as a bee whose selfish and calculating behaviour works to the overall benefit of the hive (Mandeville 1997: 27). But the account, Mauss suggests, is a product of its age, the early European Enlightenment: an abstract theoretical, which is to say metaphysical, construct, rather than an anthropological given. Mandeville and those who follow him fail to account for the complex social bonds that must be seen to determine the scope of individual agency. In neglecting the question of social conditioning, they also neglect the historicity of the subject, of what Foucault would later call the 'recent invention' of man, whose existence is nothing more than 'a new fold in our knowledge, and [who] will disappear again as soon as that knowledge has discovered a new form' (OT, xxiii/15).

Mauss anticipates this so-called death of man and the anthropologist will ironically be decisive in awakening philosophy from what Foucault diagnoses as its 'anthropological slumbers' (OT, 340/351). As it is outlined in *The Order of Things*, Foucault uses this *sommeil anthropologique* to characterise the increasingly lazy, dogmatic stance of philosophy with regard to the conceptualisation of man, who by the end of the nineteenth century was taken for granted as an analytic point of departure from which to understand the world, a rational-transcendental given awkwardly imposed on experience. Philosophy, in other words, had lapsed into a kind of anthropocentrism, or 'Anthropology': 'And so we find philosophy falling asleep in the hollow of this Fold [in our knowledge]; this time not the sleep of Dogmatism, but that of Anthropology,' understood as 'the pre-critical analysis of what man is in his essence' (OT, 341/353). Calling into question the analytic credentials of the rational, calculating and sovereign 'I think', Mauss writes:

> *Homo œconomicus* is not behind us, but lies ahead, as does the man of morality and duty, the man of science and reason. For a very long time man was something different, and he has not been a machine for very long, made complicated by a calculating machine. (G, 76/272)

In place of the pre-social, metaphysically individuated essence, or residual soul, of the modern subject, Mauss's study of gift exchange suggests the very opposite: a complex network of obligations, commitments and blurred identities from which there no more emerges a concept of the individual than there does an isolable market place.

In the gift economies of archaic societies, operations of exchange are not confined to transactions between individuals, nor are they primarily economic in nature. On the contrary, Mauss writes: 'First, it is not individuals but collectivities that impose obligations of exchange and contract upon each other' (G, 5/150). The exchange of gifts is not limited to the distribution of scarce resources, but occurs at every level of society, as a '*system of total services* [système des prestations totales]' (G, 5/151), a total social fact able to account for the whole of society: a military structure; a structure of politics and intertribal diplomacy; a legal technique for the dissemination of law (encoded in myths and songs that assert the necessity of giving), in addition to the more obvious religious (sacrificial) and ceremonial connotations. Mauss describes a scenario in which the giving of gifts cannot be reduced to any logic of individualistic, utilitarian rationality. Gifts given are not in themselves economically desirable or necessary, but rather tend toward the materially useless, the purely symbolic. The motive for exchange is not internal to the objects exchanged, but a product of the social imposition of obligation, according to which it is not enough just to reciprocate gifts given:

> The institution of total services doesn't merely carry with it the obligation to reciprocate presents received. It also supposes two other obligations just as important: the obligation on one hand, to give presents, and on the other, to receive them. (G, 13/161)

The threefold obligation to give, to receive and to reciprocate locks participants into an interminable series of obligations by demanding that gifts 'follow around this circle a regular movement in space and time' (G, 22/176 [TM]). The public sphere is thus all-encompassing, structured by laws and myths endowed with the task of reiterating the notion that adhesion to the rules of gift exchange is 'in the final analysis [. . .] strictly compulsory, on pain of private or public warfare' (G, 5/151). Underlying this logic is the fundamental claim that to receive a gift is to become indebted to its giver. Mauss draws on Germanic etymology to show that the gift, inseparable from the debt it engenders, is *poison* (Mauss 1997: 28–32/243–7), to be cured or expiated only by ensuring its constant circulation. Every gift given compels a countergift of equal or greater value, in order to prevent the accumulations of power that would threaten communal stability by introducing inequality back into the structure of society. In the extreme example of the Amerindian *potlatch*, this is taken to the point of competing to establish who is 'the most madly extravagant' (G, 37/200), ritually destroying vast quantities of possessions *prior* to the requirement to give them away. In exchange for the material wealth that could see them acquire power over others, tribal members receive dignity and prestige as a reward for embracing poverty.

In a study that situates Mauss in a long line of social contract theorists from Grotius and Hobbes to Rousseau, the economic historian Marshall Sahlins famously describes the *Essai* as Mauss's 'own gift to the ages', 'a source of unending ponderation for the anthropologist *du métier*', whose work 'in fact only renders the due of the original' (Sahlins 1972: 149). For Sahlins, then, it is as if one could look to Mauss's text, above all to his claim that it is the very nature of the gift to compel reciprocation, to explain the extent of subsequent engagements with his work. An apparently similar claim is made by Jacques Derrida, who repeats Sahlins's point, yet subtly radicalises it, posing the question of whether 'the gift is not first of all the essay titled *The Gift*, precisely insofar as it finds it impossible to speak of the gift that is its theme?' (GT, 57/79 [TM]). The gift of Mauss's *Essai*, in other words, would not lie in its recognisability, in the generation of a sense of recognition that one would feel impelled, obliged, to reciprocate, but rather in its very refusal of recognition, in the difficulty of identifying it explicitly with any gift. To respond to Mauss out of obligation would in fact be to negate the gift, to subsume it under a law of exchange, an economy in which it would become both conditional and predetermined.

Derrida's argument lies in extending the Maussian logic of the gift

beyond the conclusions at which Mauss himself arrives. By emphasising the anthropologically irreducible relationship between the gift
and poison, the gift and obligation, Mauss endeavours to expose the
occidentalism of a (Christian) concept of giving that valorises the gift
as inherently virtuous, given unconditionally, without expectation
of return. But his critique of *homo economicus* ultimately falls short
because it remains rooted in anthropology. By asserting the impurity
of the gift to be constitutive, a by-product of its inseparability from the
contaminated relations of human exchange, Mauss sacrifices unconditional generosity to a modern logic of the subject. In a much earlier
essay, to which we shall return presently, Derrida writes of Claude
Lévi-Strauss that, 'whether he wants to or not', the ethnologist 'accepts
into his discourse the premises of ethnocentrism at the very moment
when he denounces them' (WD, 356/414). The claim is equally applicable to Mauss, who anthropocentrically defines the gift in relation
to the subject, and not *vice versa*. For Derrida, it is not the gift that is
contaminated, but the economic logic of subjectivity. We see this in the
way that, rather than sacrifice the purity of the concept, Derrida insists
on an irreducible discrepancy between the promise of the gift and the
possibility of fulfilling that promise. Mauss's *economy* of the gift testifies to the excess of our concept of giving over any instantiable instance
of giving. But it does not in and of itself suffice to preclude the possibility that there could still be an unconditional gift, a gift that would fulfil
the promise implied by its concept. The crux of Derrida's argument is
that the gift cannot exist where its giving is merely conditional; where,
that is to say, it risks generating a sense of debt, a perceived obligation
to reciprocate, on the part of the recipient. Nor can it exist even if it is
given unbeknown to the recipient, so long as there is a giver who would
stand to experience some kind of pleasure or *jouissant* return on his or
her (or its) investment:

> For there to be a gift, *it is necessary* that the donee not give back, amortize,
> reimburse, acquit himself, enter into contract, and that he never contracted
> a debt. [. . .] It is thus necessary, at the limit, that he not *recognize* the gift as
> gift. If he recognizes it *as* gift, if the gift *appears to him as such*, if the present
> is present to him *as present*, this simple recognition suffices to annul the gift.
> Why? Because it gives back, in the place, let us say, of the thing itself, a sym-
> bolic equivalent. [. . .] If the other perceives or receives it, if he or she keeps
> it as a gift, the gift is annulled [*Si l'autre le perçoit, s'il le garde comme don,
> le don s'annule*]. But the one who gives it must not see it or know it either,
> otherwise he begins at the threshold, as soon as he intends to give, to pay
> himself with a symbolic recognition, to praise himself, to approve of himself,
> to gratify himself to congratulate himself, to give back to himself symboli-
> cally the value of what he thinks he has given. (GT, 13–14/26–7)

Irrespective of whether it is given in the explicit context of an (archaic) gift economy, the gift, Derrida argues, is inherently economic – so long as it is identifiable as a gift. The mere intention to give or recognition of a gift serves to inscribe the gift within an economy that annuls its supposed unconditionality. For there to be a gift, it would by definition have to break with the economy in which it finds itself inscribed in the very act of being given. It would have to take place in the absence of the subject, in the absence of any supposedly self-identical giver or receiver who might recognise obligation or benefit in the giving or receipt of a gift. It is accordingly impossible:

> If the figure of the circle is essential to economics, the gift must remain *aneconomic*. Not that it remains foreign to the circle, but it must *keep* a relation of foreignness to the circle, a relation without relation of familiar foreignness. It is perhaps in this sense that the gift is the impossible.
>
> Not impossible, but *the* impossible [*Non pas impossible mais l'impossible*]. (GT, 7/19)

Not just impossible but *the* impossible, the gift would be the very definition of impossibility simply because it could never admit of subjective experience. Derrida repeatedly insists on the qualification, '*s'il y en a*', 'if there is any' (GT, 7/18), in order to emphasise that in speaking of a pure gift we depart from the realms of the experientiable and enter into the domain of an event that can be neither verified subjectively nor communicated in language (Derrida, Nouss and Soussana 2001: 89).

The counterintuitiveness of the gift's impossibility is one of several objections raised against Derrida's argument. The most prominent and sustained version of the criticism comes from the phenomenologist Jean-Luc Marion, who remains sympathetic to the deconstructive position, but criticises Derrida for failing to see that the gift does admit of conscious, phenomenal experience – even if it remains subjectively ungraspable. In *Being Given* (1997), Marion argues that Derrida's analysis of the gift does not go far enough, because Derrida fails to see that the conditions of the gift's impossibility serve as the very conditions of its possibility, by preventing its recuperation within any kind of economy. The gift, according to Marion:

> would be accomplished not *despite* the threefold objection made by Derrida, but indeed *thanks to it* [grâce à elle]. In effect, the so-called 'conditions of the impossibility of the gift' (no givee, no giver, no object given) would become precisely the conditions for the possibility of its reduction to and for a pure givenness. (Marion 2002: 84/122)

This defence of the experientiability of the gift revolves around the notion that it can exist, albeit not as the object of an identifiable exchange. Rather than defy experience outright, Marion suggests that the gift yields itself to experience of a kind that defies conceptualisation, refusing any appropriative synthesis or assimilation by what he, following Kant, calls transcendental subjectivity. The gift, in other words, would give itself in an experience that does not require, and would moreover be incompatible with, an active, preconditioning subjectivity. Not only does pure donation not need a subject to recognise its existence, but it is also of such intensity that recognition is rendered impossible, because it pacifies the conceptual mechanisms of its would-be recipient. Far from it withdrawing from or not yielding to experience, as if somehow deficient, Marion describes the gift as a 'saturated phenomenon', a phenomenon whose intuition exceeds the ability of any concept to grasp it, and which occasions a beatific encounter that cannot be traced to any cause, or identifiable giver (2002: 214/299). For the openly Christian Marion, who sets out to redeem a negative theology he detects at work in Derrida, phenomenology thus opens on to a 'mystical theology' that leaves open a space for (divine) revelation (Derrida and Marion 1999: 40). Responding to this in a dialogue with Marion, Derrida expresses doubt that such an asubjective experience is conceivable within the horizons of phenomenology. He suggests that Marion 'wants to free the gift and givenness from being' (1999: 59). Derrida is, for all that, clear that our inability to experience the gift *as such* does not amount to saying that it could never exist in excess of the horizons of subjectivity, yielding itself to the desubjectified (1999: 57–8).

One might hazard that the difference between the two philosophers ultimately comes down to the relation of the aneconomic gift to the economic structure of consciousness. In seeking to articulate the experience of the gift as one of the sublime pacification of subjectivity, Marion seems less interested than Derrida in the gift's violent, poisonous dimesion. For Derrida, this violence is what necessitates the gift's rupture with both consciousness and phenomenology. Where Marion's subject is left pacified but essentially intact by an encounter with the gift, we shall see that Derrida's emphasis on the gift's ability to unground, or break down, subjectivity becomes crucial to an understanding of its politics.

By claiming to draw out and extend the implicit Christianity of the Derridean account, Marion renders it more susceptible to another series of criticisms, this time hailing from the opposite end of the spectrum. For the philosopher and anthropologist Marcel Hénaff, the decoupling of the gift from the social dimension of recognition reveals the Derridean treatment of giving to be formed by a restrictive Judeo-Christian perspective that is simply incommensurable with the logic of gift giving in archaic society. Preferring a vocabulary of 'ceremonial giving' to the language of 'archaic' gift 'economics' employed by Mauss, Hénaff denies that the giving of gifts entails the kind of creation of obligation that would generate an economy of debt. Defining economics more narrowly than either Mauss or Lévi-Strauss, as 'a relation between men through the intermediary of things' (2002: 204), he argues that the ceremonial giving analysed by anthropologists is not economic but *symbolic*, a gesture intended less to subordinate than simply to present a 'mark of respect, as the expression of a desire to know the other in his existence, in his status and finally as evidence of an alliance' (2002: 204). The gift is thus above all *political*, pertaining to 'the originating gesture of *reciprocal recognition* between humans, a gesture found in no other living beings in that it is mediated by a thing' (Hénaff 2009: 230). It is in this affirmation of an intentional politics of recognition that Hénaff's reading becomes critical of Derrida, whom he accuses of reading the gift not just overly *economically* and insufficiently *politically*, but as too exclusively *moral* (2002: 188). His principal concern is that Derrida's construal of the anthropological gift retroactively projects capitalist notions of exchange and debt back on to non-capitalist societies. Derrida's second mistake, according to Hénaff, is to make the gift contingent upon its unconditionality, upon the absence of any attenuating recognition. In so doing, Derrida undermines his own claim to have established the non-self-identity of the gift by rendering the deconstruction of its essence dependent upon 'the only voice recognizable and recognized by our entire religious and moral tradition: purely generous gift giving' (2009: 218). This alone is what accounts for and sustains the 'impossibility' of the gift being given in and to experience.

Where Marion is ultimately in broad agreement with Derrida, the weight of Hénaff's charges is potentially devastating and he is not the only one to make them. We shall see in Chapter 2 that Jean-François Lyotard proffers a similarly occidentalist critique, suggesting that 'the whole problematic of the gift, such as [we] receive it from Mauss [. . .] belongs in its entirety to Western imperialism and racism,' as a fantasy produced by capitalism, which leads us to idealise anything that might escape the totalising logic of exchange-value (Lyotard 1993a: 106/130). Hénaff and Lyotard can none the less be shown to labour under a number of misapprehensions about what is at stake in Derrida's engagement with the gift, all of which are linked to the assumption that it abstracts itself from politics in favour of a naïvely idealistic ethics. It might be argued in response that Derrida's engagement implies a deeper appreciation of politics than Hénaff's conception of the intentional creation of alliances allows, and moreover explains how and why we might arrive at the overly simplistic formulation of politics as symbolic recognition. The question of an unmediated giving is not one of *moral* generosity so much as of generosity as an expression of the spontaneous and unmediated, of that which precedes and thereby establishes the conditions of mediation and exchange. In other words, Derrida wants to know what it is that precedes the giving of any recognisable gift, what it is that elicits the initial act of giving. The same question is posed by Hénaff in response to what he perceives as a lacuna in Mauss: namely, the question of what occasions the giving of a gift prior to any form of obligation to reciprocate. His solution again rests on the idea of recognition, above all on the idea that recognising others through the giving of gifts finds its origin in some kind of human nature. 'The ceremonial prestation of gifts puts on display a fundamental structure of reciprocity as a condition of all social life in the human species' (Hénaff 2002: 181). However interesting, the hypothesis is one that Derrida – along with the majority of thinkers to be discussed over the course of the next four chapters – would regard with considerable suspicion of essentialism.

In the Derridean account of giving, the (human) subject is not the privileged site of aneconomy, of a spontaneity and generosity unmediated by the calculation of interest, but the very opposite. As will perhaps become clearer through readings of Derrida's contemporaries, aneconomy is reserved for the giving of existence, which is to say for the event of a giving that precedes the subject, and in relation to which subjectivity is moreover habitually and even constitutively in a relation of tension, *economically* seeking to preserve itself against a giving that is also poisonous to its subjective integrity or identity. The economic should not, in the first instance, be conflated with the more conspicuous and conscious calculations of the materially self-interested *homo economicus*, which would only be an extreme version, a recently emergent caricature, of a more basic economy of subjectivity. Nor should it be deemed independent of, or incommensurable with, the aneconomic, since the two exist in a relation of interdependent tension. An instance of deconstruction's conceptual minimalism, which rids language of its metaphysical baggage, Derrida's concept of economy should be read as a literal interpretation of the Greek *oikonomia*: the management, or rather the law (*nomos*) of the *oikos*, meaning household or hearth, a place of identity (GT, 6/18; PC, 299–300/320–1; Johnson 1993: 57–64). Economy thus refers to the law of identity, to that which returns or attempts to return to its perceived point of origin, its *oikos*.

Despite the connotation of being prior or external to the sphere of politics, in a familial *chez soi* distinct from the public space of the *polis*, this identification of economics with the law of the *oikos* does not quite entail that it is pre-political or uncontaminated by politics. Exemplified by Jean-Jacques Rousseau's entry on 'Œconomie' in the 1755 edition of the *Encyclopédie*, the modern, Enlightenment thinking of economics moves away from its supposedly pre-political origin in housekeeping by distinguishing itself as *political* economy, the study of 'the great family that is the state' and, increasingly, of a market place whose brutality contrasts with the sanctuary of a private-sphere *oikos* thought beyond the reach of politics (Rousseau 1986: 16). The modern tradition culminates, in the mid-nineteenth century, with Karl Marx, for whom the horizons of politics are framed and moreover caused by the economic 'superstructure', with political struggles determined by the relations between economic classes and the ownership of the means of production (Marx 2000: 425/8). As is illustrated by the feminist movement's demands to repoliticise the *oikos*, the advent of postmodernity brings with it the reversal of the modern situation of economics prior to politics. To paraphrase the prominent slogan of the feminist writer Carol Hanisch (1969), Derrida argues that the personal is always already political. The site of a purportedly inviolable, domestic seat of identity is constitutively violated, shot through with an (aneconomic) alterity that the economic logic of identity retroactively seeks to keep at bay: there is economics because there is politics. A major influence on Derrida, Emmanuel Levinas sets out the logic of this position in *Totality and Infinity* (1961), where he argues that 'economic existence remains within the same. [. . .] Its movement is centripetal,' because it constructs a dwelling place for identity through the exclusion of anything construed as threatening (TI, 175/191). Derrida elaborates on this in a late essay on hospitality, arguing that the subject comes into being as the site of a permeable *oikos* (Derrida and Dufourmantelle 2000: 29/37). The economic return-to-self is occasioned by the ungrounding of economy by aneconomy, and consists in the reassertion of identity against the incursions of difference from which it cannot and should not secure itself definitively. Understood as the law of identity and its continual reinscription, economy also thus functions as a working definition of the subject. Construed by modernity as a self-identical ground of privileged, transcendental consciousness, subjective self-identity is now recognised as being preceded and made possible by alterity, constructed through the management of anything that undermines the *nomos* of its *oikos*.

In shifting the site of giving away from the economics of the subject and on to an unrecognisable, aneconomic event, Derrida's critique is less of Mauss and more of the modern philosophical tradition, of which Mauss remains a part in spite of *The Gift*. Phenomenology in particular has conceived the gift as an indubitable, isolable locus of sense-certainty and presence on which to ground the subject. Somewhat ironically, given Mauss's critique of modern (Cartesian) subjectivity, his illustrious contemporary, the German phenomenologist, Edmund Husserl, uses the idea of gift as sense *datum* to reground a Cartesian philosophy of consciousness and privileged, transcendental structures of subjectivity. In the *Cartesian Meditations* (1931), Husserl writes of a 'principle of pure "intuition" or evidence' pertaining to 'what we find actually given (and, at first, quite immediately) in the field of the *ego cogito*' (Husserl 1960: 24/64). This thesis on the 'givenness' of the world in consciousness is later reworked by Heidegger, who, initiating the interrogation of giving subsequently assumed by Derrida, criticises the residual 'anthropologism', the residual privileging of consciousness in Husserl. Heidegger differentiates ontologically between that which is recognised as given and that which gives it, positing the necessity of an impersonal event of giving that cannot be grasped simply in terms of what *es gibt* (TB, 21–2/22). For Derrida, however, Heidegger – like Mauss – is still too committed to representation, still too wedded, in spite of himself, to the idea of a gift that can be conceived and identified independently of those who would receive it. Through its residual commitment to thinking the gift in terms of an essentialised presence-to-self, phenomenology continues to endorse the idea of an authentic, legitimate recipient. This is particularly problematic when it comes to Heidegger's politics, where his conviction that Germany stands in a philosophically privileged relationship to Ancient Greece, as the *proper* heir, the recipient of Greek *Heimischwerden*, gets caught in a drift toward Nazism (see, for example, IM 40, 213/208 [152]). Contemporary phenomenology moves away from this, notably in the case of Jean-Luc Marion, who concurs with Derrida that the gift cannot be received, in the sense of being recognised as such (even if it can be experienced). But one might wonder in passing whether there is not still a problem of politics in Marion; whether, like Heidegger, Marion does not see the wholly benign, unpoisonous gift as short-circuiting politics, giving itself to philosophical or phenomenological analysis in a way that sublates any politics of gift and receipt.

Marcel Mauss was deeply suspicious of Heidegger, dismissing him, in a letter to Roger Caillois, as 'a Bergsonian held back by Hitlerism, legitimating a Hitlerism infatuated with irrationalism' (Fournier 2006: 327/710; Fournier 1990: 87). An unswerving proponent of the modern ideals of rationality, humanism and positivism, he was equally

suspicious of the anti-Enlightenment counterculture, 'this sort of absolute irrationalism' that a number of his more experimental students,
most notably Caillois and Michel Leiris, under the influence of Georges
Bataille, took to be the natural progression of his work (2006: 327/710;
1990: 87). For Derrida, however, the point is that in seeking to separate
out his own legacy from that of Heidegger, Mauss is ultimately complicit in the same kind of essentialist, politically dubious thinking of the
gift in terms of self-presence, the inheritance of which would amount to
a mimetic repetition of the same. We see this, on one hand, in terms of
Mauss's nostalgic claim that 'we can and must return to archaic society
and to elements in it [*on peut et on doit revenir à de l'archaïque <sic.>*]'
(G, 69/263); on the other, in his reliance on a concept of homecoming
not dissimilar to that of Heidegger. To the disappointment of many
of his legatees, including Lévi-Strauss (IMM, 47–8/xxxvii), the Maori
ethnographer, Firth (1959: 419), and the anti-Lévi-Straussian political
philosopher, Claude Lefort, who describes the move as 'incomprehen-
sible' (1978: 30), Mauss's rationalism appears to desert him once he
draws on the Maori myth of the *hau*, 'the spirit of the thing [*l'esprit des
choses*]', to explain the intrinsic power of the gift to compel response.
'Ultimately, it is the *hau* that wishes to return to its birthplace, to the
sanctuary of the forest and the clan, and to the owner' (G, 12/160).
An early essay by René Major (reprinted in Major 2001) attempts a
Derridean reading of this myth, anticipating Derrida's retention of the
Maussian language of the ghost. Derrida, however, rejects the central
tenet of the *hau*, the idea of centripetal homecoming (GT, 40–3/58–60).
Read through Derrida, the spectres of Mauss are defined not by homecoming and rhythm but by rupture and the refusal of economy, the
gift's escape from the law of the place of identity. The gift does not
return economically to itself, but refuses conflation with presence by
always returning to and from the future. Its legacy is not programmed
in advance, predetermined in its destiny by the intrinsic qualities of the
bequest, but rather defined by the absence and moreover the impossibility of teleology.

    What compels us to respond to Mauss's offering is not the self-iden-
tity of the work, not the ease with which, as Sahlins implies, we are able
to recognise it as a gift, but the *aporia* of the gift, the impossibility of
recognising it as such, the impossibility of disentangling its essence from
a whole host of other legacies and spectres. Rather than a straightforward affirmation of the *Essai*'s self-evidence, the question of Mauss's
legacy becomes caught up in a problematic of inheritance that serves
to undermine it, refusing it conceptualisation in terms of the gift and
receipt of a self-identical, essentially recognisable object. The gift and

the spectre alike come to exist amidst the instability, the groundlessness of a bequest that is constituted discontinuously, in the act of a repetition that breaks with the original. In an interview conducted to coincide with the publication of *Spectres de Marx* (1993), Derrida remarks that: 'To inherit is not essentially *to receive* something, a *given* that one could then *have*. To inherit is to select, to sort, to highlight, to reactivate' (Derrida 2002: 110–11; see also PC, 299/320, on 'The Legacy of Freud'). Governed by the *aporia*, by the impossibility of receiving, that is, of identifying the gift we supposedly receive, to inherit is rather to respond to and reanimate a life in excess of any phenomenal object, to participate in a repetition of difference that exceeds mimesis. Through the continual renegotiation of what it is of the gift that lives on, we unleash a life that resists confinement to finitude, to a finite proper name, such as Mauss. In attempting to name the gift, in attempting to select, to *decide*, what of Mauss's gift survives, however, we are also called upon to give death, to sacrifice one (reading of) Mauss in order that another might live on beyond and as a result of this sacrifice.

> Life – being-alive – is perhaps ultimately defined by this tension internal to a heritage, by this reinterpretation of what is given in the gift, and even what is given in filiation. This reaffirmation, which both resembles and interrupts, resembles (at least) an election, a selection, a decision. (Derrida and Roudinesco 2004: 4–5/16 [TM])

It is through the decision that life is conferred and restored that the proper name of the author gives way to a multiplicity of spectral incarnations. The citation describes deconstruction as a strategy that, rather than 'kill off' its chosen texts and authors, seeks to reanimate them, to disclose how they live on, suspended between life and death by a sacrifice that can never be definitive.

In emphasising the necessity of decision, the citation also serves to disclose the political dimension that deconstruction, despite Derrida's assertions to the contrary (R, 39/64), has so often been accused of eliding. In place of inheritance as a private matter, a concern for the familial *oikos*, it becomes a question of political, *an*economic exchange. There is a politics of inheritance in which giver, receiver and gift cannot be rigidly delimited but rather contaminate one another, rendering lines of filiation indistinct, overflowing any notion of an *oikos* that would precede the public sphere of the political. In place of the 'economic', 'marketised' model of politics as a form of exchange or 'competitive struggle' between pre-given individuals (Mouffe 2005: 13; Schumpeter 1976: 269), we encounter politics in an event that – like the gift – eludes identification, moreover as the response to this elusiveness: the tension between a gift that continually takes flight and the decision that attempts to name it, to delimit the sacred site of that which refuses recognition. To speak of a politics of the gift is therefore to speak of a politics of decision, a decision about what it is that withdraws from experience. At least one critic has queried the extent to which this can really be considered political, whether 'a description of deconstruction as a viable analysis of the political' would not rely upon 'deconstruction taking up a definable position within political discourse' (Williams 2001: 132): in other words, consenting to work within a field whose terms are already defined, contributing to existing debates within political philosophy, rather than seeking to redefine the relation between philosophy and politics through a questioning of what politics *is*.

The present work is an attempt to reject this concern, by beginning the (impossible) task of naming in what politics would consist once, following Derrida following Mauss, we refuse to reduce it to a description of economic relations and seek instead to discern the relationalities, the *an*economic exchanges by virtue of which the political comes into existence.

TO RETURN (ETERNALLY) TO THE GIFT

In *The Delirium of Praise*, her formidable study on the intellectual relationships of Bataille, Klossowski and Deleuze, amongst others, Eleanor Kaufman writes of 'the peculiarities of a twentieth-century French context' that gives rise to a philosophical moment, an 'atopic space' of aneconomic exchange that 'certain historicizing impulses not only would not do justice to, but might not even notice as existing at all' (Kaufman 2001: 6). Kaufman argues that the contingent, historical relationships between various figures in and around poststructuralism contribute to a fundamental change in the way we think about the nature of intellectual exchange. This account of an idea that participates in, yet is irreducible to, the history from which it develops is strongly prefigured by Deleuze, who, in *What Is Philosophy?* (1991), differentiates between scientific descriptions of actual 'states of affairs [*états de choses*]' and the philosophical project of extracting from the sciences in order to create concepts that stand in for the impossibility of experience (WIP, 21–2/26–7). This creation presupposes scientific changes, but crucially also goes beyond science. To create a concept is to *repeat* the event by creating a language adequate to the expression of that which refuses representation, a language that gives consistency to experience beyond the point at which subjectivity begins to unravel.

One can discern in the philosophical legacy of Mauss the repetition of a concept of the gift that derives from and yet cannot be reduced to either anthropological or phenomenological accounts. Following Kaufman, the aim of the present work is not to give a history of ideas, however, even if such a history is on occasion inevitably offered. Nor is it to produce Lacanian, Deleuzian or Nancian readings of (what Mauss calls) the gift economy, though these too may creep in on occasion. Rather, reading the gift through Derrida as that which refuses experience, the project is to extract a concept of the gift as event, as a Deleuzian 'line of flight' or becoming, freed from both its anthropological confinement to a particular moment in space and time, and from the constraints of subjective representation, and to ascertain how the deployment of this concept generates a new paradigm of postmodern, poststructuralist political economy. The tracing of this concept is organised around a series of repetitions, which, while in a sense beginning with Mauss and Maussian problematics, move increasingly further away from the conclusions of *The Gift*, notably from the relatively conventional political morality Mauss espouses. Mauss believed the potential of his analyses lay in their contribution to a reassessment of the welfare state (G, 67–70/261–4), in a promotion of the social values of obligation and reciprocation. His derivation of moral conclusions about the denigration of reciprocity in twentieth-century Western society has received considerable criticism, though. As Mary Douglas observes, in the foreword to *The Gift*'s English translation:

> his own attempt to use the theory of the gift to underpin social democracy is very weak. Social security and health insurance are an expression of solidarity, to be sure, but so are lots of other things, and there the likeness ends. (G, xv)

The difficulties of transposition have not deterred Hénaff, who traces the politics of symbolic recognition in ceremonial giving through modern institutions of law and government embodying a *'public procedure of reciprocal recognition between human groups'* (2009: 227). Read through Derrida and other poststructuralists, however, Mauss's legacy is marked by a far broader interrogation of these very institutions and of the liberal democratic politics of modernity as a whole.

Despite the claims of Jürgen Habermas, amongst others, this invocation of poststructuralism should emphatically *not* be taken to connote an irresponsible politics of relativism guided by 'normative intuitions' rather than philosophical rigour. Nor should it be thought to descend from a critique of reason that shows 'reckless disregard for its own foundations' (Habermas 1987: 337/391). As James Williams has recently argued, poststructuralism is not inherently *'against'* anything – except perhaps the naïve claims to certainty that would lead us to take something for granted, its self-evidence immunising it from critique (Williams 2005: 6). By challenging the rigour of ontology and the sup-posed self-evidence of modern ideals, so-called poststructuralists have not sought to collapse the tradition that bequeathed them, but rather to create the conditions for its reaffirmation through an interrogation of its limits. Poststructuralism implies a 'politics of the left', Williams argues, only in so far as it demands that ideas be subject to scrutiny, re-evaluated, exposed to the new (2005: 4–6). One might say, only in so far as it subjects thought to trial by an eternal return of the new and different.

The choice of a language of eternal return is not incidental, here. Central to the question of the poststructuralist politics of reaffirmation is the French legacy of Friedrich Nietzsche, whose scathing critique of the abstract, idealised thought of modernity broadly lent itself to – and for one commentator even 'anticipated' – the (admittedly theoretical) empiricism of Maussian anthropology (Schrift 1995: 87). Jacques Le Rider has noted how, between the 1920s and 1960s, the reception of Nietzsche in France is marked by 'a reversal of political perspectives', the increasingly radical deployment of Nietzsche, reappropriated from the ideologues of Nazism by, amongst others, Georges Bataille and Pierre Klossowski – who were also amongst the first readers of Mauss (Le Rider 1999: 181). The alignment of Nietzsche with the gift would be a central theme of this radicalisation. The philosopher and intel-lectual historian, Alan D. Schrift, has observed how for Bataille, in particular, Nietzsche's critique of debt, in the *Genealogy of Morality*, and valorisation of the 'gift-giving virtue [*schenkende Tugend*]' in *Thus Spoke Zarathustra* 'place him firmly on the side of *those who give*' (Z, 100–2/93; Schrift 1995, citing HES, 370/404). Le Rider also points to an exegetical shift of emphasis towards Nietzsche's idea of eternal return which, decoupled from a more problematic concept of the will to power and reaffirmed as a will to *chance*, lent itself to a renewed thinking of politics in terms of time. Reworked by poststructuralist phi-losophers as an ontology of the non-linear temporality of the event, the thought of eternal return provides an alternative to the then dominant anthropocentrism of thinking time as the linear progression of human history (1999: 172–4). The argument is put most succinctly by Michel Foucault, who posits Nietzsche's eternal return as another name for the death of man, hence the basis for the new *épistémè* – the 'fold in our knowledge' – that would supersede the framing of philosophy by 'Anthropology' and 'mark the threshold beyond which contemporary philosophy can begin to think again. [. . .] If the discovery of Return is indeed the end of philosophy, then the end of man is the return to the beginning of philosophy' (OT, 342/353). The eternal return becomes synonymous with the gift both as a name for the intensity that breaks down the accepted identity of the human, and as the promise of something (a future, the *Übermensch*) in excess of the *homo economicus*. Through its implication in a selective process of interrogation and affirmation, the politics of the gift is inextricable from poststructuralist readings of Nietzsche's eternal return, the thought experiment in which identity is continually ungrounded through the challenge to affirm repetition. Seeking to confront the nihilism of living in anticipation of an afterlife, Nietzsche defies us to contemplate life as an interminable repetition of the same:

> This life as you now live it and have lived it, you will have to live once more and innumerable times more; and there will be nothing new in it, but every pain and every joy and every sigh and everything unutterably small or great in your life will have to return to you, all in the same succession and sequence. (GS, 273/250, [§341])

For Nietzsche, those unable to bear the prospect of finitude without redemption simply collapse under 'das grösste Schwergewicht', the utmost weight of the thought experiment, thus filtering out the weak from the strong. For his *héritiers*, as we shall see, this process of selection becomes the mark of the repetition of difference, of a singularity that cannot be absorbed without remainder into the economic structures of consciousness (Klossowski 1963: 206–8). The recognition of the limits of consciousness gives rise to the idea of a life of the gift beyond man, beyond the limit of corporeality. The gift exists as an irreducible, spectral remainder that exceeds any attempt to delimit it as a phenomenologically appropriable object. More than just an affirmation of the past, the inheritance of *The Gift* becomes an affirmation of the future, of the inexperientiable, unpredictable life of a gift whose legacy consists in its undecidability, multiplicity and spectrality.

In excess of any 'legitimate', or what Johnson has called 'paradigmatic' reading of Mauss (Johnson 1996: 314), there is a life of the gift that survives the eternal return, lives on because it escapes determination by the proper name, Mauss. If every attempt to engage with Mauss is a repetition of Mauss's initial engagement, the repetition is not one of sameness, but of a minimal difference that simultaneously preserves and transforms its meaning. Mauss's work is no longer a gift because it conforms to his own description thereof, but precisely because it generates a concept of the gift that resists such a description. It succeeds because it fails. As Derrida writes in his own study of Mauss, *Given Time* (1991): 'One could go so far as to say that a work as monumental as Marcel Mauss's *The Gift* speaks of everything but the gift' (GT, 24/39). The tone of the statement reverberates across the eighty years that have passed since the *Essai*'s 1923–4 publication.

The anthropologist, Maurice Godelier, has already written extensively on 'the legacy of Mauss', tracing the history of the development of Maussian ideas from the *Essai* to the present, through a broad discussion of recent work in sociology and anthropology (Godelier 1999: 10/17). Yet, like Sahlins, Godelier continues to work from within a traditional concept of inheritance. This exclusive emphasis on anthropology prevents him from extending the legacy to account for Mauss's bastard progeny, to emphasise his influence on other disciplines, not least philosophy, which he helped to liberate from the strictures of 'Anthropology'. According to Schrift, writing in his collection, *The Logic of the Gift* (1997), in addition to Mauss's incalculable, even founding, contribution to the fledgling disciplines of ethnology and anthropology, 'the theme of the gift [. . .] can be located at the centre of current discussions of deconstruction, gender, ethics, philosophy [. . .] and economics.' It is, furthermore, 'one of the primary focal points at which contemporary disciplinary and interdisciplinary discourses connect' (Schrift 1997: 3). While acknowledging more distant origins in Nietzsche and phenomenology, Schrift initially suggests the cause of the recent upsurge in interest to reside in a combination of Derrida's engagement and the growth of feminist discourses within the social sciences (1997: 1–3). Particularly significant in this respect are the Algerian writer and philosopher, Hélène Cixous, and the Belgian psychoanalyst, Luce Irigaray, whose work sets out to rethink society around a feminine economy, in contrast to the phallocentrism of traditional political economy. A point of departure for both is the positive revalorisation of a long-standing identification, observed ethnographically by Claude Lévi-Strauss of woman as gift, an object of exchange who does not herself participate in exchange (Lévi-Strauss 1969: 65/76). Cixous differentiates between a 'masculine' economy of possession, of the return of the 'Selfsame [*Propre*]', and a 'feminine' economy of giving, which consists in the return of difference. In a passage recalling the ethos of withstanding eternal return, she writes: 'It all happens as if man were more directly threatened in his being by the nonselfsame [*non-propre*] than woman' (Cixous 1996: 87/117). Where man behaves in line with Mauss, treating giving as a kind of investment, a 'gift-that-takes' and brings in a 'return [*revenu*]', linked to the imposition of obligation, the accretion of status and profit, woman, by contrast, 'gives for [*donne* pour]', without trying to ' "recover her expenses [*rentrer dans ses frais*]" '. She is not able to return to herself, never settling down, pouring out, going everywhere to the other' (1996: 87/117–18). The distinction is repeated by Irigaray, who appeals to woman not to let herself be reduced to the commodity, to a work of man's labour, whose circulation furnishes the basis of society. She argues that in excess of 'the reduction of her sensory, corporeal and material qualities to an abstract exchange-value, moreover the reduction of the whole sensory world to the concrete practical activity of men' (Irigaray 1985: 184/180 [TM]), there is a feminine nature that cannot be appropriated, and whose potential threat man attempts to control by mediating woman's access to herself. She identifies this nature with a utopia, 'where nature could expend itself without exhaustion; could be exchanged without labour; could give itself – beyond the reach of masculine transactions – for nothing; free pleasures, well-being without pain, enjoyment [*jouissance*] without possession' (1985: 197/193 [TM]).

This notion of containing the gift's subversive potential also comes into play in the reception of Mauss. Drawing on Schrift's more recent work on the organisational set-up of post-war French academia, one might point to institutional and broader social factors to understand how Mauss's *Essai* has become a philosophical *point de repère*, a gift to which, at some point, almost every major French philosopher and theorist would want to be seen to respond. Derrida's claim regarding the essential undecidability of the gift is illustrated by this reception among philosophers, who were undoubtedly threatened, but also freed, by Mauss's assault on the Cartesian tradition: more specifically by what his intervention spelled for the security of philosophy atop the hierarchy of academia. The discipline had long occupied a position of seniority, even superiority, in the institutions of French academia (see, for example, Fournier 2006: 113–14/240–1), but, by the end of the Third Republic, this position was being assailed by a combination of political, epistemological and institutional factors (2006: 260–2/559–61; Schrift 2006: 40–3). Foucault's analysis of the rise of the human sciences offers a useful broader backdrop for what Schrift will portray as a 'crisis' in twentieth-century French philosophy. *The Order of Things* paints an image of philosophy as having arrived, by the end of the nineteenth century, at the limit point of the then dominant paradigm, or *epistémè*, of Anthropology. Philosophy-as-Anthropology, which is to say, philosophy construed, increasingly pejoratively, as an abstract 'analytic of man', would be challenged by a combination of Nietzsche and the positivism of the human sciences, which called into question the apriority of the transcendental subject. The growth of new disciplines, including ethnology and psychoanalysis, generated the crystallisation of a new *epistémè* around the 'death of man', which would liberate philosophers to fill 'the void left by man's disappearance' through a reworking of eternal return as an ontological description of the event of existence giving itself (OT, 342/353). But this process was not without complications. Under threat of being eclipsed by the new disciplines, philosophy emerged battered and bruised from wars that it had not only failed to prevent, but in which, through such politically dubious figures as misappropriated Nietzsche and the Nazi-sympathising Schmitt and Heidegger, it had also, moreover, arguably been complicit. Philosophers could thus hardly ignore the challenge that Mauss posed, both in his own right and as the figurehead, post-Durkheim, of *la sociologie française*, but nor were they willing to accept him without a fight, without reasserting the (ontological) priority of philosophy over anthropology. The evidence of this is borne out in a series of broadly philosophical attempts to renegotiate the gift, to incorporate it within philosophical and psychoanalytic traditions of thinking about giving that both echo and supersede the findings of Mauss. It has been suggested by Gasché that Mauss, too, was ill-prepared for the impact of his work. On the verge of a thinking through which 'Western thought would be thrown back, for once at least, onto itself and would remain alone with its wretchedness', it is as if he pulled back from the ontological implications of his discoveries, fearful of what they would entail for the project of modernity he was not yet ready to abandon (Gasché 1997: 102–3/73).

An anthropologist running up against the limits of 'Anthropology', Mauss thus occupies a liminal position, the site of an undecidable line separating the apogee from the zenith of the modern project. If contemporary French philosophy is defined by the critique of the subject, then Mauss not only anticipates but is exemplary of its subsequent trajectory. The essay on *The Gift* becomes a battlefield for the future of the subject of philosophy – in both senses of the term: the site of an encounter between the insurgent anti-humanism of Lévi-Strauss and the last stand of the existentialist-humanists, Sartre and Lefort; between the scientific sociology and psychoanalysis of the structuralists and the more avowedly experimental *sociologie sacrée* of Bataille and Klossowski; between the Deleuzian gift of eternal return and the Badiousian politics of grace; between the *ethical* gift of Levinas and Nancy's unrepentant ontology of an offering that abandons us to being political.[1] In sociology, Jean Baudrillard's critique of the meaningless

---

1. See, in the order in which they are referred to above, Lévi-Strauss's *Savage Mind* (1966: 245–58/292–305); Sartre's posthumously published *Notebooks for an Ethics* (1992: 373–8/387–91); Lefort's *Les Formes de l'histoire* (1978: 21–4); Merleau-

hyper-reality of symbolic exchange develops out of an early reading of gift economics in which he asserts the need to 'play Mauss against Mauss' (1993: 1/8), while Pierre Klossowski's description of the exiled Walter Benjamin as an 'assiduous auditor' of the Collège de Sociologie (cited in Hollier 1988: 389/586) means that further links present themselves between Mauss and the Frankfurt School, though the potential influence has downplayed by one commentator with expertise in both areas (Jarvis 1998: 86; see also Jarvis 1999).

The effect of Mauss's influence and the growing interest in gift theory is also tangible in the English-speaking world, where Lewis Hyde's Mauss-inspired bestseller, *The Gift*, has left a lasting and public contribution to the history of art, despite frequent criticisms of its overly romantic theorisation of giving (Hyde 1983: xii-iii; Osteen 2002: 28). Elsewhere, in the wake of the aforementioned Cixous and Irigaray, an extensive literature has developed around the exploration of the relationship between giving and corporeality. What Judith Still has called 'feminine economies' and Rosalyn Diprose 'corporeal generosity' merits a more sustained discussion than can be offered here; as does Lisa Guenther's *The Gift of the Other* (see, in particular, Still 1997: 13–24; Diprose 2002; Guenther 2006: 53–4). Their emphasis on the body as the site of giving – and Diprose's suggestion that there is a politics of non-linear, non-volitional, corporeal exchange, in particular (2002: 48) – presents the prospect of a dialogue with Jean-Luc Nancy, whose reworking of giving in terms of the passive exposure of finite bodies is discussed in Chapter 3.

The proliferation of different and even incommensurable concerns is also reflected in a number of recent edited collections, notably the aforementioned *Logic of the Gift* (Schrift 1997) and Mark Osteen's *The Question of the Gift* (Osteen 2002). Both volumes capture the explosion of interest generated by the intersection of anthropology with contemporary philosophical and theoretical approaches. Schrift's brings together, from the most substantial interventions in philosophy, sociology and anthropology, material suggestive of a coalescence of modern and postmodern thought around the gift. He stops short,

Ponty's essay on Mauss in *Signes* (1964: 114–16/143–6); and Lacan's comments on Mauss in the *Écrits* (E, 223/269). The more experimental, Bataillean and Klossowskian, notions of 'sacred sociology' and giving are outlined in Hollier (1986: 11/34) and Klossowski's novelistic trilogy, *Les Lois de l'hospitalité* (1997: 55–8). For Deleuze and Badiou, respectively, see the former's (DR, 1/7; LS, 328/334; AŒ, 207/224) and the latter's comments on grace (2000, 97/142–3; 2003, 65/69); for Levinas, see 1991 (168–77/182–92); and for Nancy, EF (73/99) and FT (237–8/185–6).

though, of suggesting any convergence around a unified theory of giving. Osteen's collection is deliberately more varied and interdisciplinary, insisting on the prematurity of any attempt to reconcile empirical practice with what the editor (not always accurately) perceives as the lacunae of French theory. According to Osteen, if gift theory is to avoid the 'trite polarities' of idealised generosity and the utilitarian logic of self-interest, 'the Scylla of sentimentality and the Charybdis of economism' respectively (2002: 35), then it must, for the time being at least, renounce its Mausso-Lévi-Straussian pretensions to offer a totalising theory of social relations. The spirit of the gift, of Mauss's legacy, should be identified less with a romanticised notion of receipt than with an acceptance of the 'risk and danger' that the gift's poisonousness poses to established disciplinary boundaries (2002: 35). This view contrasts with that of those identifying themselves more explicitly as Mauss's *héritiers*, Jacques Godbout and Alain Caillé, associated with the *revue du MAUSS* ('Mouvement Anti-Utilitariste en Sciences Sociales), who sound a note of caution against the current vogue for 'epistemological' (theoretical) sociology and argue that Mauss's greatest contribution continues to be his 'renewal of economic sociology' and empirical social science (Godbout and Caillé 1998: viii–x). The caution hints at the complexity, even the opacity, of Mauss's philosophical heritage.

REPETITIONS OF DIFFERENCE

The legacy and spectres of Mauss are intertwined with those of Hegel, Nietzsche, Freud and phenomenology, amongst others, but it is possible to trace the process of this contamination, the unfurling of the gift as concept through both its anthropological and phenomenological lineages, and its culmination in a new understanding of politics. Propaedeutically, a distinction needs to be made between those, in the first instance, who take their lead directly from Mauss and those who, though working primarily from within phenomenology, find themselves framed or implicitly informed by the crisis in philosophy to which Mauss both contributed and responded. This book is accordingly split roughly into two halves, the second of which looks at the defence of philosophy against the perceived threat of anthropology: in particular at how philosophers – Martin Heidegger and Jean-Luc Nancy – attempt to overturn the framing of philosophy by anthropology through a purely philosophical conceptualisation of politics. The first half, by contrast, traces the more explicit legacy of Mauss through his 'legitimate' and 'illegitimate' heirs, the structural anthropologist,

Claude Lévi-Strauss, and the writer of heterology, Georges Bataille. Both men stood outside the established institutions of French philosophy and, despite their differences, contributed substantially to the intellectual development of the psychoanalyst Jacques Lacan. Lacan's influence in turn paved the way for Deleuze and the latter's radical reconceptualisation of the relationship between philosophy and the human sciences. Between them, these three would give rise to a legacy that incorporates at least three major philosophical events, each one of which directly draws on *The Gift* to renegotiate the relation between philosophy and its other.

In terms of its recognisability and broader intellectual impact, the first major event in the post-Maussian history of Mauss arrives with the structuralism of Claude Lévi-Strauss. Driven by the desire for a 'progressive mathematisation' of the social sciences (IMM, 43/xxxvi), Lévi-Strauss shared Mauss's commitment to the project of transforming philosophy into a more rigorous anthropology, and receives the latter's blessing as 'the hope of French Americanism', one who would 'professionalize' the Durkheimian tradition as an American-style empirical social science (Mauss, in Fournier 2006: 300/648). Lévi-Strauss's fundamental move was to raise Mauss's 'total social fact', the all-encompassing culture of gift exchange, to the level of an *a priori* synthesis of society in which the gift is a mere subjective misperception of an unconscious process of structurally guaranteed symbolic exchange. Mauss's counter-legacy, by contrast, is defined by the refusal to identify the gift with exchange, an insistence on the gift's singularity, inexchangeability. At the other pole from Lévi-Strauss's extreme modernity, we find Georges Bataille and his avowedly secretive forum for sacrifice, Acéphale, and the loosely associated Collège de Sociologie, convened between 1936 and 1939, and attended, amongst others, by Alexandre Kojève, the Russian *émigré* famous for introducing Hegel to France through an 'anthropologisation' of *The Phenomenology of Spirit* (IRH, 6–8/12–14). Both within the Collège and in his later, sole-authored writings, Bataille invokes themes from Nietzsche and Freud in a critique of the Hegelianism of Kojève and, subsequently, structuralism. Above all, he rejects the Hegelo-Kojevian diagnosis that we have reached the end of History, 'the end of human Time or History [*la fin du Temps humain ou de l'Histoire*]' (IRH, 159n/435n). The modern Hegelian tradition, with its affirmation of nation-state theodicy, completely overlooks a field of politics and experience that cannot be conceived within the terms of the phenomenological self-presence yielded by dialectics. Bataille articulates this excluded horizon of experience in terms of a 'general economy' of the exuberant giving of life, which cannot be reduced to the 'restricted economy' of (capitalist) exchange between sovereign institutions and individuals. He defines the latter's exclusion of the former as the characteristic trait of modern politics (HES, 34/41). Bataille thus opens the way for a third event in Mauss's *differantial* legacy. Poststructuralism ceases to depend upon a direct engagement with Mauss but can broadly be seen as the site of a series of encounters between the *exchangist*, structuralist Mauss of Lévi-Strauss and the Nietzschean, aneconomic Mauss of Bataille. In spite of Slavoj Žižek's (primarily political, oppositional) insistence that the 'rationalist', 'modern' Jacques Lacan should *not* be thought poststructuralist (Žižek 1989: 7), the focus of Chapter 1, Lacanian psychoanalysis, is arguably the most explicit example of this, counting amongst its multiple influences close personal engagements with Lévi-Strauss and Bataille. The effects of this are borne out in Lacan's theorisation of multiple strata of giving, corresponding to the imaginary, symbolic and real registers of his pre-ontology of the unconscious.

The equation of gift and event is central to Derrida's reading of the gift. In one of his earliest conference papers, now recognised as one of the first important critiques of structuralism, 'Structure, Sign and Play in the Discourse of the Human Sciences', Derrida returns to Lévi-Strauss's hugely influential introduction to Mauss and, in the presence of Lacan, takes Lévi-Strauss to task for neglecting 'the structurality of structure'. He pays particular attention to the idea of something that 'while governing the structure, escapes structurality' (WD, 352–3/410–11). This raises the question of how the structures that oversee symbolic exchange could be independent from the effects of exchange in a way that would guarantee their supposedly transcendental status. In place of a self-contained, logical totality, traceable to a central origin, or *archè*, Derrida evokes the figures of Freud, Heidegger and Nietzsche, neglected by Lévi-Strauss, to assert the existence of an 'event of rupture' in excess of structure. He argues that Mauss's concept of the *hau*, the 'spirit of things given' supposed to ensure the gift's homecoming, must be susceptible and indeed made possible by a type of repetition that could not be confined to a transcendentally determined path of movement. In other words, it presupposes an *aneconomic* repetition of difference prior to any *economic* repetition of identity. For the gift to be reciprocated, returned to its sender, there would have to be the possibility of its *not* being reciprocated, a flaw in the structure that would function as its condition of (im)possibility. In reducing gift exchange to a synthetic *a priori* structure, in other words, Lévi-Strauss fails to think the unconditionality and spontaneity that would form a constitutive part of any gift. When *Given Time* is reread in light of Derrida's earlier essay, its claim that Mauss 'speaks of everything but the gift' (GT, 24/39) means that, anticipating Lévi-Strauss, Mauss speaks of a structural totality, *le tout*, the total social fact, but neglects the aneconomic 'event of rupture' through which the gift escapes the economic law of identity. In both earlier and later engagements, Derrida concludes in favour of philosophy, against the anthropological attempt to supersede it, by arguing that the structuralist 'step "outside philosophy"' continues to be governed by philosophical presuppositions regarding the nature of man in general, and language in particular (WD, 359/416; GT, 62–70/86–94).

As we shall see in Chapter 2, a similarly, though more sustainedly Nietzschean critique of Lévi-Strauss is staged by Deleuze and Guattari, who argue in *Anti-Oedipus* that 'The great book of modern ethnology is not so much Mauss's *The Gift* as Nietzsche's *On the Genealogy of Morality*. At least, it should be' (AŒ, 207/224). In deploying Nietzsche's conjectural history of exchange to cast doubt on the supposed apriority of social structures, Deleuze and Guattari set about organising a far-reaching rehabilitation of philosophy, reconceptualising it in a way that prevents its usurpation and supersession by anthropology. Their analysis of the archaic gift economy as an attempt to stave off the eternal return of the gift generates an understanding of politics as that which emerges in response to the excessive giving of the event. By emphasising the inappropriability of this giving, Deleuze and Guattari also reject the possibility of successful (Marxist) revolution, the revolutionary reappropriation of a metaphysical foundation, which would allow the grounding of political institutions in philosophy. This has seen them accused, notably by Alain Badiou and Slavoj Žižek (Badiou 2000: 12/22; Žižek 2004: 20), of elucidating a philosophically overdetermined account of the political that reinforces the political structures they set out to criticise. The problem is not merely incidental, but, from Bataille and Heidegger onward, has plagued almost every attempt to politicise the gift, to think politics philosophically, in relation to the event.

With this in mind, Chapters 3 and 4 depart from the explicit legacy of Mauss in order to return, via Heidegger, to the problematic ontology of the political: namely, the question of whether politics admits of ontological description. Chapter 3 begins with an analysis of Heidegger's understanding of the relationship between the gift of the event and politics, which he deems coextensive with anthropology as a technique for the suppression of being in excess of the human. Heidegger's attempt to bypass politics through ontology, to supersede politics through philosophical as opposed to political revolution, famously gets entangled in Nazism, on account of his belief that the institutional politics

of democracy is inadequate to a thinking of the giving of being beyond
the horizons of subjectivity. The recent and relatively unexplored
work of Philippe Lacoue-Labarthe and Jean-Luc Nancy examines the
charge that Heidegger's elision of politics is a necessary by-product of
a philosophy of the gift. Like Heidegger, Lacoue-Labarthe and Nancy
do not engage explicitly with Mauss at any point, but they can be seen
to respond to a problematic he triggers: namely, the question of the
relationship between politics, philosophy and anthropology. Motivated
by a commitment to the legitimacy of the ontological analysis of the
political, and an insistence similar to that of Deleuze and Guattari on
the priority of politics to subjectivity, the irreducibility of politics to a
form of exchange between subjects, the explicit task of their project is
to reassert a non-anthropological philosophy of the political without
repeating Heidegger's dismissal of politics, without treating politics as a
symptom of the anthropology that takes place in the absence, or forgetting, of a philosophy of the event. Both Deleuze and Nancy specifically
differentiate a politics of the event from the calculable transactions
of traditional political economy, regarding the latter as an attempt to
conceal the absent ground by which politics is made possible. They furthermore show how a politics of the gift, through its trenchant critique
of the politics of homecoming and identity, overthrows rather than
legitimates totalitarianism.

It has none the less been argued by Alain Badiou, Peter Hallward
and Simon Critchley, amongst others, that Deleuze and Nancy go
too far in this respect, treating all institutional, organised politics as
inherently contaminated by totalitarianism, collapsing the distinction
between democracy and totalitarianism in a way that idealises their
own, non-institutional concepts of the political. We see this in Deleuze
and Guattari's apparent disdain for democracy, which they regard as
constitutively opposed to the singularity of the event (WIP, 108/104),
and moreover in their affirmation of eternal return as a philosophical
supplement to the insufficiency of institutional politics (WIP, 99/95).
For Alain Badiou, this amounts to a 'profoundly aristocratic' arrogation of politics by philosophy (Badiou 2000: 12/22), the assertion of
philosophy as the solution to politics, which thus implicitly reaffirms
the prospect of theodicy criticised by Bataille. By effectively believing
that ' "All" *is* grace [*"Tout" est grâce*]', Badiou argues, Deleuze, too,
naïvely sublates political struggles in the redemptions of thought (2000:
97/142–3). Staying on the theme of how we *receive*, or respond to, the
offering of the event without thereby sacrificing its singularity, Chapter
4 discusses whether Nancy is similarly hasty in relying on philosophy,
rather than politics, for redemption, on account of a critique of sacri-

fice that forecloses the prospect of meaningful political action. Nancy's work on the political is shot through with a rejection of sacrifice, which, in contradistinction to Bataille, he thinks is inherently predisposed to a totalitarian subordination of difference and inescapably bound to the attempt to appropriate an ontological ground. But his later work on democracy has brought him closer to Derrida, for whom there is no alternative to sacrifice, no possibility of *not* sacrificing the event to representation. Derrida argues that politics *is* this impossibility of escaping the contamination of difference by a logic of identity, the reinscription of the aneconomic gift within a restricted economy of the subject. This is also why politics is irreducibly marked by sacrifice, which seeks to separate out the sacred from the profane, while also affirming the impossibility of theodicy. Sacrifice consists in the making of decisions, in the selection of what can and cannot be named, counted as existing, in a world of compromise that precludes the theodical giving of everything. It is sacrifice that preserves the possibility of democracy – and the gift. By recognising the impossibility of the capture of the gift in actuality, sacrifice is what enables the gift to live on beyond any identifiable instantiation thereof; what enables the eternal return of its promise.

*   *   *

This tension between the gift and its sacrifice becomes the decisive moment in the politics of the gift. As another name for politics, sacrifice becomes the means through which we respond to the offering of the event. But it is destined to fall short of the inappropriable gift it reciprocates, condemning politics to return, eternally.

Is this not the message of von Trier's *America* trilogy, laid bare in the transition between its first two instalments? We see this already at the end of *Dogville*, where becoming-gift is perhaps never as straightforward as was earlier implied. As Dany Nobus has also observed (2007: 25), from the moment of Grace's arrival, the politics of Dogville plays itself out in reaction to the gift, as a question of how best to receive it; whether to try to absorb and integrate it into the community, or rather keep it at a safe distance – maybe even refuse it altogether. Rather than being welcomed as a gift, Grace, an unknown, unidentifiable quantity, is treated progressively worse as an object, a commodity to be circulated through the town, exploited and enjoyed as the townsfolk see fit. The further she descends into the life of the commodity, the more her subjective integrity, her identity and even her humanity are eroded; the closer we come to an unleashing of the intensities that exist in excess of the individuations of subjects; the closer we come to the arrival of a gift so different, so unanticipated, so violent that its recipients are destroyed in the moment of receiving it.

Yet having ceased to be a subject, having been raped, dehumanised, offered up for sacrifice, Grace is reterritorialised as a moralising angel of death in the very moment she could become gift. Moments prior to embarking on a slaughter of the townsfolk, she gives a speech that signals an appropriation of her name, a willingness to bestow herself as poison, to recognise herself as gift. 'If there's any town this world would be better without, this is it,' because the people of Dogville fall short of the gift's purity, have failed to become worthy of its receipt. This totalitarian arrogation of sovereignty, this essentialisation of the gift as something for which one should willingly die, is carried over into the sequel, where it masquerades under the name of democracy. Throughout *Manderlay*, in place of the ingénue at the start of the previous film, Grace now seems only too aware of the promise her name bestows. The subtitle of the film, *A Case of Mistaken Identity*, forewarns us of the perils of imaginary misrecognition, of both attempting to name the gift, identifying oneself with the site of the event, and of seeing tyranny where there is the promise of democracy and democracy where there is only a hypostatised fantasy thereof. With hindsight, perhaps, we can say again that Grace ceases to be the gift in the very moment of recognising herself as such, in believing herself the designated recipient of the slaves' call for redemption. The slaves she emancipates come to resent the groundless anomie of the democracy she bestows on them, unaccustomed to the responsibility it demands in their exercise of sovereignty. When, at the end of the film, they force her to oversee a return to the 'old ways' of slavery, it is revealed that these old ways, too, were designed with the complicity of the slaves themselves, fearful of 'the greatest weight' of the freedom they would otherwise be forced to bear. Yet if the people of *Manderlay* thus show themselves to be unworthy of the event, so too does Grace. Her eventual sacrifice is tragic, in the sense of being programmed from the instant she assumes the role of messiah. Equally, however, it embodies the way sacrifice resacralizes, preserves the integrity of the promise. At the heart of her tragedy is a conflation of the gift with what Grace takes to be democracy, a fixed and inflexible ochlocracy that, with its aestheticised ideals of absolute equality and corporate sovereignty, reveals itself simply inappropriate to the life of the *polis* it represents.

The problem is precisely the belief in the possibility of definitively identifying a spectre of democracy, a gift that, like Grace, ultimately evades capture. Grace is governed by a residual faith in the human, a fantastical concept of a humanity that exists to be emancipated, to be sublimated by a gift for which people will henceforth radiate gratitude. In place of an essential humanity whose emancipation would entail the sublation of political struggle, however, there are only the multiple becomings of a gift that, like Grace, repeatedly takes flight. This flight demands that the gift be repeatedly renegotiated, subjected to the decisions – the sacrifices – entailed by the attempt to name it in an affirmation of eternal return. The findings of von Trier thus repeat those offered by the pursuit of Mauss's spectres, revealing a politics of the gift, of the impossibility of recognition, which gives rise to the repeated attempt to name, to identify, the excessive offering that eludes us, an event that compels and yet refuses our hospitality, by which the gift is destroyed or deferred in the very attempt to receive it.

1. *Speech, Sacrifice and Shit: Three Orders of Giving in the Thought of Jacques Lacan*

Between the publication of the *Essai sur le don* in 1923–4 and its author's death in 1950, Georges Bataille and Claude Lévi-Strauss did more than most to reciprocate the gift of Mauss's legacy. This reciprocation takes place through an extension of the Maussian critique of *homo economicus*; Lévi-Strauss and Bataille alike reject the notion of an ontologically grounded, transcendentally individuated human subjectivity. Simultaneously following and radicalising Mauss, both men regard this subject as nothing more than the product of exchange, but also criticise Mauss for an insufficiently 'general' understanding of exchange as a 'total social fact'. Yet to some extent, their respective treatments could hardly have been more different, signalling what one commentator has called 'a major split in the interpretation of the Maussian gift' (Pefanis 1991: 22). The split, as Pefanis (somewhat reductively) notes, originates in the shifting emphasis between two different instances of the gift, between the *kula*, on one hand, and the *potlatch*, on the other, the circulation and exchange of gifts versus the competition between rivals in which, on occasion, 'one must expend all that one has and keep nothing back' (G, 37/200 [TM]). Lévi-Strauss concentrates on the former to articulate a distinctly 'symbolic' social reality, in which subjectivity is determined extrinsically, intersubjectively, by unconscious structures of language and linguistic exchange that lie outside and in excess of the subject. Bataille broadly corroborates this account of subjectivity, but praises the destructive ritual of the *potlatch* precisely for its intimation of a heterogeneous '*intimacy* of the divine world' in excess of the symbolic order (TR, 44/308). He traces the gift not to culture – language – but to an understanding of *nature* as 'le don d'une énergie exubérante', 'the gift of an exuberant energy', an 'effervescence of life' that cannot be conceptualised within a capitalistic understanding of economic utility (HES, 41/34). Beyond the 'restricted economy' of *homo economicus*, life itself functions in accordance with a more *general*, less anthropocentric, economy, an aneconomy of excess and 'unproductive expenditure [*dépense improductive*]' that 'brings into contradiction [. . .] the entirety of the existence of man' (AS, 73/75). This idea serves as the backdrop for Bataille's fascination with sacrifice, a practice in which he sees the potential to overturn man's bondage to commodified, material things and accede to a hitherto inaccessible position of sovereignty. Through sacrificial giving without return, he argues, it becomes possible to attain a paradoxically impossible, and hence 'sacred', unconscious experience of the effervescence of life that exceeds the subject.

Both Lévi-Strauss and Bataille thus initiate a shift away from thinking the gift as a question of simple empiricity and toward an understanding of the gift as an unconscious, transcendental 'event'. There none the less remain profound differences in the nature of this event, not least with regard to whether the gift is symbolic or heterogeneous to the symbolic order, cultural or natural, economic or *an*economic, which is to say constitutively antagonistic to any overarching law of identity.

A friend and colleague of both men, Jacques Lacan was uniquely positioned to take advantage of and thrive on the tensions between the two. He did not do so uniformly, however. Although a confidant of Bataille from the early 1930s, the trace of the latter's influence does not become apparent until the seminar of 1959–60, on *The Ethics of Psychoanalysis* – in other words, not until after the engagement with Lévi-Strauss, whom Lacan knew only later. As a consequence, though the occasional commentator has recognised the 'constant though implicit presence of Bataille in Lacan's evolving work' (Roudinesco 1997: 136/188), there has until recently been a tendency to privilege the influence of Lévi-Strauss, reading Lacan primarily as a structuralist, a thinker of the gift in terms of the economics of symbolic exchange, to the exclusion of the transgressive, aneconomic gift of Bataille (see, for example, Kurzweil 1996: 146; Pefanis 1991). The oversight is no doubt partly attributable to the almost total absence of Bataille's name in Lacan's published work, the extent of which is atypical even by the standards of a man for whom, on account of there being no such thing as 'symbolic ownership', 'plagiarism does not exist' (SIII, 80/93).

Even less has been said about Lacan's own thinkings on the gift and its relation to the unconscious, which arise as a result of sustained negotiations between Bataille and Lévi-Strauss, not to mention other, most notably Hegelian influences. The aim of this first chapter is to redress this imbalance. As indicated by the use of the plural – thinkings – Lacan's engagement with the gift is often fragmentary and rarely

sustained; it also evolves over time, including a decisive epistemological break that coincides with a turn toward Bataille in the late 1950s.
More importantly, however, the plural points to there being three different, albeit overlapping and often blurred, conceptions of the gift,
pertaining to each of the three registers of Lacan's 'pre-ontology' of the
unconscious (SXI, 29/38): the *symbolic* order of speech and language;
the *imaginary* site of an ego in search of an ontological ground; and the
ungrounding *real* of the libidinal drive.

Expressed simply, the argument to be pursued can be summarised as
follows: Lacan borrows from Lévi-Strauss a theory of the gift as symbolic exchange, while the idea of the gift as a gift of shit, experienced
in the failure of symbolic exchange, emerges from the work of Bataille.
These also correspond to two different conceptions of the unconscious,
first as symbolic, regulative social reality, then as unpredictable excess
of the real. A third tier of imaginary giving emerges from a combination
of Freud and Lévi-Strauss's criticisms of Mauss, but is developed in a
way that might also serve as a critique of Bataille. The symbolic 'gift
of speech [*le don de la parole*]' describes how the subject comes to be
through the exchange of recognition. The imaginary gift – also referred
to as 'the gift of love', 'the gift of what one doesn't have [*le don de ce
qu'on n'a pas*]' (E, 580/691; SVIII, 419) – reflects the fact that speech is
never enough to satisfy what Lacan, following Alexandre Kojève, calls
the 'desire to have his desire recognised' (E, 285/343). This imaginary
gift of what one does not have encompasses the offerings, the sacrifices
one makes in a bid to supplement and guarantee this recognition, which
is exposed as illusory by the gift of the real. The gift of the real pertains
to an experience of the impossible – namely, the impossibility of satis-
fying the desire for recognition; it is also the impossibility of achieving
an experience of intimacy in which sovereignty is regrounded in being.
Arguably *contra* Bataille, Lacan invents the concept of 'extimacy' to
explain how that which is most intimate to the subject also lies irreducibly beyond its grasp (SVII, 139/167). In a move that recalls Bataille's
vividly literary disquisitions on the 'horror of *excreta*' (HES, 53/44),
he elaborates on this as a 'gift of shit [*un cadeau d'une merde*]' (SXI,
268/299), an excremental remainder that lives on after the subject's
fantasy of a metaphysically grounded existence has dissolved.

Taken together, this triplicate understanding of giving radicalises
the critique of *homo economicus* initiated by Mauss and continued by
Lévi-Strauss and Bataille. Initially seen as an expression of the agency of
the subject, the gift becomes an expression of desire's impotence, of its
bondage to an extimate, excremental object. It ceases to be identifiable
as a benign offering and becomes redemptive only in so far as recog-

nised as poison – as that which falls outside and moreover prevents the completion of symbolic exchange. Lacan thus traces the gift's passage from tangible offering to a transcendental structure of intersubjectivity, to an intangible event – a name for life as such – that we recognise only in the ungrounding of privileged subjectivity.

THE CULTURE OF EXCHANGE

A combination of ethnographic fieldwork and an enforced wartime exile in New York meant that the Belgian Lévi-Strauss did not meet Lacan until 1949. By this time, with the recent publication of *The Elementary Structures of Kinship*, also in 1949, he had already set out on the project of 'structural anthropology', a project of returning via Mauss and the linguistics of Saussure and Jakobson, to study the excessive, inexperientiable form of social reality. Lacan's involvement with Bataille had begun much earlier, by at least 1933, when the latter published an article on the *potlatch*, 'The Notion of Expenditure'. Lacan would also play a supporting role in the projects the essay anticipates, notably the Collège de Sociologie, the institution of 'sacred sociology' that embarked on a programme of excess, sacrifice and the recovery of the sacred. Inspired in part by Bataille's encounter with Mauss, the Collège was co-founded with Leiris and Caillois in 1937, and functioned as a more open intellectual forum than the associated but secretive sacrificial cult of Acéphale lurking in its shadows. The Collège and its associated activities proved central to Bataille's work throughout this period, which sought to affirm the 'transgressive', disruptive 'aneconomy' of a gift so excessive that it could not be comprehended within a capitalistic, utilitarian conception of exchange. Like his fellow 'rationalist', Mauss, who remained suspicious of the Collège throughout its brief existence, Lacan was not himself an active participant, though he was present at its inception (Hollier 1986: 4/22) and 'Bataille can be assumed to have kept him scrupulously informed about [the] activities' of Acéphale (Surya 2002: 252/306). By the time Lacan met Lévi-Strauss, he was also engaged to Bataille's soon-to-be ex-wife, Sylvia, and effectively sharing his children. He and Bataille also shared a *maître à penser* in the form of the Russian philosopher, Alexandre Kojève, whose legendary seminar on Hegel's *Phenomenology of Spirit* they attended together as self-confessed 'disciples' (SXVII, 169/197; Stoekl 1995: 89n). Yet despite – or, perhaps, because of – the proximity of this rapport, Lacan rarely shows any sign of Bataille's influence. Even noting his tendency not to acknowledge his intellectual sources, relative to the influences not just of Lévi-Strauss, but also those of

Saussure, Heidegger and Kojève, Bataille seems to have made little
impression on his earlier work. Roudinesco posits rivalry over Sylvia
as the predominant factor in this, with Lacan's refusal to acknowledge
intellectual debts indicative of a desire to establish an existence independent of Bataille (Roudinesco 1997: 136–7/188).

By contrast, when in 1950 Lévi-Strauss's 'Introduction à l'œuvre
de Marcel Mauss' appeared at the opening of Mauss's *Sociologie et
anthropologie*, its impact on Lacan was both decisive and immediate.
The essay, hailed as 'the foundational act of structural analysis' (Major
2001: 170), outlined a theory of the symbolic that would serve as the
point of departure for Lacan's own reading of Mauss. It would also set
the tone for a structuralist reworking of psychoanalysis in which, as
one commentator puts it, 'Mauss and Boas must be accorded virtually
the same status as Freud' (Macey 1988: 155). The resulting output,
most notably the so-called 'Rome Discourse' of 1953 – 'for all practical
purposes the manifesto of the structuralist reinterpretation of Freud'
(Schrift 2006: 149) – is largely responsible for creating the impression
of Lacan as a Lévi-Straussian who thinks the gift only at the level of
symbolic exchange.

CLAUDE LÉVI-STRAUSS

Mauss set out what has been the programme of modern ethnology [. . .];
at the same time, he perceived the most significant consequence of this new
orientation of research, which is the bringing together of ethnology and
psychoanalysis.

(Claude Lévi-Strauss)[1]

Given both the undoubted influence of Mauss on Bataille and the likely
influence of Bataille on Lacan during the 1930s, it would seem probable
that Lacan read Mauss's essay on the gift first-hand. Macey has suggested the presence of Mauss in one of Lacan's earliest works, *Family
Complexes* (*Les Complexes familiaux dans la formation de l'individu*),
published in 1938, though the fleeting mention is not followed through
in a subsequent, more detailed discussion of the text (Macey 1988: 33,
215–16). *Family Complexes* contains a tangible but unreferenced strand
of sociological and anthropological thinking that could have come
from any one of Durkheim, Frazer, Malinowski and Mauss (Lacan
1984: 15–16, 66). Based on the ambiguity of this evidence, it would
seem safer to say that Lacan's encounter with Mauss's *The Gift* is less
independent than mediated by the structuralist anthropology of Claude

1. IMM, 4–5/xi.

Lévi-Strauss. When he engages and refers most repeatedly to the anthropology of gift economics in 'Function and Field of Speech and Language in Psychoanalysis', the so-called 'Rome Discourse' of 1953, it is Lévi-Strauss and Lévi-Strauss's work on Mauss that receive the attention; Mauss himself is not even named. Even the explicit references offer little to suggest a first-hand reading – let alone a Bataillean one. Unconcerned by any potential difference between Mauss and Lévi-Strauss, a slightly earlier conference paper on 'The Functions of Psychoanalysis in Criminology' (1950) has Lacan affirm 'Marcel Mauss's clear formulations, which his recent death has once again brought to our attention: The structures of society are symbolic' (E, 108/132).

Scarcely thematised by Mauss, this emphasis on symbolic structure is *the* central theme of Lévi-Strauss's 'Introduction to the Work of Marcel Mauss'. As Georges Gurvitch's prefatory note to *Sociologie et anthropologie* implies, the essay that opens Mauss's selected writings is less a proleptic *reprise de textes* than a 'highly personal interpretation' (SA, viii), less an introduction than a conclusion. Christopher Johnson suggests that it is an introduction, if anything, not to Mauss but to Lévi-Strauss's own work, from which 'structuralism seems to emerge as the only logical point of conclusion of Mauss's work' (Johnson 2003: 70). Lévi-Strauss sets out from the assumption that Mauss's *œuvre* is incomplete. On the verge of uncovering objective laws that would facilitate the 'progressive mathematisation' of the social sciences, 'enabling the use of deductive reasoning in a domain which seemed subject to the most total arbitrariness' (IMM, 43/xxxvi), Mauss 'halt[ed] at the edge of those immense possibilities', ultimately collapsing back from 'science' into anecdotal empiricism (IMM, 45/xxxvii).

The possibility of understanding archaic society through the universal matrix of the total social fact was nevertheless a decisive breakthrough. Lévi-Strauss argues that Mauss's identification of the threefold obligation to give, to receive and to reciprocate represents a starting point for deciphering the otherness that separates tribal from Western culture, a mechanism for identifying objective social structures that underlie both. He moreover credits Mauss with insights that directly facilitate the discovery of a radical new theory of the unconscious, one that links psychoanalysis to social organisation. Through Mauss, he continues:

> I arrived at the hypothesis that the psychical and the social are complementary. That complementarity is not static [. . .]; it is dynamic and it arises from the fact that the psychical is both at once a simple *element of signification* for a symbolic system which transcends it, and the only *means of verification* of a reality whose manifold aspects can only be grasped as a synthesis from without. (IMM, 28/xxvi–xxvii [TM])

In an essay on 'Symbolic Efficiency', published roughly simultaneously with the introduction to Mauss, Lévi-Strauss asserts that the unconscious exists not simply within and as the property of individual subjects, as 'the ultimate haven of individual peculiarities – the repository of a unique history' theorised by Freud (Lévi-Strauss 1963: 202–3/232). Treating the unconscious as a privatised faculty of the individual mind has the effect of propagating the modern subject whose ontological privileging Freud set out to decentre, because it neglects the way in which subjectivity is situated within culture. For Lévi-Strauss, and Lacan after him, the existence of the unconscious is rather extrinsic, to be located in the symbolic community that intersubjectively creates its members through systems of reciprocal exchange.

The earliest form of this argument is developed in the monolithic study of exogamy undertaken in *The Elementary Structures of Kinship*, where Lévi-Strauss arrives at his hypothesis of the social reality of exchange through a study of the exchange of women – 'the supreme gift' (Lévi-Strauss 1969: 65/76) – in relation to incest taboos. Previous work had sought to show these taboos as the decisive factor in distinguishing between 'nature' and 'culture', with exogamy serving to prevent incest. Lévi-Strauss instigates an inversion, suggesting that the prohibition of incest actually originates as a strategy to ensure exogamy: in other words, to justify the continuity of exchange (1969: 62/72–3). It is this emphasis on exchange and reciprocity as forms of communication with the other that explains Lévi-Strauss's claim to have drawn 'inspiration' from the structural linguistics of Saussure and Roman Jakobson (1969: xxvi/xiv). Although neither language nor the unconscious receives explicit treatment in this earlier work, both concepts subsequently become decisive in the elaboration of a symbolic order that stands in contrast to pre-linguistic 'nature'. This is perhaps seen most clearly in the way Lévi-Strauss asserts the allocations of positions within the symbolic order – for example, the socially significant roles of brother-in-law, and also mother and sister – to be the outcome of the giving away of women for marriage.

From the introduction to Mauss onward, Lévi-Strauss becomes more explicit in attributing the exchange constitutive of culture to extrinsic structures of language existing in excess of individual subjects, as a distinctly collective social reality: 'Like language, the social *is* an autonomous reality The same one, moreover; symbols are more real than what they symbolise, the signifier precedes and determines the signifier' (IMM, 37/xxxii). He elaborates on this point through a reworking of the relation between signifier and signified (*signifiant* and *signifié*), the binary distinction between the 'sound pattern' (*'image acoustique'*)

and the meaning attached to it that operates at the heart of the structuralist linguistics of Ferdinand de Saussure (Saussure 1983: 12/28).
The point he wishes to emphasise is that what produces meaning – the
signifier – is prior to and in excess of the meanings, or signifieds, that it
produces; these meanings, consequently, can never fully express what
it is that expresses them, nor refer exhaustively to underlying social
reality. Similarly, the notion of an individual psyche is not a base unit
of social reality, but merely an attempt to give expression to a reality
that escapes it.

The gist of this is that the unconscious is a network of significations
whose origin, Lévi-Strauss suggests, coincides precisely and abruptly
with that of society and exceeds the comprehension of those it serves
to organise (IMM, 59–60/xlvii). Society is structured by symbols and
a symbolic order that cannot be understood solely at the level of the
culture in which they participate. The unconscious is located in the gap
between the language that the subject assumes as its own and the structures of language that are irreducibly beyond subjective manipulation.
Its presence, or rather absence, becomes tangible in the form of 'discontinuities' within everyday experience (*connaissance*) (IMM, 59–60/
xlvii). Myths arise to fill the deficit of comprehension, collectively
fulfilling the functions Freud once ascribed to the dreams of the individual. They generate meanings that cover over the void of experience
and justify the symbolic practices that societies employ but yet cannot
otherwise explain. For Lévi-Strauss, through an analysis of myth it thus
becomes possible to glean insights into the unconscious structures that
govern social reality.

Lévi-Strauss is able to credit Mauss with the discovery, or rather
near-discovery, of these unconscious structures because he identifies
the symbolic with the law of exchange. Irrespective of this praise, he is
quick to pick up on the ontological ambiguity that pervades Mauss's
account of the gift. For all the *Essai*'s emphasis on the total social fact,
and for all Mauss's coruscating indictment of the artificial narrative of
homo economicus, who 'is not behind us, but lies ahead' (G, 76/272),
at times he still seems uncertain as to whether gift exchange is ontologically prior or posterior to the subjects it organises. In other words, it is
unclear whether the subjectivity of tribal members is a product of and
preconditioned by gift exchange, or whether gifts circulate between
subjects that are already ontologically individuated, superimposing
upon them a 'collective spirit' that would not otherwise exist. Despite
Mauss's quite explicit rejection of the subject in other works, notably in
'The Notion of Person, the Notion of "self"' (see, in particular, Mauss
1979: 87; SA, 359), it is unclear whether he discovers structures that

expose the modern subject as a myth, or whether he merely reads into gift exchange the prospect of diminishing the more deleterious aspects of *homo economicus* from a subject that, stripped of its rampant individualism, is none the less essentially (metaphysically) preserved.

The ambiguity takes us to the heart of Mauss's residual thinking of the subject; it is precisely this residue of which Lévi-Strauss seeks to rid him. Repeating the argument that led him earlier to reject the privileging of incest as the cause of exogamy, he argues that Mauss is guilty of succumbing to 'a mystification, an effect quite often produced in the minds of ethnographers by indigenous people' (IMM, 47/xxxvii), regarding native myths of *mana*, the supposed substance of magic, and *hau*, the 'spirit of things given' that compels the circulation of objects through the gift economy. Focusing too specifically on the minutiae of fragmented experiences and anecdotal accounts of the necessity of giving across different cultures, he failed to see beyond the 'subjective' beliefs through which 'objective' unconscious structures of society are rendered amenable to understanding (IMM, 48–9/xxxix).

> It has to be admitted that, like *hau*, *mana* is no more than the subjective reflection of the need to supply an unperceived totality. Exchange is not a complex edifice built on the obligations of giving, receiving and returning, with the help of some emotional-mystical cement. It is a synthesis immediately given to, and given by, symbolic thought, which in exchange as in any other form of communication, surmounts the contradiction inherent in it; that is the contradiction of perceiving things as elements of dialogue, in respect of self and others simultaneously, and destined by nature to pass from one to the other. (IMM, 58–9/xlvi)

The passage makes clear the priority accorded to the structures whose objectivity is seen as a condition of subjectivity. The gift is not constituted as such in its passage between giver and receiver, but as a form of communication gives expression to a structure that is rather prior, and moreover constitutive of, these subjective positions.

The criticism that Mauss fails to appreciate the totality of the structures underlying the *hau* is extended to apply to the most basic principles of gift exchange. Lévi-Strauss argues that Mauss's holistic account of the irreducibly political, religious, economic and legal institution of giving is undermined by the division of the gift economy into three distinct obligations to give, to receive and to reciprocate. The distinction is, again, 'subjective' in its failure to grasp the totality of exchange as an event, or total social fact, irreducible to separable actions. Taken at this level, exchange ceases to be a mere empirical practice and becomes instead something akin to a (Kantian) transcendental synthesis: 'the concept of reciprocity, providing immediate resolution of the opposition between the self and the other; and the synthetic nature of the gift' (Lévi-Strauss 1963: 22/36). Like the prohibition of incest, the *hau* is not what causes the gift to circulate, but a fragmented, partial expression of this synthesis, a myth that is generated to fill the empty site of the unconscious signifiers that organise exchange. As Maurice Merleau-Ponty eloquently puts it, in an essay titled 'From Mauss to Lévi-Strauss' that signals the increasing importance of structuralism to his primarily phenomenological concerns: 'exchange is not an effect of society, but society itself in act' (Merleau-Ponty 1964: 116/146 [TM]).

Where Mauss erroneously accords agency to the *hau*, or even, ultimately, to subjects endowed with the capacity to give or not to give (hence the need for an *obligation*), Lévi-Strauss ascribes it to signifiers whose operations exceed the subject, famously rejecting the prevailing (Sartrean) humanism of the era (Lévi-Strauss 1966: 245–58; Lévi-Strauss 1966: 245–58/292–305). At the heart of the functioning of this network of signifiers, in the place where Mauss sought to locate the *hau*, he posits a point of 'inadequation' between the signifier and signified, hence a surplus of signification that cannot readily be assigned to a referent. Adopting 'Jakobson's definition of the zero-phoneme term for term' (Dosse 1997: 30/51; see Jakobson 1971: 218–19), Lévi-Strauss articulates the existence of a 'symbol in its pure state [*à l'état pur*]', 'a *zero symbolic value*, that is, a sign marking the necessity of a supplementary symbolic content over and above that which the signified already contains' (IMM, 64/l). The surplus of signification is 'the very condition of the exercise of symbolic thinking', the moment of instability whose inability to be adequately captured in language makes possible the circulation and exchange of other signifiers; a surplus, moreover, whose existence ultimately gives expression to, and *is*, 'the disability of all finite thought' (IMM, 63/xlix).

For a time, up until his engagement with Bataille, Lacan repeats Lévi-Strauss's claims about the intersubjective, symbolic nature of the unconscious, writing soon after his meeting with the anthropologist that: 'The unconscious is the part of discourse qua transindividual that is not at the subject's disposal in re-establishing the continuity of its conscious discourse' (E, 214/258 [TM]). He also famously maintains that: 'the unconscious is structured like a language' (SXI, 149/167; E, 223/269) and affirms the idea of the unconscious agency of the signifier. In the Lacanian repetition of Lévi-Strauss, however, the degree zero of signification is no longer the site of a simple indeterminacy, but of the phallus – a term denoting not the biological organ but, more generally, the complexity of translating human sexuality into the symbolic order of language. Castrated, or incomplete, the subject lacks the satisfaction of desire that would obviate the need for social existence; the fate of desire plays out through the symbolic exchange of language. The phallus stands at the centre of a chain of signifiers, which circulate around it without being able fully to grasp its excess. Like Lévi-Strauss, Lacan argues that incest is not an innate aversion, which is to say, prior to the symbolic, but retroactively introduced as a fantasy that seeks to explain castration. The circulation of signification around the phallus is compelled by the lack that generates this fantasy. As will become apparent over the course of the following sections, one sense of the gift in Lacan is as an imaginary offering that attempts to fill in for the absent phallus. This is not the same as the Lévi-Strauss-inspired 'gift of speech' by which Lacan enjoins us to come to terms with Lacan's influences. Lévi-Strauss's (Kantian) emphasis on the transcendental synthesis of symbolic exchange also passes through a distinctly Hegelian moment, re-emerging in Lacan as an ethics of recognition and a politics of its tragic failure.

HEGEL, KOJÈVE AND THE EARLY LACAN

The World changes *essentially* (and becomes human) through 'exchange'.
(Alexandre Kojève)[2]

Prior to the manifesto of the 'Rome Discourse', Lacan's work had engaged primarily with traditional Freudian and post-Freudian concepts of psychoanalysis, albeit with a clear interest in philosophy, sociology and the human sciences.[3] Most notable amongst these engagements is his work on the mirror stage, a concept 'plagiarised' from Henri Wallon and subsequently reworked into a post-Hegelian theory of subjectivity that would constitute a point of reference for Lacan throughout his career. First undertaken in 1936, as part of a collaborative project with his philosophical mentor, the Hegelian philosopher, Alexandre Kojève, the essay goes through a number of changes before settling in the form in which we know it in the *Écrits*, 'The Mirror Stage as Formative of the *I* Function as Revealed in Psychoanalytic Experience' (Roudinesco 2003: 28). By the time of its eventual publication in 1949, Kojève's name had disappeared from both the title page and the text. The short essay none the less retains strongly discernible traces of Hegel. According to one

---

2. IRHf, 179n.
3. In addition to the aforementioned *Les Complexes familiaux dans la formation de l'individu* (1938), which deals with the Oedipus complex in relation to sociological themes on the family, see also, for example, the brief essay on 'Beyond the "Reality Principle" ', published in the *Écrits*.

commentator, it even 'reads like a commentary on' the *Phenomenology of Spirit*'s Master–Slave dialectic (Williams 2001: 93).

In the subsection of the *Phenomenology of Spirit* (1807) entitled 'Lordship and Bondage', Hegel posits an encounter between two consciousnesses, unknown to one another, each of whom lives in a 'world without alterity' (Roudinesco 2003: 30), as 'a simple being for-itself, identical to itself [*sichselbstgleich*] through the exclusion from itself of everything other' (PS, 113/147 [§187]). Both believe this world to exist as an extension of their respective selves, purely as an object of consumption for the satisfaction of their desires. Their mutual encounter is accordingly unexpected, presenting itself as an obstacle to satisfaction; for the first time, the consciousnesses run up against one another as alterities that refuse to submit to the autarkic conditions of their perceived existence, resisting incorporation into the megalothymic assumption that the object of desire is already contained within the identity of the desirer. They enter into a fight until the brink of death, at which point one pulls back, accepting servitude in exchange for the preservation of life.

The newly confirmed master puts the slave to work on his behalf to maintain the impression that the world exists for his own consumption, but subsequently becomes resentful. Where the slave gets a sense of external validation through recognition of the products of his labour, the master gets no freely offered recognition. He is left unsatisfied by the ongoing attempts to establish himself as the ontological ground of his own existence and succumbs to a sense of alienation that ultimately leads him to surrender his dominion and set the slave free. From the resulting positions of equality, it finally becomes possible for each to acquire the recognition and ontological ground he initially sought. Presaging Lévi-Strauss, Hegel argues that the 'truth' of the subject is found not through unmediated reference to oneself, but through the recognition of the other as the 'truth' of oneself. The humanist, anti-Lévi-Straussian philosopher, Claude Lefort, has argued that this reciprocal, or rather dialectical, exchange of recognition is actually far closer to Mauss than to Lévi-Strauss's reading of Mauss (Lefort 1978: 21–4). The language Hegel uses to describe the act of letting the other go free reinforces the point through its explicit reference to giving, receiving and reciprocating:

> For *first*, through the supersession, it receives back its own self [*erhält es durch das Aufheben sich selbst zurück*], because by superseding *its* otherness, it again becomes equal to itself; but *secondly*, it equally *gives* the other self-consciousness back again to itself [*gibt es das andere Selbstbewußtsein ihm wieder ebenso zurück*], for it saw itself in the other, but supersedes

this being of itself in the other and thus lets the other go free. (PS, 111/146 [§181])

Lefort points to the Hegelianism of Mauss to underline the sovereignty of the subject, and to decouple Mauss from what he perceives as the abstract, idealist Kantianism of Lévi-Strauss (Lefort 1978: 42). Lacan's Lévi-Straussian reworking of Hegel generates the opposite conclusion. Rather than a sign of the sovereignty of the subject, the gift demonstrates the sovereignty of the signifier in excess of the subject and is above all illustrative of the impotence of the subject. That Lefort's position is so far removed from Lacan's is somewhat surprising, given the proximity of both to Kojève. Most distinctive about Kojève's reading of the *Phenomenology* – and something that would seem to place his interests very much in line with those of Mauss and Lévi-Strauss – is his insistence that Hegel's undertaking is a work of *anthropology* (IRH, 6–7/13–14). In more conventional interpretations, Hegel's account of history sees subjects come mutually to recognise one another through a dialectical process whose teleology risks the impression that man is a passive bystander, swept along by an impersonal, theocratic event that has no origin in human agency. Kojève, by contrast, 'reduces being to history, and excludes the dialectic from nature' (Baugh 2003: 26). Placing the emphasis firmly on man's agency *qua* desire, a 'negating negativity [*négativité négatrice*]' (IRH, 12/12), he insists upon a crucial distinction between nature and the subject, which, as Butler notes, 'is created through the experience of desire and is, in this sense, a non-natural self' (Butler 1999: 67). Rather than Hegel's '*Cunning of Reason* [List der Vernunft]' (LPH, 89/49), for Kojève it is man's desire to be recognised as desire, as negativity, that propels history forward. The capacity for the negation belongs not to the master but to the slave, pertaining to the labour through which, 'stimulated by fear of death', he or she transforms nature (IRH, 26/30). In fact, it is labour that enables the slave to work through the trauma of near-death, producing objects – and history – that fill in the void of mortality. 'It is this work and only this work that frees – i.e., humanizes – man (the Slave). On the one hand, this work creates a real objective World, which is a non-natural World, a cultural, historical, human World' (IRH, 26/30–1).

In so far as it is labour that humanises, the humanity of the slave stands in sharp contrast to the animal behaviour of the master who, suppressing the desire for recognition, merely acquiesces in the passivity of unmediated (natural) being. In contradistinction to Lefort, who writes of 'the *denaturing* cogito of gift exchange' (Lefort 1978: 45), Kojève describes this natural being as 'being-given [*être-donné*]', the 'givenness' of the world prior to any mediation by man. This strictly phenomenological, Husserlian, use of the language of giving creates tensions with Kojève's claim to be doing anthropology. Where Mauss and Lévi-Strauss work to prevent the discipline from being conflated with metaphysical anthropocentrism, Kojève espouses a broadly traditional and, by implication, *anti*-structuralist doctrine of subjectivity. Clearly aware of this, Lacan borrows Kojève's ideas on the constructedness of history and human society, while reasserting the Lévi-Straussian account of the gift as social reality.

Man, according to Lacan, is characterised by a '*specific prematurity of birth*' (E, 78/97), a motor vulnerability that sees culture come into being to supplement the meagre provisions of nature. In the aforementioned article on the mirror-stage, Lacan locates the first stage of the entry into culture, or in Kojevian terms, into history, with the infant's encounter with its mirror image, precipitating an internal struggle of identity. Played out in the register of the imaginary, in relation to the imaginary projection of the infant's psychic unity, this initial struggle precedes the passage into the symbolic order of language and recognition. The latter comes into play only later, as the infant seeks to resolve a sense of alienation from the specular image underlying the ego. The mirror-stage thus functions as 'the symbolic matrix in which the *I* is precipitated in a primordial form, prior to being objectified in the dialectic of identification with the other, and before language restores to it, in the universal, its function as subject' (E, 76/94). Lacan describes how the infant discovers its reflected image in the form of a continuous *Gestalt*, or whole. The discovery causes the presubjective *infans* to undergo a transformative process of identification, acquiring, through abstraction, a sense of identity it can retrospectively be seen to have lacked. The experience of physical integrity and unity 'symbolizes the mental permanence of the *I*' (E, 76/95), giving rise to the formation of the ego.

Despite the appearance of unity, the ego is only ideal, a product of the imagination, however; its agency transpires to be a mere fiction. The initially 'jubilant assumption of its specular image' results from the infant's narcissistic investment of libido in its own image. But the investment soon gives way to an internal dialectical struggle, marked by a sense of alienation from the psychic identity imposed on the infant by the appearance of corporeal unity (E, 76/94). The reason for this struggle is that there is a substantial part of the infant that escapes the ego's organisation of consciousness, and which is furthermore kept at bay by the ego's role as a self-defence mechanism against the excessive stimulations of the outside world. The ego thus becomes the 'armour of an alienating identity' (E, 78/97), structured around the *méconnaissance*,

or misrecognition, of the subject with the field of perception-con-
sciousness. The part of itself that it cannot recognise is desire, which
is repressed as unconscious, only to return, symptomatised in violent
behaviour and fantasies like that of *le corps morcelé*, expressing the
attempt to overturn desire's imprisonment by the ego.

The failure of the ego to capture the alterity of unconscious desire is
what pushes the child away from a purely imaginary construction of its
identity, toward the realm of the symbolic, where the (Kojevian) desire
to be recognised by others as desire is made possible by the expression
of desire in language. The direction of imaginary violence toward the
imaginary ego frees desire from its bondage to a fixed object. Its existence will henceforth be subject to the process of symbolic exchange,
determined by the movement of the signifier that enables desire,
through speech, to offer itself to the other and receive in return a recognition of its offering. According to Richard Boothby, who draws on
ideas sketched out in *Seminar X: Anxiety* (1962–3), this transition from
imaginary to symbolic is structured around the logic of sacrifice, which,
by initiating symbolic exchange, brings about 'the capture of the Other
in the network of desire' (SX, 320). Boothby writes: 'in Lacanian terms,
the general function of sacrificial practices is to establish the operation
of the signifier,' before continuing: 'what is accomplished by sacrifice
is less the engagement of any particular exchange than the establishment of the law of exchange itself' (Boothby 2001: 183, 185). The
operation of the signifier refers to the process of symbolisation through
which access to the world becomes mediated by language. At the origin
of this operation is a renunciation that is also an offering. The infant
renounces itself as an object of masturbatory pleasure, renounces the
fantasy of grounding the satisfaction of desire in itself, in order sacri-
ficially to offer up its desire to an other who might thereby reciprocate
and recognise it.

> What is sacrificed is immediate access to the objects of desire. One repeats
> the gesture of giving up in order to rehearse the possibility of regaining in
> a new form [. . .]. Sacrifice thus serves to establish the kingdom of significa-
> tion in which the objects of desire can circulate in an unending economy of
> substitutions. [Sacrifice] functions less simply to offer a gift than to found
> the very being of the gift by establishing the dimension in which the cycle
> of giving and receiving will be enacted. This cycle is consubstantial with
> the operation of the signifier. The promise of the gift is continually called
> up by the shuttle of signification but forever escapes from it. By establish-
> ing the scaffold of binary relations upon which the system of the signifier is
> constructed, while at the same time setting in motion the virtual object with
> which discourse is continually haunted, sacrifice serves to constitute the very
> matrix of desire. The essential sacrifice is less *do ut des* [the term used by

Mauss – GM], I give so that you might give, than *do ut desidero*, I give in
order that I might desire. (2001: 188–9)

Boothby suggests that this renunciation is what is at stake in the
infans's rejection of identification with the mirror image. The imaginary violence inflicted against the *imago* of the ego is a self-sacrifice,
where the infant offers itself up for socialisation, submitting to the law
of the Father in exchange for liberation from its alienating entrapment
by the ego. The gesture of giving up is premised on the possibility of
recovery through the economy of symbolic exchange. In being returned
to itself via the Other, through the other's recognition of the expression of desire in language, the subject hopes to recover the unity of the
abandoned *imago*. Ironically, as we shall see, the process of symbolisation is one that renders any such recovery impossible. Borrowing from
Hegel, Lacan states: 'the word is murder of the Thing' (E, 261–2/318).
Boothby rereads the murder as a *sacrifice* (2001: 185).

With language constituting the sacrifice of the Thing, the mirror
image marks a decisive moment in the transition between imaginary
and symbolic. But it should not be seen as the only instance of the
sacrificial logic through which symbolic order is instantiated. In a
1917 paper on 'On Transformations of Instinct as Exemplified in
Anal Erotism', Sigmund Freud discusses a similarly sacrificial process
of renunciation at the anal stage, in the lavatory training of children.
The infant undergoes socialisation by foregoing the pleasures of unregulated defaecation, offering gifts of excreta to the father in order to
forestall the imagined threat of castration.

> For its faeces are the infant's first gift [*das erste Geschenk*], a part of his
> body which he will 'give up' ['opfert' – also meaning sacrifice] only on per-
> suasion by someone he loves, to whom, indeed, he will make a spontaneous
> gift of it as a token of affection. (Freud 2001b: 130/406–7)

Once again described as a sacrifice (*Opfer*), the gift testifies to the
child's submission to a symbolic law that requires satisfaction to be
sought beyond the confines of the self. Its presentation becomes the
means through which children not yet fully endowed with the capaci-
ties of speech seek to purchase the love and recognition they so strongly
desire from the parent. The gift, in other words, becomes an instrument
for the repayment of symbolic debt.

Representing a phallus, the gift of shit is given in the hope of preventing castration, the loss of parental love. Lacan comments on this
at length in his most sustained analysis of the gift, during his seminar
of 1956–7, *The Object Relation* (*Le Séminaire, livre IV: La Relation
d'objet*). Much of the discussion revolves around a highly technical

rereading of Freud's case study on 'Dora' through the lens of Lévi-Strauss's *The Elementary Structures of Kinship*, the details of which are beyond the scope of the present discussion. Lacan makes a crucial distinction between the symbolic and imaginary functions of the gift, between, on one hand, 'the gift of speech [*le don de la parole*]' (SIV, 189) and, on the other, 'the gift of what one does not have [*le don de ce qu'on n'a pas*]' (SIV, 123). The former refers to the overall structures of language through which the subject comes to be in the symbolic order as always already castrated, the latter to the attempts of the ego to overcome castration through the offering of gifts. Particularly worthy of note in this discussion is the attention paid to sacrifice, not just at the inception of the symbolic, but as a technique of the imaginary that attempts to overturn the deleterious consequences of symbolisation.

'THE GIFT OF WHAT ONE DOES NOT HAVE' AND 'THE GIFT OF SPEECH'

The 'Rome Discourse' of 1953 constitutes Lacan's first, but not his most sustained, discussion of the gift. It does, however, offer the most pronounced demonstration of Lacan's turn toward structuralism, even if the voices of Jakobson and Lévi-Strauss at times seem drowned out by a cacophony of others, including Freud, Bichat, the *Upanishads*, Heidegger and Hegel–Kojève, to name only a few. It is this Hegelo-Kojevian influence that is most immediately apparent in the discourse's discussion of gifts, not least by virtue of Lacan's choice of vocabulary. The discussion begins with a description of gifts bound up in a process of recognition: 'the law of man has been the law of language since the first words of recognition presided over the first gifts' (E, 225/272). Taking its leave from the privilege now accorded by Lacan, following Lévi-Strauss, to linguistics, the citation makes it clear that gifts are given to supplement the exchange of words and not *vice versa*. The gift itself is a mere placeholder, something he will later describe 'as being only the sign of the gift' (SIV, 182). Symbolic, but merely of the symbolic order as such, the material offering serves to draw attention to the words whose apparently supplementary status belies their structural priority. It returns, becomes significant, only when the very symbolic order it expresses is called into question. The supplementary gift, given in addition to, or in the absence of the word, thus pertains to an attempt of the imaginary to reinforce the ego against what is perceived as symbolic instability. Rather than the object, what is given in the symbolic is 'the gift of speech' (E, 265/322), a phrase repeated on several occasions over the course of Lacan's presentation. If this privileging of the word over the thing constitutes an implicit challenge to Mauss, Lacan's call to the analytic community to return to the word and reassert its centrality to the therapeutic process reaffirms Mauss's injunction to reassert the gift as an organisational category of contemporary society (G, 69/263).

Just as for Mauss, one gives to elicit a countergift. When one speaks, according to Lacan, one does so in order to elicit a response. 'What I seek in speech is a response from the other. What constitutes me as a subject is my question' (E, 247/299). The statement must be taken within the context of the earlier, Hegelo-Kojevian, claim that it is recognition, rather than obligation, that is sought in this response: 'man's desire finds its meaning in the other's desire [. . .], his first object(ive) is to be recognized by the other' (E, 222/268). The point is confirmed by the ease with which one of most decisive, yet problematic, formulations of the 'Rome Discourse' lends itself to interpretation through the Master–Slave dialectic. Lacan writes that: 'Human language would then constitute a kind of communication in which the sender receives his own message back from the receiver in an inverted form' (E, 246/298). The wording – suggested to Lacan by Lévi-Strauss (Borch-Jacobsen 1991: 143/174) – recalls the Hegelian concept of being-one-self-through-another, according to which consciousness accedes to the full subjectivity of self-consciousness only through the receipt of recognition from another self-consciousness. It would accordingly be easy to read Lacan as constructing a Hegelian argument to the effect that it is exclusion from discourse and the right to free speech that serves as the cause of alienation.

For Lacan, however, the arch-modern temptation to lay bare the other subject as ground of one's own subjectivity is precisely the temptation to be resisted. He diverges from Hegel, rejecting the idea of grounded subjectivity, and he is at pains to emphasise that the analyst's gift of speech should in no way be used to create or indulge the impression of any such ground.

In this sense it becomes crucial to return to the distinction between the imaginary and symbolic order, and to differentiate the symbolic 'don de la parole' from another formulation of the gift as a technique of the imaginary. Throughout his career, Lacan also employs the gift to describe love as 'giving what one does not have' (E 580/691; SIV, 140; SVIII, 419). Love, he argues, is the imaginary gift of what one does not have: namely, the void of subjectivity. To put this in more conventionally psychoanalytic language, it is also the gift of the (lacking) phallus, a denial of castration, where one offers an imaginary phallus to the other in order to receive back the same in return. The gift of speech would be precisely the gift of that which creates this void – namely, language, the symbolic law that castrates the subject in the first place. In love, he argues, one denies the extrinsic structures of subjectivity by offering oneself to the other as a ground, a 'truth' that serves as an ontological support. One moreover gives and sacrifices to this other, showering them with presents one can symbolically and deliberately ill afford, in a bid to convince them – and, Lacan would say, oneself – of this truth. Love, in this respect, is the very opposite of psychoanalysis, the latter being a process whose conclusion routinely involves propelling the analysand backwards out of love with an analyst to whom they turn for emotional (*viz.* ontological) support.

On a clinical level, this insistence on effectuating a counter-transference explains Lacan's highly unorthodox and controversial refusal to adhere to the standard analytic practice of fixed-length sessions. The conventional insistence on a 'purely chronometric halt', he argues, serves only to facilitate the possibility that the analysand capture itself in the imaginary objectivation of a subjective agency that articulates its own substantial interiority (E, 209/252 [TM]). It thus runs counter to the task of psychoanalysis, which is to disabuse the analysand of this pretension. This is what Lacan hoped to achieve through the introduction of seemingly arbitrary end points, intended to confront the analysand with the real of a desire that speaks from without, a position of external, alienated lack that articulates only this alienation. Analysis, in other words, exposes desire as a gift that only gives (love) in the narcissistic hope of receiving recognition of itself in return. If treatment is expensive, the argument goes, it is in order to counteract any impression that the analyst gives to the patient the nothingness that would indicate love: 'he is paid for this nothing [*ce rien, on le lui paie*], preferably well, in order to show that otherwise it would not be worth much' (E, 516/618; see also E, 254/308). The point has been expertly developed by Forrester, who, writing on the Lacanian theory of transference, argues that: 'the signifier of signifiers, the signifier that designates the effects of the system, as Lacan describes Lévi-Strauss's zero signifier, is not *hau*, is not *mana*, is not the quantum, is not even the phallus, but – money' (Forrester 1997: 1959–60). In handing over money for treatment, the patient is exposed to the harsh reality of a transactional existence that, insisting on payment irrespective of the patient's suffering, obstinately refuses to indulge in fantasies of charity. The transferential process works through the very refusal of charity, the unreciprocated gift. The offering of the analyst should be one that leaves the subject to dwell on the groundless narcissism of any attempt at totalising self-narrative, to be achieved by 'punctuating' the speech of the analysand, exposing it to the moments of resistance it passes over in silence (E, 253–4/307–8). Through this dramatic reworking of the psychoanalytic process of transference, Lacan aims to show that symbolic gift exchange does not take place between independent, subjective agents, but unconsciously.

Underlying this is the Lévi-Straussian claim that the subject does not, as lovers tend to imagine, exist outside of and immune to society, but rather only exists by virtue of the place it is interpolated to occupy within the symbolic order. It is not – as argued by the American ego-psychologists against whom the 'Rome Discourse' is directed – the subject that articulates the unconscious, but the (symbolic) unconscious that speaks the subject. 'I will show that there is no speech without a response, even if speech meets only with silence' (E, 206/247). The claim reiterates but also extends the Lévi-Straussian emphasis on the total social fact. Lacan argues that, like the exchange described by Lévi-Strauss, at the level of its unconscious structures, dialogic speech cannot be broken down into individuated instances of speech and its response. Structurally, there is no distinction between the two. Just like the Lévi-Straussian gift, which is only a fragmentary expression of an underlying, unitary structure of exchange, 'true speech already contains its own response' (E, 255/310). 'The gift', in other words, 'implies the whole cycle of exchange' (SIV, 182).

Reiterating the above, to say that speech is a gift does not mean that it rewards its recipients by telling them what they want to hear. Nor does it simply mean that the subject does not exist, since the being that is at stake here is rather one of self-grounding *in*-sistence. 'The enunciation (the gift) of speech is what institutes and very literally gives being to what is uttered (given to be heard)' (Borch-Jacobsen 1991: 142/173). Following Kojève's argument that the truth of human history is created as 'Reality *of-which-one-speaks* [*Réalité*-dont-on-parle]' (IRH, 174/451), Lacan suggests that the reality of the subject is not pre-given, but rather gives itself in the very act of speech, in giving its word. Its existence becomes a matter of the recognition that is given in reciprocation of its own act of giving. The gift is described as a 'pact' (E, 225/272), signifying the giving of a consensus in which what is 'signified' is existence as such. The signifier is the law of the gift, presiding over the fact that what is given is not 'what one does not have', but precisely *all* that one *is*: 'the whole reality of its [the psychoanalytic experience's] effects lies in the gift of speech [*le don de la parole*]; for it is through this gift that all reality has come to man and through its ongoing action that he sustains this reality' (E, 265/322).

Before moving on to discuss the impact of Bataille upon this theory, we might note that what appears to be a relatively straightforward reworking of Hegel-Kojève is complicated by the claim that recognition is actually already presupposed in the act of giving one's word. As Forrester and Borch-Jacobsen have both argued at length, speech is 'performative', in the sense that the subject is enacted in and by its utterance, irrespective of whether anyone is listening (Borch-Jacobsen 1991: 143–8/174–80; Forrester 1990: 152–4). To quote again from Borch-Jacobsen:

> the given word [. . .] presupposes the recognition of the one to whom it is addressed. It is not what it is – a word that binds – except on condition of being given to another who is not *me*. In this respect, it does not matter whether the other accepts this gift or not, whether he in turn gives his word or not; the given word institutes in any case, by the very fact of its enunciation, a relationship that defines me in my relation to an other. (Borch-Jacobsen 1991: 141/172)

Much as 'men recognize each other by the gift of speech' (E, 265/322), the truth of the subject is that there is no truth, aside from that performatively enacted through the other, the 'big Other' of the symbolic unconscious. In a reversal of the Hegelian position, recognition is not a question of other subjects recognising a subjectivity that speaks itself. At stake, rather, is recognition by the subject of the Other, the symbolic order, that speaks *it*. This brings us back to the distinction between the imaginary gift of what one does not have and the symbolic gift of speech, implicit in which is the idea that the imaginary gift attempts to reconfigure the unconscious other as a knowable entity. The offering of the (imaginary) phallus is a sacrificial act that seeks to confer human, subjective attributes on an anthropomorphised social reality, foremost amongst which is the ability to offer love and recognition. Lacan remarks of gifts made to the gods that:

> sacrifice consisted [*le sacrifice, ça consistait*] in behaving as if they desired like us. [. . .] Which isn't to say that they will eat what one sacrifices to them, nor even that it might be useful to them, what matters is that they desire it. (SX, 321)

Manifesting itself as a 'call' to the Other (SIV, 182), the offering of what one does not have functions as a narcissistic attempt to buy the love of the Other. But it has the additional effect of reinscribing, consolidating the process of imaginary misrecognition that leads to the experience of debt in the first place. As Žižek puts it:

> In its most fundamental dimension, sacrifice is a 'gift of reconciliation' to the Other, destined to appease its desire. Sacrifice conceals the abyss of the Other's desire, more precisely, it conceals the Other's lack, inconsistency, 'inexistence,' that transpires in this desire. *Sacrifice is a guarantee that 'the*

Other exists': that there is another who can be appeased by means of the sacrifice. (Žižek 2001: 56)

To receive the gift of speech, by contrast, is to recognise that 'behind what [the subject] gives there is all that it lacks, and that the subject sacrifices beyond what it has' (SIV, 140). In receiving it, the subject comes to accept symbolic debt as an effect of the structure of subjectivity, the effect not of a superegoic law of the father, but of structures of language that generate an excess of meaning, in relation to which the subject is lacking. The debt is affirmed as constitutively unpayable.

Through his distinction between imaginary and symbolic giving, Lacan is able to move beyond Mauss's 'discovery' that the gift is always tied to the receipt of a debt. The question of debt is transformed into a question of how to perceive ourselves in relation to the symbolic order: whether we construe the other as a substantialised ground with which to exchange gifts, or whether to recognise the tendency to look for ontological support as an inbuilt effect of the extrinsic structures of language. Even if he rejects the idea of charity, one might wonder whether, in distinguishing the gift from the obligation to give, Lacan does not leave an opening for an unconditional giving of the type sought by Derrida. Whether Derrida would think he goes far enough is another matter.

LACAN *WITH* DERRIDA?

Despite Lacan's claim that the subject is merely an empty function of speech, it might be suggested that this emphasis on the performative enactment of the subject in language still collapses back into a thinking of language as an ontological ground. One variant of this argument, proposed by Deleuze and Guattari in *Anti-Oedipus*, will be studied in depth in the next chapter. Most immediately germane to the question of the gift is an argument put forward by Derrida. In the deconstruction of Lacan in *The Post-Card*, Derrida is driven to wonder whether the exchange of recognition in speech works only at the cost of restricting language to a 'metalinguistic' conveyance of the presence, or 'truth', of a transcendentally privileged signifier: 'what the Seminar insists upon showing, finally, is that there is a single *proper* itinerary of the letter which returns to a determinable place that is always the same and that is its *own*' (PC, 436/464–5). The argument amounts to a rejection of the total social fact. Indeed, it closely recalls the much earlier article, in which Derrida broke ranks with structuralism by arguing against Lévi-Strauss's hypothesis of a distinct social reality. In 'Structure, Sign and

Play in the Discourse of the Human Sciences' (1966), Derrida accuses
Lévi-Strauss of over-determining the fixity of signifiers' production of
meaning, and suggests that he remains implicitly caught up in an 'ethics
of presence', recuperating speech as a metaphysical ground. Through
his excessively rigid distinction between nature and culture, Derrida
argues, Lévi-Strauss neglects the extent to which symbolic order is
subject to and made possible by a 'play' of meaning that blurs this distinction (WD, 369/427).

In a rereading of Edgar Allen Poe's short story, 'The Purloined Letter'
(1844), initially conducted as part of *Seminar II*, but subsequently
reprinted as the opening essay of the *Écrits*, Lacan compares Poe's
detective hero, Dupin, to a psychoanalyst. The analyst's knowledge
of symbolic exchange is what leads Dupin to locate the missing letter
in between the 'legs' of a fireplace, a symbolic site to which the letter
(the phallus) will unconsciously return, undoing any attempt to assert
agency over it, to wrest it away from the logic of symbolic exchange.
Lacan concludes with the (Lévi-Straussian) assertion that 'a letter
always arrives at its destination,' offering the literary text as evidence
that 'the sender, as I tell you, receives from the receiver his own message
in an inverted form' (E, 30/41). The claim appears to emphasise the
inevitability of castration, the inevitability that the giving (enunciation)
of the subject by the signifier will be met by a countergift, a surplus
of signification that ungrounds and decentres the subject, rendering it
impotent. Derrida takes issue, suggesting that this only holds true by
virtue of an idealisation of the signifier as a self-identical phallus, an
ultimately stable referent that belies Lacan's (Lévi-Straussian) assertion of its intrinsic inadequation: 'Not that the letter never arrives at its
destination, but it belongs to the structure of the letter to be capable,
always, of not arriving' (PC, 444/472). By emphasising the artificial
imposition of unity on the signifier, what Derrida wants to preserve
is the possibility of a letter *not* arriving at its destination, of a gift *not*
being reciprocated – even if this gift would still be impossible on his
own terms. Derrida, we recall, argues that the gift, in order to qualify
as such, be unconditionally aneconomic, which is to say unrecognisable
and uncontaminated by the negative impact of reciprocity. Lacan, for
Derrida, destroys the gift by capturing it in a self-identical present.

Articles from Barbara Johnson and Slavoj Žižek have sought to
contest this. Turning Derrida back against himself, the former accuses
him of falling victim to too literal an interpretation of the letter's
arrival, of the notion of its 'destination' in particular. Johnson suggests
that Derrida presupposes a teleological understanding of destination as
something *preceding* its circulation, and in so doing fails to consider the

way the gift (the phallus, the letter) performatively enacts the reality of the recipient *qua* recipient (subject) (Johnson 1988: 248). Similarly for Žižek, in thinking that the repressed can also *not* return, that the gift can *not* be reciprocated, 'we entangle ourselves in a naive substantialist notion of the unconscious as a positive entity ontologically preceding its "returns"' (Žižek 2001: 14). The point that Derrida's critics seek to make is that the Lacanian social fact is not as totalisable, not so much of an all-encompassing ground, as it initially seems. The very fact that the reality of the symbolic order is performatively enacted is precisely what prevents it from being total, riddling it with holes that must be filled in by the imaginary. What Johnson and Žižek perhaps fail to signal is the extent to which this only becomes apparent in Lacan's later, more Bataillean work, in which he begins to distance himself from his Lévi-Straussian inheritance of Mauss.

GEORGES BATAILLE AND THE 'DON DE LA VIE'

To sacrifice is not to kill but to give, to relinquish [*abandonner*].
(Georges Bataille)[4]

Writing in *Le Souffleur* (*The Whisperer*), the final instalment of his trilogy, *Les Lois de l'hospitalité* (*The Laws of Hospitality*), Pierre Klossowski, a member of the Collège de Sociologie, parodies Lacan through the character of Dr Ygdrasil, an analyst who accuses his patient of misunderstanding the economics of the gift: 'You cling absolutely to giving without return! But you can't live without submitting yourself to the universal law of exchange!' (Klossowski 1965: 302). The recipient of the outburst is one Théodore Lacase, who, with the encouragement of his friend, the imperious Guy de Savigny, indulges in the curious practice of offering his wife up to guests in his household. By giving her away, he hopes better to possess her. Only by watching her in intimate congress with another, he thinks, can he know her intimately; know that part of her disclosed only to the other, beyond the confines of her role as wife. Upon discovering that his wife has been short-circuiting the laws of hospitality, substituting another, a spitting-image, for herself, so that it is this other woman who is given away, Théodore breaks down, perceiving his imaginary experience of intimacy never to have taken place. The psychiatrist's response is to tell him to stop being so generous – the universal law of exchange means that he will always come undone, always receive an unanticipated, poisonous countergift by way of return of his

4. TR, 48–9/310 [TM].

own gifts. Far better, then, simply to submit wholeheartedly to the law, to give up on the illusory, impossible pursuit of intimacy and accept a life of symbolic circulation, in which he, too, sleeps with whomever he pleases. Underlying this response is the Lévi-Straussian theory of the symbolic exchange of women, an account that sees subjective positions of husband and wife conferred in accordance with the logic of the signifier. This Lévi-Straussian approach is what reveals Ygdrasil to be a caricature of Lacan. As Leslie Hill has pointed out, the ethos of radically sacrificial giving suggests Savigny to be a repetition of Bataille, with Théodore repeating Klossowski (Hill 2001: 165).

The move of treating a simulacral critique of Théodore for an actual Lacanian critique of Klossowski and furthermore Bataille is fraught with problems, obviously including the conflation of two quite different thinkers, Bataille and Klossowski, to say nothing of the complexities of deconstructing Klossowski's simulacra.[5] Heuristically, however, Ygdrasil's damning indictment arguably finds no more plausible a recipient than Bataille, who can not only be seen to eulogise intimacy, but also to regard sex and sacrifice as a means to its attainment. This potential difference between Bataille and Lacan arises in spite of a shared Kojevian heritage and persists even after Bataille's reading of Lévi-Strauss. It would also seem to lend support to the hypothesis of Lacan's biographer that Bataille possibly never read the work of his supposed *protégé* (Roudinesco 1997: 136/188; see also Botting and Wilson 2001: 82–4). The opposite does *not* hold true, though one might wonder how much of what passes for a critique of Bataille is not already implicit in Lacan. It may not be immediately apparent, but something closely resembling a Bataillean thinking of giving comes increasingly to inflect the work of Lacan. The latter does not accept without qualification the Bataillean idea that, through sacrifice, one might restitute an experience of lost intimacy, 'of immanence between man and world, between the object and the subject' (TR, 44/307). More nuanced ideas of both sacrifice and intimacy none the less become crucial for the formulation of the third and final register of his 'pre-ontology' of the unconscious, a concept of psychic reality *qua* 'real', 'an idea of morbidity, of *reste* (vestige), of *part maudite* (doomed or accursed part), borrowed without attribution from the heterological science of Bataille' (Roudinesco 1997: 217/289). In place of intimacy,

5. On the not entirely harmonious relations between Bataille and Klossowski, see Kaufman (2001), Hill (2001) and James (2006b); James has written extensively on the thematic of the gift in Klossowski's *Les Lois de l'hospitalité* (James 2000), as has Deleuze, in an appendix to *Logique du sens* (LS, 321–40, 327–42).

Lacan writes of 'extimacy [*extimité*]' (SVII, 139/167), or external-intimacy, an intimacy so interior to the subject as to be 'en toi plus que toi', 'in you more than yourself' (SXI, 268–9/299), lying in excess, even, of the extrinsic structures of language. We experience extimacy not through sacrifice, but through what is increasingly being called the 'sacrifice of sacrifice', understood as a strategy for finally coming to terms with the traumatic absence of an ontological ground (Žižek 2001: 165–73; Keenan 2005: 105). Characteristic of this later, more Bataillean, Lacan is the rearticulation of the relation between the gift and castration, and of the nature of the unconscious that causes castration. For the early Lacan, the gift is understood both as the castrating symbolic exchange of speech and as the imaginary offering that seeks to reappropriate the castrated phallus. With the gift of the real, the castration effect of the floating signifier is traced to a hole in the symbolic, which comes into being as the unsymbolisable excess of symbolisation.

Bataille's first engagement with the gift occurs in a short essay of 1933, 'The Notion of Expenditure', written before his meeting with Alexandre Kojève. Bataille's later references to the gift, including those in the trilogy of *The Accursed Share* (1948–57)[6] and the *Theory of Religion* (written by 1948 but only posthumously published), are decisively inflected by, but also highly critical of Kojève and Lévi-Strauss. The earlier work extends Mauss's critique of utilitarianism, returning to archaic society to make the point that apparently disutilitarian behaviour can be rewarded and justified at the level of libidinal economy. The later works develop this further through an emphasis on the Kojevian motifs of death, desire and recognition, which Bataille challenges in what also becomes a critique of Lévi-Strauss. In *The History of Eroticism*, he accuses the latter of oversimplifying the opposition between nature and culture, animal and man, to the point of arrogating the gift to a sphere of symbolic exchange in which its intrinsic relation to the erotic – and to life in general – is foreclosed (HES, 47–58/39–48). The criticism in fact repeats the one levelled at Mauss by Lévi-Strauss: namely, the failure to appreciate the full extent, or 'totality', of the total social fact. The point this time is that, as already implied by Lévi-Strauss's lengthy analysis of the incest taboo, the apparently distinct symbolic social reality cannot but be bound up with nature. Bataille draws a distinction between '*restrictive* economy [*économie* restreinte]' and '*general* economy [*économie* générale]' (AS, 25/33), which recalls, yet is far broader than, the one Lévi-Strauss

---

6. Consisting of *The Accursed Share* (1948), *The History of Eroticism* (1957) and *Sovereignty*, written by around 1957 but unpublished during the author's lifetime.

makes between 'restricted' and 'generalised exchange'. The latter uses the contrast to distinguish between straightforwardly reciprocal and more complex, simultaneously patri- and matrilineal systems of exogamic exchange (Lévi-Strauss 1969: 178–89/189–98). Despite Lévi-Strauss's declared anti-humanism, the problem for Bataille is that this generalised exchange still only refers to disutilitarian forms of exchange between humans. What Bataille regards as the true 'Copernican transformation' (AS, 25/33) of general economy overturns this perceived bias by focusing on the energic excess of *'living matter in general'* (AS, 23/31) and even on the sun, whose continual generation of life is the archetypal figure of 'giving without ever receiving' (AS, 28/35).

Bataille's principal argument is that every living system generates an excess whose expenditure, or wastage, is fundamental to the sustenance of that system. The gift pertains to the 'unproductive expenditure [*dépense improductive*]' of this excess, which is none the less habitually suppressed as an 'accursed share [*part maudite*]', a disutilitarian and unhygienic profanity thought simultaneously unpalatable and unnecessary to human economic concerns. Modernity emerges from the ruthless exclusion of unproductive expenditure, allowing consumption only where it works directly in the service of production (AS, 132–3/126). In a repetition of Nietzsche's analysis of the ascetic priest (GM, 97–101/390–1 [III, §15–17]), Bataille argues that beyond the modern apotheosis of reason, efficiency and calculation without remainder, there lies a fetishisation of hygiene, a fear of contamination, which is ultimately to say a fear of death. Reversing the modern (Durkheimian) construal of the sacred as that which is free from the profane, Bataille affirms profanity – shit, death and menstruation, the orgiastic and intemperate, the unscientific – as that which is sacred, belonging to the exuberant general economy of 'the gift of life' (ASf: 7, 235). Sovereignty, he argues, does not reside in and with the 'clear and distinct' reasoning of a metaphysically individuated, essentially immortal Cartesian subject. On the contrary, it coincides with the spontaneous, miraculous moment in which the subject-as-object 'dissolves into NOTHING, because, ceasing to be useful, or subordinate, it becomes *sovereign* in ceasing to be' (HES, 204/255). Another way of saying this is that sovereignty is experientially 'impossible', incommensurable with the experience of the subject. Long before Derrida, it is thus Bataille who asserts the experience of the gift to be one of an impossibility that dissolves the subject. It is not entirely clear whether the impossibility of experiencing it subjectively renders it inaccessible to experience *tout court*, or whether it simply points to the fact that human experience is artificially restricted by the conditions it imposes on itself, however.

Bataille writes in *Sovereignty* that to become sovereign is to open up the horizons of experience beyond the restricted economy of the human, to witness 'the *impossible coming true*, in the *reign of the instant*' (HES, 211/261). The citation could be thought to imply the throwing off of the supposedly sovereign subject for the sake of acceding to, reappropriating, a new form of superior subjectivity. Jean-Luc Nancy suspects that this is indeed the case and has been particularly critical of the centripetalism of Bataille's language of immanence, apparently indicative of the ongoing pursuit of an ontological ground, the return of the subject under another name (IC, 22–5/60–4; FT, 63/87). A quite different reading of Bataille emerges from Maurice Blanchot, who offers a more Lacanian Bataille, for whom the inner experience of intimacy 'says the opposite of what it seems to say' (Blanchot 1988: 16/33). Blanchot emphasises Bataille's descriptions of experience at the limits of experience, 'the extremities of the possible', 'a voyage to the ends of the possible of man' (IE, 156, 7/48, 19), that is strictly neither 'inner' nor even 'experienced' as such. Rather than the becoming possible of the impossible, Blanchot argues, sovereignty implies an encounter with the limit at which experience becomes impossible, in which the subject is exposed, ek-statically, to the absence of ground, the impossibility of 'communitarian fusion' with being (1988: 11/24). At the heart of this experience of impossibility is Bataille's thinking of sacrifice.

SACRIFICE

In place of Kojève's triumphant affirmation of 'the end of History' (IRH, 159n/435n), the completion of man's historical transformation of nature through labour, we find in Bataille a lamentation of modernity as the highest point in the history of man's alienation. Despite his declared allegiance to Kojève, Bataille had begun to criticise him as early as 1937, inventing the concept of 'useless negativity [*négativité sans emploi*]', broadly synonymous with unproductive expenditure, in a letter of response to the master's address to the Collège de Sociologie ('Letter to X., Lecturer on Hegel ...', in Hollier 1986: 89–93/170–7). It is presumably in this address, the text of which is now lost, that Kojève 'effectively reproached the conspirators [*conjurés*] of the Collège, but above all Bataille, for wanting to play at being sorcerer's apprentices', for wanting to use magic tricks to make them believe in magic (Caillois, cited in Hollier 1988: 12, 86/37, 167). Much like Mauss's own reproach of the *collégiens'* 'absolute irrationalism' (Fournier 2006: 327/710; Fournier 1990: 87), the cause of concern is an obsession with using violence to gain privileged access to the 'sacred' reality of the total

social fact. Clearly aiming at Kojève's claim that labour is the means
through which man becomes human, comes to terms with his mortality,
Bataille is highly critical of Western civilisation's inability to cope with
death. In an argument that repeats, but also radicalises, Mauss's injunction to 'return to archaic society and to elements in it' (G, 69/263),
he laments the West's continual attempt to defer death through the
obsessive-compulsive production of objects designed to outlive their
producers. Such a trait, he argues, is constitutive of the essentialisation
of human identity in an abstract notion of the subject. Modernity thus
represents a far cry from the so-called 'primitive', archaic societies of
the gift economy. Where the structures of the latter reflect the natural
order of death at the heart of society, modernity bears witness to a
'hatred of expenditure' and the suppression of death, brought about
through the valorisation of production purely for its own sake (NE,
124/314). Reread both through and against the Kojevian interpretation
of the Master–Slave dialectic, the institution of the *potlatch* is offered
as a primary example of this: a ritual in which the mass destruction of
goods purports to prove participants' independence from the immortal-
ity of the object. As Leslie Hill puts it, what Mauss considered no more
than 'an extreme form of gift exchange' became, for Bataille, 'a struggle
to the death between agonistic partners, each of whom was required
by the rules of the *potlatch* to outdo the other and in the process undo
oneself' (Hill 2001: 39). The reference to undoing oneself refers to
Bataille's fascination with transgressing and going beyond the rigidity
of subjective experience.

Bataille focuses on the recognition of honour and prestige that is
staked on one's ability to waste, the annihilation of property through
which one demonstrates that one has no desire to see one's offering
reciprocated. Reciprocation is rendered unnecessary by the fact that, in
the acquisition of power, the squandering of a 'useless' excess already
generates its own reward: 'Gift giving has the virtue of a surpassing
of the subject who gives, but in exchange for the object given, the
subject appropriates the surpassing' (AS, 69/72). What appears to be a
profitless venture from the restricted perspective of a purely economic
measure of wealth appears within the perspective of general economy
as a loss that is compensated by an augmentation in status. While
Bataille celebrates the Amerindian *potlatch* as an instance of *dépense
improductive*, he does not, however, see it as an unqualified affirmation of finitude: that is, as fully exemplary of the general economy he
espouses. In the later work it becomes apparent that in destroying only
the surplus of a society's production, only that share that it does not
require to be exchanged or traded, the *potlatch* does not go all the way

in counteracting the means through which humanity extricates itself from the general economy of life and death. It falls short of the aneconomy attained by full-blown sacrifice, whose purpose is to destroy that quality of objectality, or thinghood, that is characteristic of restricted economy. The difference between the two is that 'in general, sacrifice withdraws useful products from profane circulation; in principle the gifts of *potlatch* liberate objects that are useless from the start' (AS, 76/78; see also Richman 1982: 16–22, for a more extensive commentary). The *potlatch* is not truly transgressive because it only witnesses the destruction of unnecessary, luxury items; it therefore *symbolises* but does fully act out the possibility of liberation from things. Subjectivity is only symbolically exceeded: that is, exceeded only on account of the recognition one receives from those observing the ceremony. In sacrifice, by contrast, the sacrificer arrives at a sacred experience of death by removing the object-form of subjectivity. 'The thing – only the thing – is what sacrifice means to destroy in the victim' (TR, 43/307).

Through its destruction of the thing, sacrifice amounts to a genuine *dépassement*, or overcoming, of the subject. The subtlety of this distinction between sacrifice and the *potlatch* has recently led Hill to suggest that Bataille is undertaking to 'sacrifice sacrifice', positing his own concept of sacrifice in contrast to a lesser type that is purely symbolic: 'It is as though for this second form of sacrifice to take place what has to be sacrificed is the symbolic economy of sacrifice itself' (Hill 2001: 46). The reward for this sacrifice, or sacrifice of sacrifice, is not just acclaim but a sovereignty that is independent of recognition, which laughs in the face of the death that recognition seeks to suspend. By overturning the separation between nature and object – a separation, incidentally, that Kojève insists to be a condition of the human (IRH, 158–9n/434–5n) – sacrifice transgresses the artificial barrier interposed between man and the world, returning life 'to the *intimacy* of the divine world, of the profound immanence of all that is' (TR, 44/308). A similarly privileged communication of intimacy is said to derive from sex, and also from transgressive forms of writing. Writing in general is sovereign, sacrificial, when it succeeds in overturning the aspiration to scientificity, usefulness and knowledge. 'Knowledge is never sovereign,' Bataille writes, on the ground that knowledge is always the result of an economic process, hence opposed to the sovereign instant:

> Knowledge [*la connaissance*] is never sovereign: to be sovereign, it would have to occur in the instant. We know nothing absolutely [*Nous ne savons rien absolument*] of the instant. In short, we know nothing about what ultimately concerns us, what is *supremely* [souverainement] *important to us*.

[. . .] Consciousness of the instant is not truly such, is not sovereign, except in *unknowing* [*dans le* non-savoir]. (HES, 202–3/253–4)

The 'sacred sociology' of the Collège de Sociologie would be a prime example of this *non-savoir* (see Hollier 1988: 11/34). As a result of his engagement with Bataille, so too, Lacan hoped, would psychoanalysis.

(RE-)SACRIFICING SACRIFICE

Bataille's fascination with sacrifice has been the subject of considerable criticism, both from his peers, notably including Walter Benjamin, and from more contemporary sources, not least Jean-Luc Nancy, whose work will be discussed at length in Chapters 3 and 4. Described by Pierre Klossowski as an 'assiduous auditor' of the Collège de Sociologie (in Hollier 1986: 389/586), Benjamin expressed grave concerns that Bataille's project of 'surfascism', of deploying sacred, sacrificial violence to turn fascism back against itself, risked indiscernibility from that which it wished to sublate (Surya 2002: 268/327). Maurice Blanchot, by contrast, draws on accounts of the sacrificial activities of Acéphale to read Bataillean sacrifice as the rejection of fascistic or politically extreme concepts of community (Blanchot 1988: 15–16/30–2). Aside from Surya's passing observation that 'Lacan worried [*s'était inquiété*] over the experiences and activities of Acéphale from up close' (2002: 534n/306n [TM]), which would seem to suggest little sympathy with the Blanchottian interpretation, little is known of the psychoanalyst's reaction to Bataille's experimentations. Dean has written on the shared cultural context of their early work, but she does not put the two men's later work into a reflective dialogue that would shed light on Surya's oblique statement (Dean 1986; 1992). There is thus an open question as to what extent Lacan's critique of sacrifice should be thought a sympathetic, albeit uncredited, re-elaboration, and how much it functions as a critique of Bataille.

Despite resistance from Fredric Jameson (Jameson 2006: 370), Slavoj Žižek has gone further than most in acknowledging Lacan's Batailleanism, albeit only suggestively, by pointing out that a number of themes treated in *The Accursed Share* trilogy are taken up in Lacan's seventh annual seminar, 1959–60, *On the Ethics of Psychoanalysis* (Žižek 2003: 54–5). Following Žižek, we might take *Seminar VII* as the site of a Lacanian response to Bataille, paying particular attention to its treatment of the Bataillean concepts of thinghood and intimacy. The seminar sees Lacan submit both to a reversal that simultaneously recalls and yet announces a departure from Bataille. Confronted by Bataille's postulation of a general economy of life so intimate as to be foreclosed from the alienated, reified existence of modern subjectivity, Lacan seemingly paradoxically develops it into the idea of an external unconscious, combining (sublating?) the two in a concept of 'extimacy': 'the intimate exteriority or "extimacy" that is the Thing' (SVII, 139/167). The neologism points to the increasing complexity of the linguistic structuralism of the early Lacan, signalling a shift towards what one might, *pace* Žižek (1999: 7), call Lacan's *poststructuralism*.

Lacan's son-in-law and executor, Jacques-Alain Miller, has stated that the real epistemological break does not occur until the seminar of 1963–4, *The Four Fundamental Concepts of Psychoanalysis*, where Lacan introduces the concept of the drive (*pulsion*), the primordial life of the libido: 'Lacan's first ten seminars are developed under the banner of a Freud coloured by Lévi-Strauss,' the result of this being an 'unconscious with rules, a social unconscious, which he would find in ethnology' (Miller 2003). But this regulative, universal unconscious is subsequently superseded by a *singular* unconscious, based on the impossibility of universality, sharing and appropriation. Although Lacan continues to refer positively to the work of Lévi-Strauss throughout *Seminar VII*, he follows Bataille in questioning the crudeness of the former's distinction between nature and culture (SVII, 67–8/82–3) and his subsequent discussions of the symbolic begin to alter in tone. He refers repeatedly, for instance, to the 'field of the service of goods' (SVII, 313–15/350–2), a term that more closely resembles Bataille's description of the symbolic as a rationalistic, *hyper*consciousness of commodified things than it does Lévi-Strauss's unconscious network of signifiers. Miller suggests that Lacan's Lévi-Straussian dictum, 'the unconscious is structured like a language,' is increasingly outdated, superseded by the new language of extimacy, though he denies that the symbolic simply ceases to be unconscious. The Thing, or *Das Ding*, he argues, 'is not the negation of the preceding structure,' but the reformulation of the core of the symbolic order as real (2003).

Lacan himself describes *das Ding* as the uncanny remainder of the symbolisation process, the Thing that lives on after the object of desire is murdered, or sacrificed, by the word. As the 'the absolute Other of the subject, that one is supposed to find again' (SVII, 52/65), it is also that which is most real, more real than the (performatively enacted, fantasmically supported) reality of the symbolic order. The real pertains to what desire desires but cannot have – not just recognition, but moreover the object of desire, whose sacrifice propels the infant to pursue recognition through the symbolic order. Like the symbolic before it, the real occupies the site of *hau*, the 'spirit of things' invoked by Mauss to describe the circulation of gifts. Lacan calls it 'the beyond-of-the-signified' (SVII, 54/67), since it does not itself participate in symbolic circulation. 'The real', he writes, 'is that which always returns to [*se retrouve toujours à*] the same place' (SVII, 70/85 [TM]). The non-movement results from the failure of symbolisation, but is also precisely what makes symbolic exchange possible. By the time of *Seminar XI, das Ding* is rearticulated as *objet petit a*: 'before the image of a completeness closed upon itself, [. . .] the separated *a* from which [the subject] is hanging' (SXI, 116/131). The subject is held in a state of suspension by an inappropriable object whose appropriation would spell completion, the definitive satisfaction of desire. The irreducibility of this separation is what serves as the cause of desire (SX, 326).

Lacan's denial of Hegel's dialectical *Aufhebung* means that desire never achieves complete symbolic integration, never translates without remainder into the language of symbolic order. The Thing is what remains of desire after symbolisation, the empty structure of the object deprived of content, a real void, the existence of which endures beyond the fantasies imposed in the attempt to conceal it, and whose constant return to the same place has the effect of ungrounding, exposing the fantasy for what it is (SXI, 185/207). In line with Bataille's account of the gift, this lost object is by definition inaccessible to the generalised structures of exchange and substitutability introduced by the movement of the signifier.

Miller's identification of an epistemological break is based on a reading of Lacan in terms of his 'return to Freud', a project he takes to be abandoned at the start of *Seminar XI*. In emphasising Freud, however, there is a sense in which he neglects the continuity of Lacan's negotiation between Lévi-Strauss and Bataille. Rather than a radical departure, the seminar marks a fine-tuning, a consolidation of this negotiation. *Seminar VII* refers only in passing to the unconscious as 'un champ d'un *non-savoir*', 'a field of *non-knowledge*' (SVII, 236–7/277 [emphasis added]), but the idea decisively returns three years later. Lacan opens the seminar of 1963–4 with a discussion of the epistemological status of psychoanalysis, posing himself the question of '*whether psychoanalysis is a science*', or whether it is rather a form of 'religion' (SXI, 7/15). The two poles, such as they are posed, articulate precisely the division between Lévi-Strauss and Bataille, between 'mathematisation' and sovereign 'non-knowledge', the possibility of symbolising, rationalising the unconscious, versus the affirmation of its *im*possibility.

The seminar's dominant theme of a distinction between desire and drive can also, broadly speaking, be mapped on to the one between a Lévi-Straussian symbolic and a Bataillean real that 'we would be led to define as impossible' (SXI, 167/188). Repeating Bataille's attempt to communicate the general economy of life in excess of the restricted economy of the subject, Lacan reworks the real as libidinal drive. The excessive remainder of the real is now described as a:

> pure life instinct, that is to say, immortal life, or irrepressibe life, life that has need of no organ, simplified indestructible life. [. . .] And it is of this that all the forms of the *objet a* that can be enumerated are the representatives, the equivalents. (SXI, 198/221)

A life that exceeds subjectivity, he describes it moreover, in explicitly Bataillean terms, as acephalous: 'what I have metaphorically called an acephalous, headless subjectification [*subjectivation acéphale*], a subjectification without subject' (SXI, 184/206). The insistence on metaphor reiterates that what is at stake is not an appropriable form of sovereignty. Lacan does not so much reject sovereignty as resituate it beyond the prospect of subjective reappropriation, in a type of pleasure – *jouissance* – that is irreducible to desire (SXI, 183–4/205–6). *Jouissance*, he argues, names the pleasure the drive extracts from the constant deferral of satisfaction, the frustration of desire.

Where Bataille tends toward a centripetal language of immanence and intimacy, Lacan is less ambiguous in opening up what might be described as a pre-ontological cut, a rupture that prevents the totalisation of being in any form of self-identity. Rather than a unified general economy, his pre-ontology of the unconscious revolves around an opposition between two different economies, an economy of desire on one hand and, on the other, the economy of the drive, whose autarkic self-enclosure disrupts the return-to-self of desire, rendering its satisfaction impossible (SXI, 166–7/188). The drive's 'aim is nothing other than the return into circuit [*son but n'est point autre chose que ce retour en circuit*]' (SXI, 179/201 [TM]), the attainment of self-identity in the form of the *jouissance* experienced in the short-circuiting of desire. In constantly returning to the same place, it achieves for itself the very closure of identity it renders impossible in desire. Paradoxically, subjective self-identity is shown to be impossible through the rupturing of symbolic order by the drive's constant and autarkic return to the site of *jouissance*. In place of the transcendental subject of modernity, it is thus *jouissance* that furnishes the 'substance' of Lacanian psychoanalysis (Žižek 1989: 68).

'UN CADEAU D'UNE MERDE'

If Bataille's valorisation of an intimacy with being fails to recognise the fantasmic support structure that underlies sexual relations, the impossibility of accessing the real through the other, he thus remains caught up in a thinking that preserves the possibility of privileged subjectivity in the very gesture by which he denies it. Lacan never states this explicitly, but the tenor of his argument unveils in the details. Over the course of *Seminar VII*, Bataille is named only once, and in passing – ' – *il s'agit de Georges Bataille* – ' – initially praised but immediately chastened for failing to grasp the radicality of libidinal economics in Sade (SVII, 201/236). Anticipating Nancy and Derrida rather than Blanchot, more revealing still is Lacan's analysis of the *potlatch*. *Potlatch*, for Lacan, ceases to be privileged for its proximity to a lost intimacy and becomes instead a witness to its absence:

> The potlatch bears witness to man's retreat from goods, a retreat which enabled him to link the maintenance and discipline of his desire, so to speak – insofar as this is what concerns him in his destiny – to the open destruction of goods, that were both personal and collective property. The problem and drama of the economy of the good, its ricochets and rebounds, all turn on this point. (SVII, 235/275–6)

Far from destroying or offering a privileged experience of the life of the drive, or even the hollowed-out transcendental structure of *objet petit a*, sacrifice is reconfigured as a fantasmic means of keeping them at bay, a gesture necessitated and moreover made possible by the very impossibility of intimacy. The final pages of *Seminar XI* make this claim in a way that revives the aforementioned criticism of Bataille by Benjamin. In a passage that equates 'the most monstrous and supposedly superseded forms of the holocaust', 'the drama of Nazism', with a resurgence of sacrifice, Lacan too now cautions against the temptation toward supposedly sacred violence. Equally worthy of note is the allusion to Hegel-Kojève that directly precedes this caution. Far from testifying, as Hegel suggests, to a sublime moment in the *Aufhebung* of *Geist*, sacrifice testifies to the failure of the dialectic and the impossibility of recognition:

> I would hold that no meaning given to history, based on Hegelo-Marxist premises, is capable of accounting for this resurgence – which only goes to show that the offering to obscure gods of an object of sacrifice is something to which few subjects can resist succumbing, as if under some monstrous spell. [T]here are certainly few who do not succumb to the fascination of sacrifice in itself – the sacrifice signifies that, in the object of our desires, we try to find the presence for the desire of this Other that I call here *the dark God*. (SXI, 275/305–6)

The passage repeats the criticism of the sacrificial gift of what one does not have, revealing it to be not so much a form of expenditure in which we repeat the general economy of life, but rather the means of giving birth to a fantasmic construction through which we conceal it. Rather than 'succumb to the fascination with sacrifice', the alternative Lacan proposes is to *sacrifice* it, to sacrifice the fantasy through which desire sustains the illusion of satisfaction. This sacrifice of sacrifice conforms to the ethical imperative of psychoanalysis, an imperative that is once again differentiated from the subject's imagined obligation to repay the symbolic debt incurred in the misrecognition of the gift of speech. The attempt to repay this debt only ever increases the sense of indebtedness, performatively reinscribing the existence of the big Other to whom one sacrifices. The only solution is to escape the vicious circle, the vicious economy of repayment. 'The only thing of which one can be guilty is of having given ground relative to one's desire' (SVII, 318/370). The claim is similar to but perhaps more radical than the ethical imperative implied in the receipt of the gift of speech. In his later work, Lacan goes on to argue that the symbolic order is itself a fantasy, the 'fundamental phantasy' of an Other that confers recognition and self-identity (SXI, 273/304).

Commenting on the fate of the heroine in Sophocles' *Antigone*, Lacan describes how, in accepting exile-until-death as the punishment for burying her brother, Antigone is driven to 'sacrifice her own being in order to maintain this essential being' (SVII, 283/329). Despite impending marriage to the king's son, she knows that only by sacrificing herself can she preserve the possibility of what she knows to be impossible: namely, desire. Knowing that the satisfaction of desire, the impossible desire for the recovery of *objet petit a*, is irretrievably beyond her, she refuses to compromise, renouncing the prospect of an illusory satisfaction out of fidelity to the impossible object. The logic is one of forced choice, of '*Your freedom or your life!*', to recall Hegel's life or death encounter (SXI, 212/237). Alenka Zupančič summarises it elegantly as a situation:

> where the only way you can choose A is by choosing its negation, not-A; the only way the subject can stay true to the Cause is by betraying it, *by sacrificing it to the very thing that drove her to make this sacrifice*. It is this paradoxical logic which allows subjectivation to coincide here with the 'destitution' of the subject. While the subject constitutes herself as a subject through the act of choosing, the nature of the choice renders her destitute as a subject. (Zupančič 2000: 216)

This rejection of identification equates with what Lacan describes as the experience of having 'traversed the radical phantasy [*traversé le fantasme radical*]' (SXI, 273/304). Through her refusal of the symbolic order of law, Antigone effects the traversal of the fundamental fantasy. The cave wherein she dwells until her demise represents the entry into 'the zone between life and death' (SVII, 280/326), between what, in light of the later work on the drive, we might call a biological death that is yet to arrive and a symbolic death that coincides with the recognition of the impossibility of its arrival – the impossibility of bringing an end to the endless circulation of the libido. It is moreover the site of *objet petit a* as a remainder that lives on after the fantasy's traversal.

When the fantasy dissolves, the object ceases to appear as something worthy of love, leaving in its wake only an unrecognisable, shitty remainder: '*I give myself to you* [. . .], *but this gift of my person – as they say – Oh mystery! is changed inexplicably into a gift of shit* [cadeau d'une merde] – a term that is also essential to our experience' (SXI, 268/299). The gift of shit is no longer the attempt of the child, at Freud's anal stage, to purchase parental affection through a sacrificial offering; no longer the imaginary gift of love, the gift of what one does not have to give, through which we seek to recognise and thereby ground the existence of the Other. Lacan refers elsewhere to his 'essential term' as 'le fruit anal' and 'le *a* excrémentiel' (SX, 353, 371), reprised by Žižek as the 'excremental kernel of the Real', the innermost kernel of being, stripped of the fantasmic support that rendered it palatable to subjective experience. As the unconscious surplus of what is consciously desired, it is always given in excess of what is consciously demanded. Its excess lies in confronting the subject with the hitherto unknown real of desire, destituting it by depriving it of the possibility of the recognition that would satisfy desire. In the place of the subject there is only *objet petit a* as an excessive and ineliminable trace, the stain of 'the "undead", a strange, immortal, indestructible life that persists beyond death' (Žižek 1999: 294). As Lacan writes, discussing Freud:

> I have already said and repeated that oblation is the fantasy of an obsessive. Of course everybody wants genital union to be a gift – *I give myself, you give yourself, we give ourselves to one another*. Unfortunately, there is no trace of a gift in the copulatory, genital act, however successful you might imagine it. There is only a gift precisely there where we have always marked it, at the level of the anus. At the genital level, something emerges, pricks itself up [*se dresse*], that stops the subject over the realisation of a gaping chasm, a central hole, and prevents whatever might function as an object of the gift, an object destined to satisfy, from being captured. (SX, 371)

The formulation anticipates and provides an explanation for Lacan's later claim, made in *Seminar XX: On Feminine Sexuality, The Limits of Love and Knowledge* (1972–3), that 'there is no sexual relation [*il n'y a pas de rapport sexuel*]' (SXX, 126/114). There is no sexual relation because there is no 'real' gift exchange, no giving and receipt of recognition that would raise the extimate, excremental object to the dignity of a recognised and grounded subject.

To return to the film that opened this book, Lacan's gift of shit is illustrated in the *dénouement* of Lars von Trier's *Dogville*, which illustrates the catastrophic consequences of the protagonist's request for a gift. Thomas Edison, Jr's request that the people of Dogville have something 'to accept. Something tangible, like a gift' initially appears to be granted with the arrival of Grace, a beautiful woman who works tirelessly to integrate herself and repay a symbolic debt to townsfolk who only reluctantly received her. When in due course it becomes apparent that they got more than they asked for, they attempt to sacrifice her to the perceived forces of law, the gangsters to whom they fearfully look for the ontological support of love and recognition. The sacrifice fails, multiplying the town's own feeling of symbolic guilt. It fails, moreover, because sacrifice of this sort only ever reinforces the relation between law and *jouissance*, law as the instantiation of the drive's frustration of desire. Having survived her attempted sacrifice, Grace becomes the embodiment of the real, a persistent stain of life beyond death, returning to the town in the form of a monstrous, violent excess and visiting death (the impossibility of recognition) upon its inhabitants. Behind the gift of what one does not have, the attempt to give away the heterogeneous surplus that never belonged in the first place, we are confronted with a *cadeau d'une merde* that always returns to the site of its attempted and ultimately futile expenditure.

In *Seminar XX*, Lacan proposes the formulation of '*I ask you to refuse what I offer you – because it's not that* [ça – also meaning 'id'],' because what I offer you will never be the object of your unconscious desire – only the Thing that stands in for its absence (SXX, 126/114). Yet it is not so much a question of refusing receipt as of recognising exactly what it is that is given. Rather than trying to sacrifice the drive, or confronting it head-on, challenging it to expend itself in some form of *potlatch* that the subject is destined to lose, the only option is knowingly to choose to accept the gift of shit, and, by affirming the impossibility of choosing, to *become* it. In accepting the gift, the tragic hero affirms the extimate part of him- or herself in excess of the symbolic order and, renouncing the pursuit of subjectivity, becomes identical to, *repeats*, the object. 'The act [of acceptance, of traversing the fantasy] is a repetition', writes Kay, 'because it repeats the moment of our entry into the symbolic' (Kay 2003: 111), because it passes us backward through the subjectivising process. There is a clear repetition here of the transferential process of passing backward through love, receiving the gift of speech that announces one as a pure effect of symbolic exchange. But now, however, the symbolic is also seen as underwritten by the imaginary, performatively enacted through the sacrifice of the object of desire to the big Other. The receipt of the gift of the real is therefore a repudiation of sacrifice, 'a *repetition* of the sacrifice of sacrifice' (Keenan 2005: 113). The repetition is an ungrounding of the gesture by which the infant gives the object away in order to recover it in another form. The sacrifice of sacrifice pertains to a 'real' sacrifice, in which what is sacrificed is the imaginary sacrifice that generates faith in the efficacy of symbolic exchange. To accept the gift of the real is therefore to recognise the first two orders of giving for what they are: a sacrificial offering through which we seek to bring about the possibility of ontological recognition, and the symbolic exchange whose constitutive incompleteness repeatedly undermines the prospect of recognition. It is also to affirm the intangibility of a gift of the real that takes us further than ever from the realms of *homo economicus*, toward a thinking of the gift as an event that undercuts the Western philosophical pretension to metaphysical privilege. In receiving it, we encounter the excremental kernel of what Lacan diagnoses as a modern European obsessional fantasy of turning shit into soap, or nothingness into a substantial ground of subjectivity (SX, 348).

CONCLUSION

In the final paragraphs of the 'Rome Discourse', Lacan briefly turns to the Hindu *Upanishads* to articulate three meanings attached to the root, 'Da-': ' "*Damyata*, master yourselves", – the sacred text meaning that the powers above are governed by the law of speech'; ' "*Datta*, give", – the sacred text meaning that men recognize each other by the gift of speech'; ' "*Dayadhvam*, be merciful", – the sacred text meaning that the powers below resound to the invocation of speech' (E, 265/322). It would, perhaps, be pushing it to suggest that these three meanings – the impossibility of an agency independent of the law of the signifier; the recognition of the *don de la parole*; grace – map directly on to a threefold understanding of the gift as imaginary, symbolic and real. An initial problem stems from the fact that the first two apparently refer to the symbolic, with less immediate relevance to the imaginary and real. One might, however, note the blurring of the distinction between imaginary and symbolic in the later Lacan, where, with the discovery of the real, he shifts away from the Lévi-Straussian structuralism that led him to identify the subject as nothing more than an effect of language. The delayed but none the less growing influence of Bataille leads him to locate the origin of the subject in the failure of symbolisation, the breakdown of symbolic exchange, for which sacrificial offerings and the performative gift of speech merely compensate. Symbolic and imaginary are intertwined in a gesture that simultaneously renounces and seeks to recover the object of desire, creates the symbolic and compensates for the castration it bestows at the (missing) core of the subject. Their effect is moreover to displace and conceal an originary gift of shit, a traumatic, poisonous offering that exceeds the symbolic order – and which is accordingly unrecognisable as a gift.

It is here, paradoxically, that we might also look for redemption. John Forrester has suggested that Lacan leaves open the space for a concept of giving that exceeds relations of exchange, in the form of grace. This 'gift as pure gift, as grace', he argues, would satisfy the unconditionality – one might also add: the unrecognisability – required of the gift by Derrida (Forrester 1997: 159). The closing remarks of the 'Rome Discourse' thus anticipate the ethical imperative to traverse the fantasy, to affirm receipt of the (excremental) gift of the real. In *Seminar VII*, the tragic hero is defined as 'someone who may be betrayed with impunity', someone who is mercifully unfettered by the disappointment of desire. In contrast to 'ordinary man', whose betrayal 'has the effect of decisively throwing him back into the service of goods' (SVII, 320/370 [TM]), the hero is one who accepts the betrayal of desire to be inevitable; whose traversal of the 'fundamental fantasy' of identification leads him or her to see through the interminable exchange of signifiers, of gift and countergift at the level of the symbolic, and recognise the impossibility of repaying one's symbolic debt to the Other. The ultimate gift therefore takes place only in breakdown of the recognisable offerings and gifts of the imaginary and symbolic, in sacrificing the sacrificial gesture that inaugurated the symbolic order, in recognising oneself as defined by the extimate '*a* excrémentiel', the gift of shit that lives on beyond the attempt of the imaginary to present it as a benign gift of love. The hero asserts his fidelity to desire by repeating the object, recognising himself not as the generous Samaritan, a bestower of love providing the ground of the Other, but rather as the excremental absence of any redemptive offering. Redemption paradoxically lies in recognising that everything turns to shit and the obscene pleasure we take in it: namely, the *jouissance* we derive from desire's frustration. The negativity of this image maps on to criticisms of Lacan by Derrida, but also Deleuze and Guattari, all of whom effectively accuse him of reinscribing the gift within an economy of inevitable repayment, in an eternal return of the same that fails to capture the heterogeneity – hence also the politics – of the event. Having opened up the question of

Mauss's legacy, tracing the reception of his ideas through the self-styled anti-philosophical endeavours of structuralism, sacred sociology and psychoanalysis, we are in a position to see the effect of this on philosophy and a philosophical thinking of the political.

2. The Eternal Return of the Gift: Deleuze (and Derrida) contra Lacan

Eulogising in the immediate aftermath of his contemporary's suicide in 1995, Jacques Derrida describes 'the flustering, really flustering experience of a closeness or a nearly total affinity' evoked by the work of Gilles Deleuze (Derrida 2001a: 192/235). Deleuze was, he continues:

> the one among all those of my 'generation' to whom I have always considered myself closest. I never felt the slightest 'objection' arising in me, not even a virtual one, against any of his works, even if I happened to grumble a bit about one or another of the propositions found in *Anti-Oedipus* [. . .] or perhaps about the idea that philosophy consists in 'creating' concepts. (Derrida 2001a: 192–3/236)

For all Derrida's knowingly Deleuzian language in the above citation, the idea of an affinity, or complicity, between the two is belied by the merely fleeting references to each other's work. Despite the intimacy of Parisian intellectual circles, there is also only a single recorded exchange between the two, a brief discussion on the politics of eternal return in Nietzsche, instigated by Pierre Klossowski in 1972 (Klossowski 1973: 111–16). Although there were other encounters, and even a promise of dialogue left unfulfilled by Deleuze's death (Nancy 2005: 8n), it seems safe to say that Derrida was never 'volé', stolen, by Deleuze in the way that Félix Guattari was 'volé'. 'I stole Félix [*J'ai volé Félix*] and I hope he did the same for me,' Deleuze intriguingly states of the political activist and psychoanalyst with whom he collaborated for over twenty years (D, 17/24). The verb *voler*, to steal, also means *to fly* and Deleuze will repeatedly play on the double meaning. For Derrida, at least, the *vol* appears to be cause for a mild concern, 'a grumble [*un murmure*]'. Commenting on the passage cited above, both Stivale and Colombat have noted the contrasting praise for the single-authored works and the somewhat diminished enthusiasm with which he receives Deleuze's major collaborations with Guattari (Stivale 2000: 9; Colombat 1996:

236). A similar criticism has been made by Slavoj Žižek, who describes the turn toward Guattari as an 'alibi', a way for Deleuze to avoid coming to terms with the unbearable weight of his own thought (Žižek 2004: 21). Underlying Žižek's provocation is a rejection of the anti-Lacanianism, the politics of reverse-castration that Guattari brings with him. The reasons for Derrida's 'grumbling' are less clear-cut and have at times been obfuscated, rather than clarified, by a small but often partisan literature, not least that of Žižek, for whom it is a matter of 'fact that Derrida and Deleuze speak different, totally incompatible languages, with no shared ground between them' (2004: 47). Against the wilful hyperbole that seeks to reappropriate Deleuze as a Lacanian, the aim of this second chapter is to take Derrida's remarks at face value – perhaps naïvely, but in the sense that Deleuze himself was avowedly naïve, not at all interested, as Derrida notes, in the philosophy of 'objections', conjecture and refutation. The concept of the gift, in particular, will be read as exemplary of this affinity between Derrida and Deleuze, but also Derrida and Deleuze *and* Guattari. Interesting to note is that Nietzsche and the politics of eternal return emerge as fundamental components in the elaboration of this affinity. So too does the concept of theft.

Like Derrida, Deleuze seeks to differentiate the gift from anything resembling an economy of exchange, anything that would subsume it under laws of identity and equivalence. He finds the potential to overturn these laws and break free from the economic, 'circular figure' of the time of the subject in Nietzsche's thinking of eternal return (DR, 113/120). From its initial reworking in *Nietzsche and Philosophy* (Deleuze 2003: 23/32–3) and subsequent re-elaboration in *Difference and Repetition* (1968), Nietzsche's thought experiment figures throughout Deleuze's work as a superior repetition, the name for a life in excess of subjectivity, chronology and castrated desire. Deleuze describes 'theft/flight and gift', 'vol et don', as the 'criteria' of this repetition (DR, 1/7). The double meaning of *vol* as theft and flight affirms the gift as an expropriation and moreover a liberation, a theft of identity that frees thought from the repressive regimes of economic subjectivity. Much of this resonates with Lacan, above all with the ethics of repeating a drive whose eternal return to the same place expropriates the subject of its desire. Like Bataille, however, Deleuze and Guattari affirm the immanence that Lacan denies, and moreover use it as the basis for a critique of the Lacanian distinction between desire and libido, the castrated life of the human and the acephalic life of the drive. Deleuze offers an ontological (or pre-ontological) reading of the eternal return that radicalises the concept of life, identifying it even more explicitly with the impersonal, aneconomic repetition of a gift that defies exchange, ungrounding the recipient in the moment of its receipt. 'In the gift, repetition surges forth as the highest power of the unexchangeable' (LS, 329/334).

This Nietzschean influence is carried over into the reading of the gift economy in *Anti-Oedipus* (1972), where Deleuze and Guattari argue: 'The great book of modern ethnology is not so much Mauss's *The Gift* as Nietzsche's *On the Genealogy of Morality*. At least, it should be' (AŒ, 207/224). Underlying this claim is a conviction that the total social fact of Durkheim, Mauss and Lévi-Strauss is totalitarian in its subordination of difference to identity and disequilibrium to equilibrium (AŒ, 202–4/220–1), its reduction of the gift to supposedly transcendental structures of exchange. Following Bataille and anticipating Derrida, Deleuze articulates the gift as a name for the event of existence as such, the eternal return of an excessive giving of life that is effectively diametrically opposed to the gifts characteristic of the archaic gift economy. Rather than an *a priori* synthesis of society, read through a Nietzschean thinking of economics as the creation of memory and habit, the ritualised exchange of gifts becomes a way of containing this excessive event, a contingent technique for the imposition of laws (*nomoi*) of identity that serve to inscribe bodies with a homogeneous experience of time and desire. Deleuze and Guattari draw a subtle – perhaps too subtle, often ambiguous – distinction between the gift as a virtual, unrepresentable event, and the gift as an (overstated) category of archaic society; the gift as a future that brings about a forgetting, an erasure of the memory of the past, and the gift as a mnemotechnique for the formation of subjectivities. As in Lacan, where the imaginary gift of love, the sacrificial offering, is given to stave off the unpredictable, ungrounding excess of the real, so in Deleuze and Guattari, the actual, recognisable gift appears as a dilution of the intensity, a constraint upon the aneconomy, of the virtual giving of the event, which it endeavours to repress through contingent practices of coding. This contingency, however, means that the gift can break free; that the virtual gift of eternal return can be glimpsed in the breakdown of the actual gift economy, in the emergence of lines of flight that escape the subsumption of life under economics. Through this crucial distinction between virtual and actual gifts, Deleuze and Guattari lend credence to Derrida's later claim that 'a work as monumental as Marcel Mauss's *The Gift* speaks of everything but the gift' (GT, 24/39).

The argument is shot through with politics and a rethinking of the political. By returning to the tension between the virtual and actual conceptions of the gift – between what, following the distinction of *What is Philosophy?*, we might call the gift as concept, teased out from the gift

as an economic 'state of affairs [*état des choses*]' (WIP, 154–7/147–9) –
we see politics come into existence as a response to the impossibility of
receiving the eternal return of the gift. Thought conceptually, as a way
of coming to terms with the unfolding of life in excess of the human, the
affirmation of an eternal return to (and of) the gift becomes a strategy
for reasserting the inherent politicity of philosophy as an alternative to
a politics that struggles to free itself from the tyranny of the economic.
The task of philosophy becomes to think the eternal return of the event
– to attempt to recuperate in thought the excessive, aneconomic giving
that is held at bay by the economic structures of representation, and to
seek to translate this back into politics.

LIFE, IDENTITY, DIFFERENCE

> The highest virtue is uncommon and useless, it is shining and mellow in
> lustre: the highest virtue is a bestowing virtue [*eine schenkende Tugend ist
> die höchste Tugend*]. [...] Lead, as I do, the flown-away virtue back to earth
> – yes, back to body and life: that may give the earth its meaning, a human
> meaning!
>
>   (Friedrich Nietzsche)[1]

As we saw at the end of Chapter 1, Lacan's pre-ontology of the real
poses something of a paradox, in that the source of aneconomy, the
aneconomic gift of the real, coincides with the economic return-to-
self of the drive, which autarkically sustains itself on the *jouissance*
derived from the short-circuiting of desire. The libidinal drive is pure,
undifferentiated life, an oppressive self-identity from which otherness
is excluded. It might be preferable to say that aneconomy, in Lacan,
is caused by the disjunction between two economies: on one hand,
the fantasmatically supported economy of symbolic exchange; on the
other, the autarkic, *auto-jouissant* libido, which in always returning to
the same place prevents the closure of the circuit of desire. The theme
of Lacan's failure fully to pursue what we are calling aneconomy resonates throughout the work of Gilles Deleuze, most notably in the sole-
authored *Difference and Repetition* (1968) and *Logic of Sense* (1969),
but also in the co-authored *Anti-Oedipus* (1972). A critique of Lacan
can be drawn from Deleuze's reworking of Nietzsche's eternal return
of the same, which repeats but also extends a similar reworking undertaken by the psychoanalyst.

Recent work by Alenka Zupančič has opened up a dialogue between
Nietzsche and Lacan, drawing particular attention to the considerable

---

1. 'Of the Bestowing Virtue', Z, 100–2/93.

degree of overlap in their ethical projects (Zupančič 2003). For all the considerable merits of the ambition, one quite obvious similarity passes unnoticed, however. Even if only indirectly, as a result of the mediating presence of Bataille, Nietzsche's challenge to dare to assume *'das grösste Schwergewicht'* of living the same life 'once more and innumerable times more' finds a distinct correlate and is metaphysicalised in the circulations of the Lacanian drive (GS, 273/250 [§341]). As the relentless 'return into circuit' of a libidinal life in excess of the subject, the drive is nothing less than a pre-ontological staging of the eternal return. The ethical imperative to affirm repetition is repeated in the traversal of the fantasy, with the ethical act described as precisely a repetition, an affirmation of the impossibility of escaping the short-circuiting of desire by *jouissance*. To traverse the fantasy is to repeat the birth of the symbolic order, while recognising the impossibility of receiving substantial recognition of one's existence from the Other. Rather than clinging to the fantasy of substantial subjectivity, it is to recognise the futility of the sacrificial offerings that sustain this fantasy, and to become identical to the object they seek to conceal.

It was argued in the previous chapter that the real is *an*economic, the unrepresentable excess that supervenes on the economy of symbolic exchange. The argument is complicated, however, by the problem of how to reconcile this aneconomy with the following paradox: to accept the gift of the real, the excremental kernel of the subject, is to traverse the fantasy and thereby escape the eternally frustrated economy of desiring subjectivity. Yet far from giving rise to further aneconomy, the receipt of this gift implicates the recipient in a becoming that is merely becoming-economic, regrounding the subject as a subject of the drive, in the substance of *jouissance*. Deleuze, by contrast, paves the way for an understanding of the aneconomic gift that, while avoiding the paradoxes of Lacan, lends itself to a re-evaluation of the political, affirmed as the question and site of difference.

Despite Lacan's positing of an energy that is prior to human subjectivity, by continually aligning the drive with an object, *objet petit a*, Lacan reinscribes it within the dichotomous language of subject and object that Deleuze takes to be symptomatic of metaphysical transcendence. The criticism is developed into a full-scale critique in *Anti-Oedipus*, albeit in a way that has met with considerable resistance from both the philosophical and the psychoanalytic communities. Žižek, in particular, has sought to defend Lacan against the common accusation of a transcendent master-signifier by emphasising the immanent emergence of the real from the failure of the symbolic order (Žižek 1999: 296). Broadly anticipating subsequent criticisms from Lacoue-Labarthe

and Nancy and Derrida, the crux of Deleuze and Guattari's argument
is that Lacan idealises desire as lack, reducing its inherently excessive
force to the desire for what is absent, *objet a*. The real does not refer to
reality as such, but is reduced to its evacuation, to the fact that reality
is always fantasmically supported. In its wake, frustrated desire is left
capable of producing only the fantasies that mask the ontological void
(AŒ, 27/33). Impotent, castrated, it has no bearing on the actual production of reality.

   Deleuze's solution to this problem is to reject Lacan's implicit recuperation of identity in the form of a negative ground. In an argument
that, *mutatis mutandis*, applies as much to Kojève and Lévi-Strauss
as to Lacan, he rejects the idea of life as an undifferentiated, homogeneous nature into which differences are introduced symbolically,
through language, and at the price of introducing an irreducible gap
between nature and culture. He also rejects Lacan's threefold distinction between imaginary, symbolic and real as an anthropocentrism
that reduces the concept of life to a surplus of the (human) symbolic.
Underlying the rejection is the sense that Lacan fails to break free from
what Deleuze diagnoses as a persistent failure of Western philosophy
to treat difference in itself, without 'subordinating difference to the
supposedly initial powers of the Same and the Similar' (DR, 155/166).
Lacan, in other words, is guilty of privileging identity, the real of the
drive, while reducing difference to the extrinsically determined differences between signifiers in the symbolic order.

   In place of the Lacanian registers, Deleuze invokes an originally
Bergsonian distinction between 'virtual' and 'actual', between a virtual
'plan(e) of consistency' and an actual 'plan(e) of organisation', as the
basis of what he unashamedly 'naively' calls his metaphysics (Deleuze
1995: 136/122). The exact nature of the relation between the two has
been the subject of considerable debate. In one of the most important
challenges to Deleuze's philosophy, Deleuze's most eminent critic,
Alain Badiou, accuses him of Platonism, by arguing that 'the virtual is
the ground of the actual' (Badiou 2000: 43/65), an ideal and moreover eternal programme that the actual passively strives to instantiate.
This argument has been recently reiterated by another Badiousian,
Peter Hallward (2006a), but finds strong contestation in the work of
Keith Ansell-Pearson. The latter accuses Badiou of reifying the virtual,
oversimplifying Deleuze's complex presentation (Ansell-Pearson 2002:
98–105). He argues alongside Deleuze that the difference between
actuality and virtuality is essentially *perspectival* rather than metaphysical. As 'two aspects' of existence (D, 151/185), virtual and actual do
not exist apart, but are rather implicated in one another, inverse sides

of the same surface, separated out only by an (unconscious) tendency to subsume experience under general laws of identity and predictability – structures of representation that organise the world as a field of discrete, substantialised and apparently transcendent entities. Although not metaphysically distinct, they are, for all that, irreducible to one another. Crucially, there is no relation of resemblance between the two. The virtual is a 'transcendental field' that conditions the possibility of actuality, but cannot be re-presented in actuality without sacrificing its constitutive singularity; nor can it be construed as a mere negation of actuality, as if hierarchically inferior, which is to say less real than the actuality it conditions. Where actuality refers to a plan(e) of representation and identity, virtuality refers to a plan(e) of pure positive differences, prior to any concept of identity, whose singularity is foreclosed by the filtration of experience in consciousness. Deleuze develops a methodology that enables an understanding of the conditions of possibility of subjective experience without recourse to the anthropologism of a transcendental subjectivity: 'the transcendental is resolutely separated from every idea of consciousness, appearing as an experience without either consciousness or subject: a transcendental empiricism, in Deleuze's truly paradoxical formula' (Agamben 1999: 225).

The virtual is thus what exceeds the restricted economy of representation, an accursed share whose foreclusion is also the condition of the possibility of actuality. Like Lacan, Deleuze rarely gives explicit mention to Bataille, but the Bataillean terminology is not incidental here. Duns Scotus and Spinoza are routinely given as the more obvious references, but Deleuze arguably follows Bataille in thinking the immanence that Lacan rejects. The 'plan(e) of immanence' is the name more commonly given to the virtual plan(e) of consistence; the actual plan(e) of organisation is also called the 'plan(e) of transcendence' (TP, 265–6/325). What appears in actuality as the substantive and ontologically distinct *lives* of self-identical subjects, exists virtually as only 'une vie', a single life of 'absolute immanence': 'an impersonal and yet singular life that releases a pure event freed from the accidents of internal and external life, that is, from the subjectivity and objectivity of what happens' (TRM, 387/361). Immanence means that all forms of existence give expression to 'a single phylogenetic lineage, a single machinic phylum, ideally continuous: the flow of matter-movement, the flow of matter in continuous variation' (TP, 406/506). There is only a single reality, prior to hierarchical individuations between different strata of being, prior to the introduction of a distinction between materiality and ideality. Hence the description of virtuality borrowed from Proust: 'real without

being actual, ideal without being abstract' (DR, 260/269; Proust 1990:
179). Life is not composed of extensively distinct objects, but nor is it an
undifferentiated mass. The plan(e) of immanence consists in the event
of (pre-conceptual) differences in intensity: 'there are only speeds and
slownesses between unformed elements, and affects between nonsub-
jectified powers' (TP, 267/327). As a field of difference, *'une vie'* is not
to be thought in terms of self-identity, but rather as a life of multiplicity,
of multiplicities of positively construed, pre-symbolic differences, continually dissolving and reforming flows of intensities, which precede the
introduction of the negation that is inherent in representation. These
singular, or intensive, differences are also the transcendental conditions
of representation, constituting the expanded field of experience from
which our own experiences are drawn, without our having to refer
beyond them to an external, transcendent ground that explains their
existence. There is no ontological cut here, no metaphysically inscribed
distinction between virtual and actual; no irreducible tension between
Eros and Thanatos, desire and drive. Deleuze rejects Lacan's claim that
the object of desire is constitutively and ontologically inaccessible to
the subject in favour of a thesis of univocity, according to which there
is no incompatibility or incommensurability between different modes
of being:

> The univocity of Being signifies that Being is Voice; that it is said, and that is
> said in the same 'sense [*sens*]' of everything about which it is said. [. . .] One
> and the same Being for the impossible, the possible, and the real [*Un seul
> et même être pour l'impossible, le possible et le réel*]. (LS, 205–6/210–11)

The thesis is reasserted in *Anti-Oedipus*, where Deleuze and Guattari
write explicitly *contra* Lacan: 'The real is not impossible, within the
real everything is possible, everything becomes possible' (AŒ, 29/35).
Ansell-Pearson suggests that Deleuze's idea of the experientiability of
the impossible comes originally from Bergson, rather than Bataille, but
works to similar effect in extending experience beyond the restricted
horizons of subjectivity, beyond reference to sets of circumstances
that already exist in actuality, where 'the possible only precedes the
real through an intellectual act that conceals its own illusion' (Ansell-
Pearson 2002: 79). Deleuze sets about reversing the intellectual acts that
give rise to the illusion of a world composed of metaphysically, transcendentally distinct entities, by locating the moments where subjective
experience reveals itself as incomplete. The incompleteness provides an
opening through which to trace the event that is 'necessarily given at the
same time as that to which it gives rise', though crucially not given in
consciousness (TP, 268/326–7). It follows from this that on the virtual

plan(e) of immanence, even the impossible gift becomes possible, albeit in a form that does not yield itself to phenomenal experience. As the giving of the plan(e) of immanence, in a time of life that cannot be reduced to the transcendent, chronological time of the subject, the gift names a virtuality that bears no resemblance to its configuration as a discrete, essentially identifiable object in actuality.

DELEUZE, ŽIŽEK AND A LIFE OF THE POLITICAL

In the collaborative works with Guattari, Deleuze moves to explore the political implications of the univocity thesis by articulating the multiplicity of life as a political ontology, in both senses of the term. Beistegui has described Deleuzian ontology as '*onto-hetero-genesis*': 'a discourse on the way in which systems and phenomena of various types come into being', where moreover 'the "principle" presiding over the process of generation is not one of identity and resemblance, but of difference and dissimilarity' (Beistegui 2004: 223). Under the influence of Guattari, onto-hetero-genesis is politicised to the point of becoming a manifesto: 'PLURALISM=MONISM' (TP, 20/31), developed from the relationality of differences on the plan(e) of immanence. The philosophy of immanence translates into a politics of inclusivity and the embracing of difference. The same perhaps cannot be said for Lacan, whose distinction between life, defined as the self-identical drive of the libidinal real, and a desire conceived symbolically as a political sphere of exchange, means that the bare force of life is always pre- or proto-political.

The evidence of this is seen in Lacan's privileging of the heroic exception, the tragic figures of Antigone and Oedipus, who make the forced choice of withdrawing from the symbolic sphere of politics. Lacan and, after him, Žižek emphasise the possibility of using this withdrawal to renew the political through a 'sacrifice of sacrifice' that recreates the symbolic order. There is no conception of any community preceding the symbolic. A similar point has been made by Judith Butler, who, in *Antigone's Claim*, writes of being struck by the traditional nature of Lacan's reading of Antigone, 'not as a political figure, one whose speech has political implications, but rather as one who articulates a prepolitical opposition to politics, representing *kinship as the sphere that conditions the possibility of politics without ever entering into it*' (Butler 2000: 2).

The problem is exposed in Lacan's attempt to construct an alternative basis of community and collective coexistence in light of the collapse of the fantasmically supported big Other, which he does by reintroducing a residual form of difference back into the undifferentiated economy of the drive. According to Žižek, Lacan:

> insists that 'going through the fantasy' is not strictly equivalent to the shift from drive to desire: there is a desire that remains even after we have traversed our fundamental fantasy, a desire not sustained by a fantasy, and this desire, of course, is *the desire of the analyst* [. . .] the desire of someone who has undergone 'subjective destitution' and accepted the role of the excremental abject [. . .]. This unique desire is what, even after I have fully assumed 'the big Other's non-existence' – that is, the fact that the symbolic order is a mere semblance – prevents me from immersing myself in the self-enclosure of the drive's circuit and its debilitating satisfaction. The desire of the analyst is thus supposed to sustain the analytic community in the absence of any phantasmic support; it is supposed to make possible a communal big Other that avoids the transferential effect of the 'subject supposed to ... "know, believe, enjoy"'. (Žižek 1999: 296)

One cannot help but wonder, in light of this, whether politics is reduced to little more than a fantasy, albeit a necessary fantasy, required as an antidote to the nihilistic temptation toward acquiescence in libidinal *jouissance*. As Butler suggests, there is the suspicion of a residual Hegelianism. Reworked into the displaced identity of a real that is supposedly posterior to the politics of symbolic order, the *oikos* still essentially precedes the political. The Lacanian real comes to resemble the family in Hegel's *Principles of the Philosophy of Right*, where it is both prior to and an antidote to the deleterious effects of a civil society defined as 'Differenz' (EPR, 220/339 [§182]). We are presented with the prospect of withdrawing from (symbolic) politics into the 'debilitating satisfaction' of *jouissance*, construed as a kind of pre-political, self-enclosed *oikos*, as if the decision to withdraw were not itself already political.

It is worth noting that Žižek's more recent work moves away from indulging any fantasy of pre-political retreat. Rather than pertaining to any particular one of Lacan's pre-ontological registers, it is increasingly apparent that politics is generated by their mutual imbrication, by the impossibility of self-enclosure. In his self-declared *magnum opus*, *The Parallax View* (2006), Žižek appears to distance himself from a conception of the real as the self-identical life-beyond-death of a metaphysicalised drive. In its place, he proffers the idea of an irreducible discrepancy between experience and the underlying fabric of reality. The 'parallax of the *Real*' refers to how the 'Lacanian Real has no positive substantial consistency, it is just the gap between the multitude of perspectives on it' (Žižek 2006b: 7). This reassertion of the primacy of minimal difference, of the irreducible gap between real and symbolic, brings Žižek closer to Deleuze and Guattari, but also, he recognises, closer to Derrida, his criticisms of whom – to which we shall return in Chapter 4 – begin to be mixed with praise (Žižek 2006b: 11).

Deleuze and Guattari posit politics as irreducible, the brute fact of a life that consists in a field of virtual, singular multiplicities, prior to any concept of identity. Rather than reduce politics to a fantasy (and by implication, we might say, to ideology), they reinvent the political as a problem of the actualisation of the virtual and the way virtual singularities are invested in, which is to say condition, the social. Deleuze and Guattari stress that 'politics precedes being': *'avant l'être, il y a la politique'* (TP, 203/249). Underlying this claim is a form of virtual relationality that is pre-subjective and pre-individuated, pertaining to the interactions of the flows of life. Deleuze describes this relationality as a process of 'differen*t*iation', where the lines of becoming that constitute the excess of the virtual emerge from the 'differential relations' in which singularities differentiate themselves intensively from one another (DR, 274/285). Differen*t*iation translates into a corresponding process of differen*c*iation, which refers to the actualisation of virtual becomings in representable reality.

The question of translation, of how the activity of the virtual is translated into the lived experience of the actual, is the central question of Deleuze's reworking of Nietzsche's eternal return. In conversation with Klossowski, Lyotard and Derrida, amongst others, in the 1972 colloquium on Nietzsche at Cérisy-la-Salle, Deleuze poses this question in terms of whether 'it is possible to conceive links between singularities whose criteria would ultimately be the eternal return, implying the loss of identities, and yet not returning to any individualism, forming on the contrary societies and groups' (Deleuze, in Klossowski 1973: 120). Whereas the Lacanian traversal of the fantasy introduces us to the sameness that exists beyond the symbolic order, and the impossibility of pre-symbolic politics that this implies, the legacy of Nietzsche achieves the opposite effect in Deleuze. By affirming the different and the multiple against the illusions of transcendent identity, the eternal return is what Hallward has felicitously described as a 'principle of ontological discrimination' (Hallward 2006a: 206). It is the experience of eternal return, configured not as identity, but as the return of difference and multiplicity that generates a new concept of the political. The supposed impossibility of an inclusive politics of life re-emerges as the already existing community of the virtual.

REPETITION, THEFT, GIFT

The initial and most concentrated development of Deleuze's reworking of the eternal return takes place in *Difference and Repetition,* a
book that speaks, from the very first page, of inexchangeable excess.
Deleuze begins by corroborating Lacan's claim that symbolic exchange
is based on substitution rather than repetition. Once again he goes
much further, however, making it clear that repetition, with its inherent
singularity, can never be a question of identity and, by implication, the
eternal return of the same:

> Repetition is not generality. [. . .] Generality presents two major orders: the
> qualitative order of resemblances and the quantitative order or equivalences.
> Cycles and equalities are their respective symbols. But in any case, generality
> expresses a point of view according to which one term may be exchanged
> or substituted for another. [. . .] Repetition as a conduct and a point of view
> concerns non-exchangeable [*inéchangeable*] and non-substitutable singu-
> larities. (DR, 1/7)

As the citation suggests, repetition pertains to precisely that which cannot
be exchanged, namely the singular, the uniquely different. It is immediately following this that, implicating the structuralist thinking of symbolic
exchange, Deleuze makes the first, albeit fleeting, reference to the gift to
appear in his major writings: 'If exchange is the criteria of generality,
theft/flight and gift [*vol et don*] are those of repetition. There is therefore
an economic difference between the two' (DR, 1/7 [TM]). What he calls
the 'economic difference' between the two orders of exchange and repetition might more usefully be defined as the difference between economy
and aneconomy. As repetition and not substitution, he argues, the trace
of a gift can never be eliminated by the presence of a countergift that
seeks to reinstate equivalence. Nor, it follows, can the gift be subjected
to any overarching law of identity and exchange. Its irreducible singularity means that it will always be in excess of the particular, resisting the
attempt to subsume it under universal principles governing its behaviour.
As a criterion of repetition, giving is thus diametrically opposed to the
law-governed substitution of terms, the synthetically inseparable gift and
countergift of Lévi-Strauss's symbolic exchange. 'The true repetition is in
the gift' (LS, 328/333–4), because in the reciprocation of gifts the virtual
offering is never simply annulled by the countergift. On the contrary, the
countergift exceeds the initial offering, compelling the opening gift to be
repeated in an interminable cycle that sees the gift acquire 'the highest
power of the inexchangeable' (LS, 329/334).

The claim that '*vol et don*' are the criteria for repetition is, for all that,
ambiguous and receives no immediate qualification. On one hand, the

formulation raises the prospect of gift and flight/theft as distinct events, brought together under the concept of repetition. On the other, the two can be read as complementary, as inverse faces of the same event. In what is to date one of only two works that look explicitly at Deleuze's thinking of the gift, Constantin Boundas draws on the seminal anthropology of Annette B. Weiner to argue for complementarity and emphasise that the gift is indeed bound up with theft (Boundas 2001: 107).[2] Writing in *Inalienable Possessions: The Paradox of Keeping-While-Giving*, on the gift economy of Western Samoa, Weiner challenges the Lévi-Straussian idea that identity is a product of the circulation and exchange of gifts by suggesting that the giving of gifts is intended to reinforce rather than blur the boundaries between public and private spheres. Where Lévi-Strauss follows Mauss in asserting the identity of the giver to be embedded in the given object, Weiner points to the existence of 'inalienable possessions', 'possessions that are imbued with the intrinsic and ineffable identities of their owners' (Weiner 1986: 6), as evidence of a distinction between *oikos* and *agora*, domestic and political economy within archaic society. Gifts, she argues, are never items of the highest value, but rather substitutes for items that are withheld from circulation, for fear that giving them away would amount to an irretrievable loss of the owner's identity (Weiner 1986: 6).

The thesis is seen by Godelier to present considerable difficulties for Lacan's theory of symbolic intersubjectivity, the idea that the subject is constituted through circulation, with no substantive existence outside this intersubjective symbolic economy (Godelier 1999: 25–7/41–2). One might also argue the contrary, however: namely, that Weiner illustrates the way the (imaginary) ego clings to the prospect of interiority, the loss of which would be experienced as traumatic, inextricable from the loss, or theft, of identity. When, in a late interview, Deleuze eventually elaborates on the meaning of 'vol', he links it to an encounter that entails the expropriation of subjectivity. *Pace* Weiner, the theft is affirmed, not just as theft but as flight, an 'encounter' that takes the subject beyond the restrictive confines of the self. If traumatic, it is because it opens experience on to the possibility of multiple different becomings:

> An encounter is perhaps the same thing as a becoming or nuptuals. [. . .] It designates an effect, a zigzag, something that passes or happens between

2. The second is Claire Colebrook's introductory but none the less superlative essay on 'Exchange, Gift and Theft' (Colebrook 2006), which, despite the name, dwells for only the briefest of moments on Deleuze's thinking of archaic society and says nothing about Deleuze's concept of eternal return.

two, as though under a difference in potential. [...] It is not one term that becomes another, but each encountering the other, a single becoming that is not common to the two, since they have nothing to do with one another, but which has its own direction, a bloc of becoming. [...] To encounter is to find, to capture, to take flight and steal [*voler*]. [...] Taking flight/stealing [*voler*] is the opposite of plagiarising copying, imitating or doing like. (D, 6–7/13 [TM])

Hélène Cixous similarly draws on the ambiguity of *voler* to see in expropriation the possibility of affirmation, the potential for a flight that escapes from (masculine) economy (Cixous 1996: 96/134). Rather than a repetition of identity, theft pertains to a repetition of difference that cannot be conceived in terms of substitution and exchange. What needs to be emphasised, perhaps, is that for Deleuze the theft only appears as such from the perspective of the actual plan(e) of consciousness, where life is broken down into appropriable, hence violable, identities. It makes no sense from the standpoint of the virtual plan(e) of immanence, where life is precisely pre-individuated, hence inappropriable. The opposite is true of the gift, which, following Derrida, we know to take place only where it cannot be recognised as such, where it cannot be recuperated into an economy of subjectivity that would see it negated. Theft exists as the inverse face of the gift, as what Mauss calls the gift of poison, or rather the gift *as* poison (Mauss 1997: 28–32/234–7). Like poison, which works by transgressing the established thresholds of life, theft also resonates as an expression of the subversiveness of a life of excess that resists subsumption under law, constantly finding new ways to overturn the established order of identity.

THE LIFE OF TIME AND THE REPETITION OF THE GIFT

From *Difference and Repetition* to *Logic of Sense* and the late work on cinema, *Cinema II: The Time-Image* (1986), Deleuze's work is marked by a persistent critique of the attempt to conceive time in terms of presence. Predominant since Aristotle, if not even earlier, with Zeno, and remaining so at least up until Kant, this view regards time as a punctilinear series in which past and future exist as mere modalities of the present: 'Past, present, and future are not three dimensions of time; only the present fills time, whereas past and future are two dimensions relative to the present in time,' reduced respectively to presents that have already passed and those which are yet to pass (LS, 186/190). For Deleuze, to conceive time thus is to frame it in terms of human subjectivity, privileging (as did Kant) the idea that time is imposed on being by the subject. His initial argument, outlined in *Difference and Repetition*, proceeds by way of a distinction between three distinct 'syntheses' of time, one pertaining to each of the present, past and future respectively. Each synthesis also bears witness to the influence of one of three very different philosophers, united, Deleuze argues, by a commitment to the thinking of difference in excess of the supposed identity of the subject. The synthesis of the present is founded on the anti-inductionist empiricism of Hume; that of the past on the (Proustian) intuitionism of Bergson; that of the future on the eternal return of Nietzsche, dramatically and influentially restaged by the *collégien*, Pierre Klossowski, as an eternal return of difference. Each synthesis is said to be 'passive', which is to say prior to any operation of subjective, human agency. The syntheses of the present, *habitus*, and of the future, the eternal return, prove to be particularly important for the analysis of the gift as repetition, and the relation of the virtual to the actual gifts of archaic society.

The first synthesis of time is *habitus*, a term Deleuze borrows from Hume's description of the imagination as a faculty of habit formation (Hume 1975: 43). Hume argues against the possibility of objectively knowing whether relations of nature are bound by necessity, or whether they are merely contingent, derived from an experience of consistency that ultimately has no metaphysical basis. He suggests that our experience of their supposed necessity is psychological, the product of the human mind, rather than transcendent in origin. The impression of necessity is not simply disclosed in experience but rather unconsciously imposed on it, or synthesised, through a psychological principal of induction. Deleuze goes further than Hume, positing that every appearance of transcendence, of logical necessity and essentiality, is the product of a similar process. He denies that this process is simply psychological, however, since this would still be to imply a privileging of the human mind as the site of synthesis. The 'contraction' of life into general laws and identities is in fact the most primordial form of pre-human organisation: 'Every organism [...] is a sum of contractions' (DR, 93/99). The human subject is but one instance of a universal process of contraction, inherent to the actualisation in consciousness of an unconscious life of immanence.

When Deleuze writes that 'the event [...] has no present' (LS, 73/79), it is because presence must be created. It exists only as (an effect of) *habitus*, the synthesis that organises time into a punctilinear experience of presents passing through consciousness. This process of organisation is said to take place in the withdrawal of difference from repetition: 'Habit *withdraws* something new from repetition – namely difference

[...]. In essence, habit is contraction' (DR, 95/101 [TM]). By extracting difference from repetition, the synthesis of the imagination creates the economic order of generality wherein one instance can be exchanged or substituted for any other. It falls short of full-blown repetition for the same reason.

The time that precedes this time of habit and presence, Deleuze argues, is a time of repetitions of difference and a futurity that cannot be conceived in terms of consciousness and presence. In *Logic of Sense*, this is described as the 'non-chronological time' of *Aiôn*, the event, which stands against the linear, habitual temporality of *Chronos* (LS, 74–5/80–2). In the slightly earlier *Difference and Repetition*, this repetition of pure difference constitutes the third synthesis of time, the impossible time of the eternal return. 'The eternal return is the same of the different, the one of the multiple, the resemblant of the dissimilar' (DR, 154/165). The formulation strongly recalls that of Pierre Klossowski, to whom Deleuze devotes a substantial appendix in *Logic of Sense* (LS, 321–40/325–50), and whose influence is also quietly discernible throughout *Difference and Repetition* and *Anti-Oedipus*. Published contemporaneously with the latter, but incorporating earlier material to which Deleuze (to whom it is dedicated) had access, Klossowski's seminal *Nietzsche and the Vicious Circle* (1969) challenges the idea that Nietzsche's thinking of eternal return could consist in a repetition of the same, the repetition of this life 'once more and innumerable times more' (GS, 273/250). According to Klossowski, the description of the thought experiment laid out in §341 of *The Gay Science* expresses not so much the unconscious reality of the eternal return as a 'simulacrum' of this reality, an attempt to reconfigure the unthinkable in terms that render it amenable to representation. The truth of the greatest weight is not the persistence of identity, but its very opposite – namely, the opening up of experience to a body that, despite being given cohesion and continuous identity by the imagined subject, is anything but continuous and coherent: 'this body *dies* and is *reborn* numerous times – deaths and rebirths that the self [*le moi*] claims to survive in its imaginary cohesion' (Klossowski 2005: 23/55 [TM]). Through the death and constant rebirth of multiple libidinal intensities, the body becomes the site of an unconscious repetition that undermines the subject's claim to unified, self-identical (*ergo*, essential) agency: 'The Eternal Return suppresses enduring identities. Nietzsche urges the adherent of the Vicious Circle to accept the *dissolution* of his fortuitous soul, in order to receive another, equally fortuitous' (2005: 55/108).

Eternal return thus describes repetition in what Deleuze takes to be the fullest sense of the term, repetition 'this time by excess' of the future, where futurity is understood as the advent of the 'absolutely new itself' (DR, 113/122). In this moment of excess, all categories of representation are overturned; all representational content is evacuated from the memory of the pure past. The economy of representation in which time is stripped of its singularity loses it *oikos*, rendering time itself 'out of joint [*hors de ses gonds*]', anarchic, no longer bound by the logic of chronological time, *Chronos*:

> Time itself unravels (that is, apparently ceases to be a circle) instead of things unfolding within it (following the overly simple circular figure). [...] It is distributed unequally on both sides of a 'caesura', as a result of which beginning and end no longer coincide. (DR, 111/119–20)

In contrast to Lacan's death drive, where the subject is destroyed through the renunciation of desire in the *répétition-en-acte* of pure identity, by the acceptance of the impossibility of the identity of desire and drive (the pure life of the libido), in Deleuze the transcendental death of the subject is brought about by the pure difference of Thanatos (rebaptised *Aiôn* in *Logic of Sense*). In this repetition of difference, time is no longer subordinate to its contents, a means of chronologically ordering or measuring the movement of things within it. It breaks with the chronology of sequential presents in a way that fractures the identity of the contractions and habits of the present. As one such contraction, the conscious, supposedly transcendent, individuated subject is destroyed. The singularities that underlie subjectivity surge up through the subject and:

> turn back against the self which has become their equal and smash it to pieces, as though the bearer of the new world were carried away and dispersed by the shock of that to which it multiply gives birth: what the self has become equal to is the unequal in itself. (DR, 112/121 [TM])

If *habitus* synthesises the identity of subjectivity, we might say that the eternal return articulates the failure of induction, the collapse of law-governed patterns (contractions) of experience. In other words, it refers to what, commenting on Klossowski, Deleuze calls a 'disjunctive synthesis', a synthesis of intensities that, for Klossowski, *'aspire only to de-individuate themselves'* (Klossowski 2005: 21/53 [TM]; see also LS, 339/342).[3] This synthesis *undoes* the synthesis of the subject, signalling the collapse of order and the opening of the world on to the underlying 'chaosmos' that is concealed by representation. The experience of pure

---

3. The reference to Klossowski in *L'Anti-Œdipe* is in fact a reprint of a slightly earlier essay, 'La Synthèse disjonctive', which, its authors note, 'isn't presented as a commentary on Klossowski, but is all the more indebted to him as a constant reference' (Deleuze and Guattari 1971: 54).

intensity propels us beyond the illusion of the transcendent subject as
the privileged ground of being and discloses, in the wake of this transcendence, the absence of a ground. There is only a 'groundlessness
[*sans-fond*], a universal ungrounding [*effondement*], which turns upon
itself and causes only the yet-to-come to return' (DR, 114/123). More
than just a collapse, an 'effond*r*ement', Deleuze calls this experience an
effondement, a reversal of grounding, an *un*grounding, in which the
experience of life on the plan(e) of organisation gives way to an experience of the world in its virtual immanence, an event of singularities
taking flight, unbound from the strictures of chronological time.

Through this experience of difference in the eternal return, the
destruction of the subject frees life from its captivity in the thought of
transcendence and opens on to a privileged experience of the world
as a plan(e) of immanence, multiple continua of differences defined as
sensation without subjectivity, experience without consciousness. The
repetition of difference returns the virtual experience of pure intensity
and transcendental death, announcing itself 'in an instant that no doubt
does not belong to the economy of time, in a time without time, in such
a way that the forgetting forgets, that it forgets *itself*' (GT, 17/30).
The citation is from Derrida, but applies seamlessly to Deleuze. The
aneconomic time of the event is the time of the forgetting of both the
subject and the representational content of memory: 'a self-effacement
that is carried off with what it effaces' (GT, 17/30). One critic has
already noted the similarity of Derrida and Deleuze on this thinking of
the temporality of the gift (Lorraine 2003: 44). Another has sought to
differentiate them on this point, however, by suggesting that the gift is
experientiable for Deleuze but not for Derrida (Bearn 2003: 181). Yet
this claim understates the extent to which for Deleuze, too, the gift does
not admit of conventional, which is to say, phenomenal experience, not
to mention the way it proves incompatible with the experience of debt
that would serve to negate it.

For Deleuze, as for Derrida, in the virtual experience of the eternal
return as gift, there can be no indebtedness on the part of the recipient
because, *qua* self-identical subject, the recipient is destroyed in the very
moment of reception. There is no longer a distinction between the giver,
the gift and its recipient. Life (time, desire) gives itself as a becoming-
other that implicates the subject in the same becoming-other. To receive
the gift, it follows, is to give up, or sacrifice, the pretension to grounded
subjectivity and recognise oneself as an expression of the event of the
giving of life. This is already to put into effect Derrida's criterion that
the gift must 'efface everything', 'leave nothing behind it' (GT, 17/30).
What Deleuze calls the 'plan(e) of organisation', of transcendence, is

populated by distinct objects and subjects, creating a set of conditions under which, following Derrida, the gift will always be annulled. It is only where the objects or actions given as gifts are themselves individuated that they become recognisable as such, and are consequently able to generate the feeling of indebtedness that reinscribes the gift within an economy. Equally, it is only where there are individuated subjects that the receiver of a gift can feel indebted to the giver, or the giver can derive a similar return on his gift by enjoying the narcissistic pleasure of having given: 'There where there is subject and object, the gift would be excluded' (GT, 24/39). Where once there was a subject, there are now only lines of flight, or becoming, each one tracing the aneconomy of *Aiôn* toward a 'becoming-imperceptible' in which one no longer perceives oneself as individuated, an identifiable giver or receiver of gifts. Even love is transformed, 'freed from bondage to the organism and to the person' (Protevi 2003: 189). No longer Lacan's imaginary gift of what one does not have (SIV, 140), the narcissistic attempt to ground oneself by offering in vain to ground another (the Other), love, for Deleuze and Guattari, names the becoming, the experimentation, of excessive desire, freed from the narcissism of the subject of lack and rendered creative, aneconomic. The one to whom one gives 'is just as selfless as I':

> One has become imperceptible and clandestine in motionless voyage. Nothing can happen, or have happened, any longer. Nobody can do anything for and against me any longer. [...] I am now no more than a line. I have become capable of loving, not with any abstract universal love, but a love I shall choose, and that shall choose me, blindly, my double, just as selfless as I [*qui n'a plus de moi que moi*]. One has been saved by and for love, by abandoning love and self. (TP, 199/244)

This love without propriety is precisely what characterises the behaviour of Roberte in *Le Souffleur*, the dynamics of which were outlined briefly in the previous chapter. In the third and final instalment of Klossowski's *Les Lois de l'hospitalité*, Théodore gives away his wife in order to know her all the more intimately, as she exists beyond the restricted economy of marriage. To her husband's despair, however, Roberte breaks with the spirit of the laws of hospitality, substituting herself for another, a simulacrum, identical to the point of undermining the idea that there exists an 'original' Roberte. While Roberte becomes what Deleuze and Guattari call an 'antiexchangist amorous machine' (AŒ, 203/219), Théodore suffers a nervous breakdown, a subjective destitution or 'theft' of identity, which is redoubled by his ensuing inability to differentiate his own self from that of another simulacrum, K. The psychoanalyst, Dr Ygdrasil (Lacan), tries to cure him

by recommending that he too submit to a circulation without beginning or end, without a higher goal that attempts to accord it meaning.
Only thus might he disabuse himself of the notion of propriety, of the
pretension that Roberte was ever his to give away. What Ygdrasil fails
to realise, however, is that the phalanstery implied by the 'universal
law of exchange' would never yield the gift that Théodore desires.
What is more, Roberte has already given her husband precisely what
he asked for. The latter simply failed to realise that the gift is theft,
poison, culminating in an experience of intimacy in excess of identity:
an experience of immanence without consciousness, of the ultimately
ungovernable multiplicity that underlies the contractions of difference
into identity. Roberte rises to meet the challenge of accepting the gift of
eternal return, actively embracing a life of multiplicity and groundlessness. Théodore, by contrast, crumbles under the weight of *das grösste
Schwergewicht*.

ŽIŽEK CONTRA GUATTARI

If Deleuze's earlier, sole-authored, efforts open us on to an experience
of time as eternal return, it is only really in the collaborative works with
Félix Guattari that this thinking of time is rearticulated as a revolutionary politics of desire, a theory of life in which the eternal return directly
plays out as a becoming that cuts across history. The idea of a discernible difference between two 'conceptual logics' in Deleuze has been
argued forcefully by Slavoj Žižek, who uses it as a basis for rejecting
the 'Guattarianised' Deleuze of *Capitalism and Schizophrenia*. Žižek
differentiates an earlier, more Lacanian, position in *Difference and
Repetition* and *Logic of Sense* from what he derisively calls the 'idealism' of *Anti-Oedipus* and *A Thousand Plateaus* (Žižek 2004: 21). In the
earlier works, the eternal return is confined to a Klossowskian experience of bodily intensity that cannot be conceived within the restricted
experiential horizons of presence and the self-consciousness of the
subject. The corresponding event is 'sterile', an intensified experience
of reality rather than a 'productive' process in which reality is actually
created by the activity of the virtual. The shift from sterility to produc-
tivity coincides with the claim that the eternal return of desire is directly
implicated in the production of social reality. It moreover coincides
with the intervention of Guattari and the onset of a sustained critique of
Lacan, in which the Lacanian concept of desire as lack is hyperbolically
dismissed as ahistorical, a formulation that characterises desire only in
light of its reconfiguration under conditions of capitalism. Žižek also
aligns it with the politicisation of a hitherto 'elitist', apolitical, or – in

the words of Alain Badiou – 'profoundly aristocratic' Deleuze (Žižek 2004: 20; Badiou 2000: 12/22).

Žižek's preference for the apolitical Deleuze is perhaps not surprising, given what was suggested above to be Lacan's restrictive conception of politics in terms of fantasy. One wonders, however, whether he does not short-circuit a politics that is already at work in the earlier Deleuze: namely, a politics of the relationality between intensive differences in a state of multiplicity, the actual political implications of which Guattari merely makes explicit.[4] In accusing Deleuze and Guattari of idealism, Žižek is rejecting the hypothesis of a 'desiring-production' capable of directly creating social reality. What his critique fails to appreciate is that the desire in question refers not simply to the generative potentiality of human desire, but rather to desire as a name for life as such.

Like the temporality of the event in *Difference and Repetition*, according to Deleuze and Guattari, 'desire knows nothing of exchange, *it knows only theft and gift* [vol]' (AŒ, 203/219 [TM]). Desire, in other words, cannot be confined to the (Hegelo-Kojevian) desire for recognition through symbolic exchange, nor to any other configuration on the plan(e) of organisation. It desires the theft of identity, the excessiveness of a gift whose receipt would undermine rather than complete identity. 'Desire lacks nothing; it does not lack its object. It is rather the subject that is missing in desire' (AŒ, 28/34 [TM]). Just as Deleuze inverts Kant by asserting that the subject is in time and not *vice versa*, so Deleuze and Guattari affirm that the subject exists within desire, albeit as a corruption of desire. Lacan said something similar through the theory of the symbolic order, but his thinking of desire as lack points to a residual framing of his work by economism. Deleuze and Guattari read him as the last stand of *homo economicus*, a figure historically defined by lack in so far as driven to make choices by the scarcity of resources within society. The prevalence of scarcity translates into the pervasiveness of lack, which leads in turn to the impossibility of satisfaction.

On the virtual plane of immanence opened up by transcendental empiricism, desire is liberated from the bondage to lack in which it is imprisoned by subjectivity and becomes manifest as the flow of intensive singularities. What desire desires is not simply an actually missing object, but rather the possibility of virtually reconnecting with its hitherto excessive dimension, where individuated objects give way to a multiplicity of intensive flows of becoming: 'What is desired is the intense germinal or germinative flow, where one would look in vain for

---

4. On this point, see also Patton (2000: 104); and Hallward, who confidently asserts that there is no radical break between *Logic of Sense* and *Anti-Oedipus* (2006a: 87).

persons or even functions discernible as father, mother, son, daughter, etc.' (ACE, 177/191). Opened on to its virtuality, desire ceases to be the castrated, impotent desire of Lacan, capable of producing nothing more than the fantasies that fill in for the impossibility of satisfaction. Through its relation to excess, desire is revealed as inherently *productive*, where this production is of reality as such:

> If desire produces, it produces the real. If desire is productive, it can be productive only in the real world and produce only reality. Desire is the set of *passive syntheses* that engineer partial objects, flows and bodies, and that function as units of production. The real is the end product, the result of the passive syntheses of desire as autoproduction of the unconscious [*Le réel en découle, il est le résultat des synthèses passives du désir comme autoproduction de l'inconscient*]. (ACE, 28/34)

Desiring-production is not expressive. When construed in terms of a general economy of life, it does not, as Lacan suggests, share a structure with language; nor does it express itself through fantasy, except when cut off from its productive aspect. It is rather a *machinic process* of creation, with no purpose – no object of satisfaction – other than the continual production of new connections with other desiring machines (ACE, 28/34). It is this connectivity that takes desire beyond the *oikos*, beyond, on one hand, the desire for identity and, on the other, beyond confinement to the familial (Oedipal) unit. By producing connections that go beyond this unit, desiring-production breaks down the modern (Hegelian, Freudian) distinction between a private sphere of desire and a public sphere of political economy.

Economics is classically defined as the distribution of scarce resources, the science of 'human behaviour in disposing of scarce means' over a limited period of time (Robbins 1945: 30). Against this orthodoxy of scarcity, for Deleuze and Guattari it is excess and *not* lack that constitutes the primary problem of the socio-political. The question is not whether there is excess, but rather how to contain the excess that is virtually always already inherent in desire. By the same measure, the principal question of revolution is not how to foment it, but, again, how to contain the revolution that is virtually ongoing. The organisation of scarce resources is but secondary to this, an attempt to forestall the excessive arrival of a future of death and instability, a future that would break from identity with the present:

> Desire is revolutionary in its essence [...] and no society can tolerate a position of true desire without its structures of exploitation, servitude, and hierarchy being compromised. [...] It is therefore of vital importance for a society to repress desire [...]. Desire does not 'want' revolution, it is revolutionary in its own right, as though involuntarily, by wanting what it wants

[*Le désir ne 'veut' pas la révolution, il est révolutionnaire par lui-même et comme involontairement, en voulant ce qu'il veut*]. (ACE, 126–7/138)

In a formulation whose potential denial of human agency has met with resistance from the more humanist of Deleuze's commentators (notably Ansell-Pearson 2004: 37; see also Hallward 2006a: 56, 162), Deleuze and Guattari argue that 'the fundamental problem of political philosophy' is 'why, after centuries of exploitation, do people still tolerate being humiliated and enslaved, to such a point, indeed, that they *actually want* humiliation and slavery not only for others but for themselves?' (ACE, 31/36). The answer they posit is that the subject is already the result of a tendency immanent yet running counter to desire: namely, repression. Repression occurs because desire is unable to cope with its own intensity, its constant production of new connections, intensities and becomings: 'there is no fixed subject unless there is repression' (ACE, 28/34). One should be wary of reading the subject as the only site of repression, however. The tendency toward repression is not just immanent to the human, but to all life. Rather than a psychic structure of a pre-given, individuated subject, it refers more generally – one might argue too generally – to the way differences on the plan(e) of immanence are contracted into the apparently transcendent entities manifest in subjective experience. As nothing more than another name for the process of filtering the virtual life of immanence into actual experience, repression is not simply a characteristic of the human, but rather pertains to every organisation of life in representable actuality. It is also, as such, one of the key concepts in Deleuze and Guattari's radically non-anthropocentric thinking of the political. The generality of the concept offers one reason as to why the above-mentioned critics suspect Deleuze and Guattari of going too far in trying to decentre politics from human need.

If politics is a question of repression, it is not an active human repression, but rather a passive operation. It refers, in other words, to the impossibility of fully actualising the virtual, of completing the breakdown of organisation that would coincide with the 'absolute deterritorialisation' of identity. According to Deleuze and Guattari, different societies are the result of differences in the way the actualisation of virtuality plays out, with different social organisations reflecting variations in regimes of restricted economy, varying techniques of repressing and containing the aneconomic, virtual potentiality of life. Deleuze and Guattari describe them in terms of different social bodies, each one the reorganisation of an underlying 'Body without Organs [*Corps sans Organes*]' which, as DeLanda notes, is roughly synonymous with the plan(e) of immanence, 'the virtual continuum formed by multiplicities'

(DeLanda 2002: 158). The socius functions as the surface on which production takes place, hence also bears witness to life's inability to cope with the intensity of excess. This becomes manifest in its inability constantly to renew itself, to repeat itself through the creation of new connections with other desiring-machines. The fixity of social life results from the organisation of the virtual flows of life into apparently transcendent, individuated bodies and partial organs, disconnected from their immanent conditions. The tension between economy and aneconomy, between the institution and breakdown of laws of identity, is thus the fundamental moment of politics. Throughout history, politics consists in the attempt to capture the excessive life of the gift in repressive regimes of identity.

In saying this, Deleuze and Guattari closely recall not only Bataille's *The Accursed Share* (1949), but also Nietzsche's conjectural, unashamedly fictional account of the birth of human society in *On the Genealogy of Morality* (1887), which Bataille's work attempts to historicise. They furthermore explicitly elevate the *Genealogy* above Mauss's *Essai* as 'the great book of modern ethnology' (AŒ, 207/224). As part of a genealogical strategy to disclose concealed values and animal modes of behaviour beneath the supposedly transcendent, *a priori* institutions of modernity, Nietzsche posits a distinction between two ideal types in the pre-history of man, which Deleuze, in an earlier work, differentiates as the 'active' noble and the 'reactive' slave (Deleuze 2003: 53/65). The behaviour of the former is distinguished by its uncontrollable instinctive spontaneity. The hypothetical noble is said to live without regard for the actions of others and is even speculatively endowed with an active 'faculty of forgetting' (*active Vergesslichkeit*) that causes suffering experienced at the hands of others to be forgotten. Able to live and face the future without fear of suffering, the noble is thus effectively aneconomic, which is to say unconcerned by identity and the prospect of losing everything. In the Bataillean terms laid out in the previous chapter, nobility roughly translates into the sovereignty of unproductive expenditure, the ability unconditionally to squander, to discharge one's instincts and energy without expecting something in return. The hypothetical slave, by contrast, is pure economy. Obsessed with death and a suffering that memory leaves it unable to forget, its behaviour seeks to minimise potential loss by holding back resources, withholding from expending energy in the present. Rational and calculating, the slave's incessant mediation of action by thought renders it fundamentally incapable of spontaneity. Whereas the noble is unaware of time, the slave lives in bondage to it, always reacts to it, as if threatened by it; servitude of this sort 'is never "through" with anything [*wird mit*

Nichts "fertig"]' (GM, 39/308 [2§1, TM]). The latter is embodied in Christianity, which sacrifices life in the present in order to invest in a future of beatitude, as if in accordance with some calculus of salvation.

Strongly anticipating what Weber, in 1905, would go on to describe as the Protestant work ethic (Weber 1992: 53–4/61), Nietzsche formulates the modern experience of time as an economic problem. Time is reconstructed as homogeneous, present, rendered suitable for investment through the foreclusion of destabilising heterogeneity. The emergence of this economic disposition towards life coincides with the 'breeding of an animal *which is able to make promises*' (GM, 38/307 [2§1]), the breeding of an animal that experiences time as stable, predictable, on the basis of which it becomes possible to regulate one's experiences within time. This in turn is traced to what Nietzsche regards as the fundamental social relationship of pre-modern (pre-Christian) society: namely, that of debtor to creditor. The former secures a loan by agreeing to the creditor's demand to extract, in the event of non-repayment, quantities of flesh commensurate with the incurred debt. In addition to affording the creditor a degree of compensatory pleasure, the inscriptions punish the failure to repay by creating a memory on the surface of the debtor's body. The presence of scars serves 'to etch the duty and obligation of repayment into conscience' (GM, 44/315 [2§5]), leaving the debtor unable to escape the memory of debt. Far from a metaphysical given, Nietzsche thus conjectures that the calculating, predictably rational figure of *homo economicus* is the product of mnemotechnical forces that have been overlooked by conventional, teleologising accounts of history.

Yet this mnemotechnical 'breeding' also conditions the subsequent (be)coming of the *Übermensch*, the one who surpasses servitude through the ability to say 'yes' to the memory of a past that has made him or her who he or she is. As the one who survives the thought experiment of eternal return, the *Übermensch* is also the one who breaks free from the economic constraints of identity; who valorises the reckless expenditure of a gift so great that it would sunder identity – and who indeed affirms the eternal return as such a gift. Hence Zarathustra's elevation of a 'schenkende Tugend', a 'bestowing virtue', above all others (Z, 100/93).

SIMULACRA OF THE GIFT (DELEUZE AND GUATTARI *CONTRA* LYOTARD)

Given Nietzsche's hypothetical location of the noble in a time prior to the onset of Western modernity, it is tempting to follow Bataille and

equate the noble with archaic society, with the capacity for spontaneous expenditure exhibited in the allegedly ahistorical societies of the
potlatch. There are, however, considerable risks in succumbing to this
temptation. Jean-François Lyotard has been highly critical of what he
sees as the fetishisation of the gift economy, the fantasy of 'ethnology's
good savage' as an untainted, idealised natural communism, prior to the
deleterious transformations of capitalism. Lyotard argues in *Libidinal
Economy* (1974) that 'the whole problematic of the gift, such as [we]
receive it from Mauss, with or without the additions and diversion of
Bataille, Caillois and Lacan, belongs in its entirety to Western imperialism and racism' (Lyotard 1993a: 106/130). Offered as an alternative
to capitalism, the gift economy reveals itself as a fantasy generated by
capital, whose logic it reinforces by positing itself as an alternative.
Judith Still argues that Derrida's awareness of 'reverse ethnocentrism'
diminishes his susceptibility to Lyotard's criticism (Still 1997: 19–20;
see also WD, 356/414, cited above, in the introductory chapter). It is
not always clear whether the same can be said of Deleuze and Guattari,
or whether they happily romanticise archaic society, purposefully con-
flating the archaic gift with a concept of the gift as the event of eternal
return. The affirmation, in *Logic of Sense*, of an 'economy of the gift
that is opposed to the mercantile economy of exchange' (LS, 328/334)
is one instance of an apparent tendency to make little effort to differentiate the virtual from the actual organisations that repress it, often
collapsing the two together. The ensuing suspicion is that Deleuze and
Guattari idealise often decidedly repressive archaic regimes, and has
led Christopher L. Miller to argue that they 'take some extraordinary
liberties' in their use of anthropology (Miller 1993: 19). The problem,
as Miller sees it, lies in their attempt to deploy anthropological concepts to characterise the event while simultaneously reading them back
into archaic society, thus transforming the latter into a utopian site
of resistance against a specifically Western history of the repression
of desiring-production. Miller offers Deleuze and Guattari's concept of
the nomad as an example of this. In *A Thousand Plateaus* (1980), they
extract the idea of nomadology from anthropological discourse in order
to recreate it as a philosophical 'concept', an expression that captures
the unconstrained desiring-production of eternal return as a *nomos*
without *oikos*, a distribution of energy unbound by the repressive formations of identity, where, to cite Ansell-Pearson, 'repetition itself [is]
the only form of "law" beyond morality' (Ansell-Pearson 1997a: 66).
Yet, Miller argues, they also characterise the nomadic 'war machine' as
an actually existing anarchic, archaic reality, prior to the social repression of desire (1993: 25–9).

In their final collaboration, *What Is Philosophy?* (1991), Deleuze and Guattari differentiate the concept of philosophy from what Deleuze perceives to be the wholly distinct and unrelated function of the sciences. To this end, they argue that the concerns of science (in which they would presumably also include anthropology and the other human sciences) lie primarily in the descriptions of 'states of affairs', the configurations and organisations of actualised, individuated entities in conscious experience. Only philosophy, by contrast, engages with the virtual, creating 'concepts' that 'survey' the plan(e) of immanence, giving expression to the impossible experience of eternal return (WIP, 32–4/35–7). Defined by its 'power of repetition' (WIP, 159/150), the task of the philosophical concept is to lend consistency to that which exists virtually, beyond the bounds of consistent, comprehensible logic. But as a repetition of difference, it also serves to unground the purportedly stable *logos* of anthropology, 'countereffectuating' the giving of the gift economy (WIP, 155–6/147).

In addition to the complaint that Deleuze and Guattari idealise the archaic gift economy, this construal of philosophy as the creation of concepts has given rise to a number of other accusations of idealism, not least of which the suspicion, already noted by Lyotard, that they legitimate capitalism. The reasons for this will be discussed at greater length in Chapter 4, primarily in respect of their understanding of the relationality between philosophy and politics. Miller's criticisms *vis-à-vis* anthropology thus fit into a broader set of concerns about Deleuze and Guattari. Taken by itself, however, the suggestion that they conflate archaic society with a site of unrestricted, aneconomic exchange is unconvincing. When *Anti-Oedipus* is reread through *What Is Philosophy?*, we see that what is at stake is not so much an anthropological description as the staging of how the archaic gift economy comes into existence. Deleuze and Guattari's aim is to extract from archaic actuality its habitually concealed relation to the event. Their iconoclastic, strategically hyperbolic writing style admittedly lends itself to confusion on this point by continually and repeatedly switching between anthropological and conceptual registers, blurring the boundaries between philosophy and the human sciences. They none the less seem to be aware of the risks of idealisation, stating pointedly in *Anti-Oedipus* that 'there is no pure nomad,' no formation of desire that is not subject to regimes of organisation (AŒ, 163/174 [TM]). Problematically, in terms of what it might imply about the trajectory of their later work, this is more apparent in the first volume of *Capitalism and Schizophrenia*, whose lengthy consideration of exogamy presents archaic society as anything but an anarchy of free desire. The distinctions that Miller accuses Deleuze and Guattari of obfuscating are also manifest in their denial of the 'especially weak and inadequate' belief that archaic society falls outside history (ACE, 165/177). This belief, they argue, is bound up in a modern (originally Judeo-Christian), teleological concept of history, which they also reject as a product of ideology and racism. Rather than a continuum of progress, Deleuze and Guattari define history in terms of rupture and discontinuity, 'the history of contingencies and not the history of necessity', whose traversal marks the breakdown of the repressive formations through which the eternal return is held at bay (ACE, 154/163). If archaic society is thought ahistorical, in this respect, it is not because it bears witness to a privileged experience of eternal return, but quite the contrary. The apparent ahistoricality stems from the success of archaic techniques in staving off the deterritorialising ruptures that would mark the entry of eternal return into history. Rather than ahistorical, archaic society is, if anything, marked by an excess of history over becoming (which is also to say a deficit of philosophy).

Nietzsche's *Genealogy* is more important than Mauss's *The Gift* not because it opens us on to a pre-Christian, ahistorical, social reality of spontaneity and aneconomy, but rather because Nietzsche's speculative account of mnemotechnicity is already implicitly at work in Mauss's account of the gift economy. Where Mauss and, moreover, Lévi-Strauss posit the synthetic apriority of an overarching total social fact, a transcendent ground of unified social reality, it is only with Nietzsche and genealogy, they suggest, that we uncover the origins of apparently pre-given social structures:

> Society is not first of all a milieu for exchange where the essential would be to circulate and to cause to circulate, but rather a socius of inscription where the essential thing is to mark and to be marked. There is circulation only if inscription requires or permits it. (ACE, 156/166)

This privileging of inscription over exchange serves as a basis for contesting Lévi-Strauss's identification of exchange with the unconscious of desire. Deleuze and Guattari actually argue the contrary: namely, that exchange functions as a technique for desire's repression, albeit one that is not repressive enough for archaic society. In place of exchange as a total social fact, the synthesis of social identity, we find a pre-exchangist economics of inscription, in relation to which the giving of gifts functions as a supplementary strategy for the circulation of debt. The archaic economy is described as a mnemotechnical attempt to regulate the 'decoded flux' of the eternal return, to repress and impose constraints upon the revolutionary potential of unconstrained desiring-production, which constitutes 'the nightmare that the primitive social machine exorcises with all its forces' (AŒ, 167/179).

In saying this, Deleuze and Guattari can be read as developing on the arguments of Lacan, who, as we saw in the previous chapter, describes the imaginary gift as a defence mechanism against the ungrounding effect of, first, the symbolic gift of speech and, later, the gift of the real. Deleuze and Guattari draw an analogous distinction between actual and virtual gifts, where the former responds to the excess of the latter in the form of a repression. In light of this, it becomes necessary to draw a distinction between the gift of eternal return and the gift as an instance of mnemotechnical repression. With this distinction in hand, it becomes clearer that the archaic gift is what becomes of aneconomic desiring-production when in so-called primitive society it is always already caught up in a process of codification, of subjection to social repression.

Whereas Nietzsche emphasised the creation of memory as a technique of individuating subjects, binding them to individual debts, Deleuze and Guattari use it to posit the archaic body as the collective body of the tribe, 'a collective investment of organs' that precedes any experience of individuated (modern) subjectivity. This is exemplified in traditions that appropriate bodies by physically marking and modifying them with signs (including tattooing, scarification, subincision, circumcision) that designate their function within the overarching tribal collective. The inscribed memory is experienced as a debt, an inability to forget the collective body to which one owes one's existence: 'Debt is the direct result of inscription' (AŒ, 208/225). 'The original subject of obligation is not the persona,' as Lingis puts it, 'it is my body, more exactly, my productive body parts, which have been incorporated into the social code by being marked' (Lingis 1994: 293). More than just an aggregate of marked individuals, the archaic social body is rendered collective through the mnemotechnical circulation of women as gifts. There is thus an explicit link between the circulation of gifts and what Deleuze and Guattari call the circular time of *habitus* (DR, 117/120). By focusing on the inscriptive power of the gift economy, Deleuze and Guattari argue that the body is not just written *on*, but moreover written into existence, produced by pre-graphic techniques of writing as forms of *habitus*, the contraction of aneconomy into iterable laws of identity.

Where the gift of eternal return breaks down the experience of chronological time, the archaic gift, by contrast, participates in the creation of this experience. Following Nietzsche, Deleuze and Guattari write of 'a memory of alliance and of words, implying an active repression of the intense memory of filiation' (AŒ, 170/182). By memory of alliance, they mean a (psychological) memory, or *habitus*, brought into existence through organisations of kinship and exogamy, techniques that restrict the potential for desire to produce new connections. The giving away of women for marriage creates a new social memory by imposing a code over another, pre-existing memory: namely, that of a genetic flux whose immanent potentiality generates a scope for reproduction and sexual activity far in excess of what the institutions of archaic society are able to absorb. Systems of exogamy code the repetition of desiring-production by imposing a patrilineal system of reciprocity on to the otherwise unconstrained possibilities of filiative (sexual) reproduction (AŒ, 173/186). The gift economy consists in the repression of differ-ence, the contraction of virtual aneconomy into economic regimes of identity. What is circulated is not just women, but debt, in the form of the obligation to reciprocate gifts given, and it is debt, Deleuze and Guattari argue, that prevents the gift economy from being configured in terms of exchange. Deleuze and Guattari praise Mauss for having kept open the question – foreclosed by the structuralism of Lévi-Strauss – of whether debt is prior to exchange, or merely a mode thereof (AŒ, 205/218–19).

Rereading the pre-Lévi-Straussian Mauss through Nietzsche enables them to go further and show how the excessive, untranslatable remain-der functions as a decisive moment in the creation of a repressive organisation. In his critique of their use of anthropology, Miller takes Deleuze and Guattari to task for over-reliance on problematically colo-nialist anthropological sources, as if to imply that their argument would find little sympathy with more contemporary, post-colonial anthropol-ogy (Miller 1993: 22–4). Yet their establishment of a relation between excess and domination suggests quite the contrary. Writing from within the discourse of anthropology, Marilyn Strathern has argued that the possibility of such a relation has been neglected by traditional gift anthropology (Strathern 1988: 166). Deleuze and Guattari not only anticipate this lacuna but moreover propose a solution to it, arguing that surplus value is central to the techniques of domination through which excessive desiring-production is drawn off and turned back against itself, rendered docile. It is always the surplus, they argue, that serves to 'organize selections [*prélèvements*] from the flows', effecting the breakdown of flows of immanence into transcendent units of iden-tity (AŒ, 165/177). Their argument – like the problematic to which it responds – is clearly Marxian in origin; like Marx's, theirs will also culminate in an analysis of surplus capital, profit, as the most advanced stage in a history of domination through excess (AŒ, 153/163).

The earliest, most 'primitive' form of surplus value, however, is the surplus value of *code* (AŒ, 164–5/176). Deleuze and Guattari identify this with the *hau*, the 'esprit des choses' described by Maori myths as the cause of the circulation of gifts throughout the gift economy. As we saw in the previous chapter, the attention Mauss pays to the *hau* leads Lévi-Strauss to accuse him of being seduced by indigenous myths. The latter reworks the *hau* as a 'floating signifier', an unconscious expression of the structures of exchange that govern social reality (IMM, 63/xlix). The *hau* is in turn reconfigured by Lacan as an expression of the lost object of desire, the empty placeholder of the real in the symbolic order, which tribal members attempt to recuperate through the sacrificial offering of gifts. For Deleuze and Guattari, the myth of the *hau* codes desire by overseeing the conversion of a virtual, inherently destabilising excess of energy into a manageable, containable surplus (AŒ, 164–5/176). By imposing the obligation that the reciprocating gift be in excess of the one it reciprocates, the *hau* generates new and more debt rather than simply extirpating debt through the establishment of harmonious equilibrium. It propagates rituals like the *potlatch* as archaic systems of taxation, skimming off surplus goods by offering honour in lieu of payment for what might otherwise have facilitated material domination. Writing on the broader 'political posture' of Deleuze, one commentator captures how this prevents the centralisation of influence in the hands of a tribal chieftain, whose 'power is held in check because the gifts he receives increase exponentially his obligation to repay them' (Valentin 2006: 195).

Far from indicating the existence of transcendental, *ergo* ahistorical and totalising structures of exchange, the regulating myths of archaic society consist in contingent and experimental *practices* (AŒ, 162/173), which through the absence of any transcendental privilege can never totally succeed in implementing a system that fully captures and codes the excess of desire. Mythopoiesis contributes to the stability of archaic society, preventing it from succumbing to a comparatively deregulated system of exchange. A similar conclusion is found in the work of Pierre Bourdieu, whose highly influential analyses of the gift economy overlap with Deleuze and Guattari's on a number of points. Bourdieu also insists on the gift economy as a 'logic of practice' revolving around a concept of habitus that prohibits a simple contrast between object and subject, society and the individual agent. Like Deleuze and Guattari, he is vocally critical of the 'exchangeism' of Lévi-Strauss, who argues that the countergift is contained synthetically *a priori* within the opening gift. Reminding us of the reasons for which Deleuze and Guattari turn toward Nietzsche, Bourdieu argues that a focus on the apriority of structures fundamentally elides the question of the relationship between

the experience of agency and social conditioning, of how people's participation in social norms is governed by unconscious ('unthinkable')
processes, which are themselves the outcome of previous practices
(Bourdieu 1990: 54/90). The attempted reversal of this elision is borne
out in Bourdieu's theory of habitus, which he describes as consisting in
'principles that generate and organise practices and representations that
can be objectively adapted to their outcomes without presupposing a
conscious aiming at ends' (Bourdieu 1990: 53/88). Drawing not from
Hume but from none other than Mauss, who uses the term to account
for culturally different 'techniques of the body' (Mauss 1979: 70–4;
SA, 368–72), Bourdieu employs the concept to explain how the sedi-
mentation of practices over time serves unconsciously to organise social
behaviour, embedding actions in habit to the point where adhesion to
social norms passes off as the result of freely chosen actions.

Of particular significance, in this respect, is the importance Bourdieu
attaches to the role played by institutions of gift giving in creating the
impression of subjective agency through manipulations of the experience of time. He accuses Lévi-Strauss of neglecting the 'temporal inter-
val between the gift and the countergift', the fact that cultures of gift
exchange almost always insist upon a delay prior to the reciprocation
of a gift. Viewed as an instance of habitus, the effect of the temporal
gap is to create an impression of agency, 'to enable whoever is giving to
experience their gift as a gift without return [*un don sans retour*], and
whoever reciprocates to experience their countergift as gratuitous and
not determined by the initial gift' (Bourdieu 1998: 94/179 [TM]). It is
in this sense of agency that we see the origin of a system of honour, a
system for channelling the instability of excess, of futurity and temporal
uncertainty, into a system of returns through which uncertainty and
unpredictability are contained. By ensuring that the gift is experienced
as freely given, the habitus creates an incentive to give. But it also thus
averts the threat of a future that breaks drastically with the established
order, converting the instability implied by the non-reciprocation of
gifts into a manageable system of surplus. Bourdieu argues that the
control implicitly exercised by the *habitus* is a fundamental prerequisite
for the harmonious functioning of a community, which falls into dis-
array once members cease to submit to the collective 'misrecognitions
[*méconnaissances*]' through which this discharge is controlled (1998:
95–6/181–2). His argument thus presents itself as a productive way of
interpreting Deleuze and Guattari's claim that the circulation of gifts
is never continual, but rather made possible by discontinuity and the
measured rhythming of time. Anticipating Bourdieu, they argue that
the repressive, mnemotechnical power of the archaic *habitus* consists

in its ability to introduce 'breaks [*coupures*]' and 'selections from the flux [*prélèvements de flux*]' that slow circulation to a stop (ACE, 163–7/174–6). It is in this slowing of circulation, the introduction of breaks allowing the accretion of honour to the giver, that we see the drawing off and encasting of excess, the conversion of potentiality into a manageable surplus that ultimately poses little threat to the metastability of the tribe.

THE PROMISE OF ESCAPE

Bourdieu's reading of the gift economy in terms of an unconscious habitus has led him to criticise Derrida for overstating the extent to which the gift is bound up in 'the free decision of an isolated individual': in other words, for presupposing the giver as a *homo economicus* whose calculations undermine and negate the supposed spontaneity and generosity of offering a gift (Bourdieu 1998: 95/181 [TM]). The criticism misses the point that, for Derrida, it would not matter whether the gift is given freely or under unconscious duress, for the simple reason that, subjectively, it is still linked to a feeling of agency, and this feeling is enough to reinscribe the gift within an economy that negates it. By emphasising that the spontaneity of a gift is a result of the habitus, Bourdieu actually reinforces Derrida's claim that the gift is never unconditional when implicated in the economics of subjectivity. But the criticism of Derrida exposes Bourdieu to an objection raised by Manuel DeLanda, who, in his recent and sophisticated elaboration of a Deleuzo-Guattarian social ontology, argues that Bourdieu's concept of habitus irreducibly differs from that of Deleuze in its failure to leave space for human agency, 'to the extent that all differences between the motivations behind social behaviour [...] disappear' (DeLanda 2006: 64). If this is transposed on to Bourdieu's reading of the gift, it would seem that he can only preserve the authenticity of gifts by denying that the giver plays any active part in the giving. Ironically, the accusation precisely mirrors one levelled against Deleuze by Hallward, whose ultimate rejection of the former stems from the conviction that he 'acknowledges only a unilateral relation between virtual and actual', thus denying 'any notion of change, time or history that is mediated by actuality' (Hallward 2006a: 162). The argument hinges on the validity of Badiou's claim that the Deleuzian thinking of virtuality collapses back into a 'Platonism of the virtual', a regrounding of existence in the metaphysics of the event (in Badiou 2000: 47/69). Without wishing to dwell too much on a question whose complexity exceeds the remit of the present exercise, one could respond provisionally in favour of

Deleuze by reprising an idea mentioned at the onset of the chapter. In looking for actuality to mediate the virtual, Hallward is perhaps guilty of a category mistake, treating virtual and actual as metaphysically rather than *perspectivally* distinct. In so doing, he conflates the rejection of a transcendent, ontologically privileged agency with a rejection of agency *tout court*.

As we shall see in Chapter 4, where it will be suggested that Deleuze's thinking of the virtual gives rise to an undue privileging of philosophy over politics, this does not mean that Deleuze and Guattari entirely escape the criticisms of Badiou and his disciple. But nor does it mean that Deleuze and Guattari deny the space for agency. On the contrary, their exposition of the relations between virtual and actual is what enables them to do this. The rejection of structuralism in favour of an analysis of mnemotechnical practices means that there is potential for members of a society actively to resist and unground the techniques through which eternal return is held at bay. This does not mean that agency is pre-given, that it can be taken for granted in its ability to override other (non-human) forces. Rather, agency too must actively be actualised, created in lines of flight that unground the restricted *habit-uses* of identity. In this respect Deleuze and Guattari are in agreement with Derrida about the possibility of the impossible, the possibility of rewriting the social order. The Deleuzo-Guattarian description of *habitus* as a technique of coding, or writing, is one of the rare instances where they refer directly to Derrida, with whom they agree that language originates in writing. Describing how the 'voice' of the *hau*, the law that compels the circulation of gifts, presupposes the appropriative marking of a tribal body through inscription, they argue: 'Jacques Derrida is correct in saying that every language presupposes a writing system from which it originates, if by that he means the existence and connection of some sort of graphism – writing in the largest sense of the term' (AŒ, 220–1/240). They go on to qualify this, noting that the relationship between writing and voice is historically unstable (Indeed, the whole of *Anti-Oedipus*'s monumental third chapter, 'Savages, Barbarians, Civilized People', can be read as a historicisation of this claim; see in particular AŒ, 220–1/240). The thesis that organisation proceeds through the introduction of breaks (*coupures*) into the aneconomic flux of life is still highly Derridean. From his earliest works, Derrida argues to similar effect that language works by creating a communicable economy of representation, which stands in for the incommunicable, aneconomic event, without foreclosing it entirely (Derrida 1988: 8, 20–1/28, 49; Derrida, Nouss and Soussana 2001: 89). Like Deleuze and Guattari, he explicitly identifies eternal return with a repetition of difference (*différance*) that prohibits the formation of closed systems of identity: 'on the basis of the unfolding of the same as *différance*, we see announced the sameness of differance and repetition in the eternal return' (M, 17/18–19). This concept of *différance*, however, describes how that which is sacrificed in the process of organisation retains a virtual potentiality through which it continues to exert influence over that from which it is foreclosed. Language is never stable, but works on account of its instability. Rather than a closed system of exchange, through which a message is communicated unambiguously and in its entirety, communication works by sacrificing this possibility, by excluding the singularity of experience in order to express it in terms of a comprehensible generality. It is only through this organisation that language can attempt to communicate the impossible: namely, the event that exceeds organisation. But the organisation is fragile, to a greater or lesser degree, which is to say it remains eternally open to the prospect of a return of *différance*, the singularity that was foreclosed in the process or organisation (1988: 20–1/49). There is always thus a future in which the impossible could conceivably become possible.

Deleuze and Guattari draw on a similar thinking of systemic instability to demonstrate the possibility of lines of flight, traces of virtuality prefiguring what, in his later work, Derrida will equate with the promise, a repetition of difference that breaks free from the economy of representation (GT, 24/39; SM, 48/126). In *Anti-Oedipus*, the effect of these virtual traces is discernible within the regimes of repression, which are never closed systems but rather open, unstable and necessarily so: 'it is *in order to function* that a social machine must *not function well*' (AŒ, 166/177).

The trace of the virtual, the gift of eternal return, is not found in the mnemotechnical gift, the gifts of women circulating throughout archaic society, but rather in the ability of tribal members to defy this circulation. Deleuze and Guattari anticipate Derrida's *Given Time* by arguing that the gift bestowing debt is in fact the antithesis of the gift as event; that the virtual gift breaks through only in the breakdown of the economy that encasts it. Paradoxically, it is in tribal members' experience of the gift as theft (AŒ, 202–3/219), for example, that we bear witness to a destabilising excess that escapes capture. Although held within a position of metastability by the practice of the countergift, the gift economy is none the less constitutively unstable, always open to the possibility that someone could successfully avoid being coded, escape the obligation to give and counter-give and accrue enough power to overturn the collective organisation of power. According to Deleuze and Guattari, this is indeed what happens. 'Primitive societies are

defined by mechanisms of prevention-anticipation' (TP, 435/542), by
the anticipation and prevention, or warding off ('*conjuration*'), of the
emergence of centres of power. They earn this definition by maintaining
circulation, by promoting the myths that nothing falls outside or resists
circulation; that production is permissible only in so far as subject to
coding, which is to say convertible into a system of surplus management that threatens its destruction (through the destruction of goods in
the *potlatch*). But archaic society succumbs to despotism through the
breakdown of circulation, when a tribal member bypasses the duty to
give away women and obtains an incestuous marriage, which in turn
creates a privileged, royal bloodline and elevates the despot as the creditor to whom all debts are owed (AŒ, 217/236).

It is in this receipt of his own gift that the self-appointed despot
appropriates the archaic 'war machine', a concept, briefly, that refers to
the possibility of a destabilising countergift, a gift that would unground
established relations of power, fracturing the monopoly of apparently
transcendent institutions and loci of power (TP, 355–60/439–46). The
birth of the State coincides with the centralisation of power in the hands
of a despot, who captures the destabilising logic of the gift by declaring himself the source of an infinite, hence ineliminable, debt, ensuring that the gifts he receives never become subject to the obligation to
reciprocate (AŒ, 215/234). The rise of despotism also coincides with
an unleashing of production and technology. In a reversal of Bataille's
reading of the gift economy as a site of unproductive expenditure, to
be contrasted favourably with the production without expenditure of
modernity (AS, 131–2/126), Deleuze and Guattari suggest that archaic
society is characterised by a repressive coding of production:

> The primitive machine isn't ignorant of exchange, commerce and industry;
> it exorcises them, localizes them, cordons them off, encasts them, and main-
> tains the merchant and the blacksmith in a subordinate position, so that the
> flows of exchange and the flows of production do not manage to break the
> codes. (AŒ, 168/179–80)

The breakdown of the gift economy paves the way for technological
lines of flight that, even if fostered and appropriated by the repressive
institutions of the State, will ultimately become forces of deterritorialisation. Decoupled from the system of honour and instrumentalised,
rendered subordinate to the despot, technology serves all the more
forcefully to add to and 'overcode' the regimes of repression immanent
to life, the better to contain the virtual potentiality of the event (AŒ,
214–15/233; TP, 419/522). The question of technology thus emerges
as another variable in a history of politics that is effectively a history
of flight from the gift, a history of the attempt to curb and encast the

unregulated potentiality of a life in excess and subversive of the social order. But the history of politics' flight from the gift is also a history of the return of the repressed, of the creation of lines of flight in which the eternal return of difference breaks through and undermines repressive social formations of identity. Much as technics may inhibit the exercise of agency, it also expands its horizons of possibility, creating new lines of flight through which a seemingly impossible agency retains the prospect of actualisation. For all that, technology remains ambiguous, both a facilitator and an obstacle to change, both a threat and a supplement to the becoming of the human (TP, 410–12/510–13).

In saying this, Deleuze and Guattari provoke comparison with another thinker of the gift who, though different in a great many ways, raises a number of questions that will need to be addressed. Like Deleuze and Guattari, Martin Heidegger advocates a politics of repetition based on a specifically – one might say overly – philosophical thinking of politics. Like Deleuze and Guattari, he writes of the ambiguous role of technology in relation to the event and is openly sceptical of democracy. If the appearance of similarity falls down on Heidegger's Nazism, one is nevertheless compelled to raise the question of whether the philosophical thinking of a politics of the gift is not inherently contaminated, liable to veer toward aristocratism through its attempt to privilege the singular and unthinkable over the general and comprehensible.

CONCLUSION

As we saw in Chapter 1, Lacan develops the idea of a tension between a (real) gift of excess and an imaginary gift that works to repress it. Deleuze and Guattari go much further, however. Reconfigured as a tension between virtual and actual, the problematic of the gift becomes the fundamental, or rather *ungrounding*, axis of the socio-political and its history, which plays out as the perennial struggle to curb the flow of virtual revolution into actuality, the attempt to forestall the repetition of eternal return. In place of a mere thought experiment, a proposition designed to challenge the Christian waiting for an afterlife, we find the eternal return ontologised, reconfigured as a name for life as such. This life, or '*une* vie', is not self-identical, undifferentiated (as it is in Lacan), but rather internally differentiating and multiple, giving rise to a temporality that cannot be confined to the mere chronology of passing presents, and to a desire that does more than just (anthropomorphically) lament its lack of self-identity. Far more than just the life of an individuated organism, '*une* vie' names the non-chronological time of a future that breaks with the present, a desiring-production that produces the continual novelty of becoming, rather than languishing in the stasis of identity. But it also, as such, names the time and generosity of a virtual giving that bears no resemblance to the anthropological incarnation of the gift. If, as Derrida suggests, Marcel Mauss's *The Gift* offers an analysis of 'everything but the gift [*tout sauf du don*]' (GT, 24/39), it is because in circulating debt and the obligation to reciprocate, and in being given in the expectation of this reciprocation, the archaic gift is precisely the opposite of a spontaneous, uncalculated, generous offering. In describing the '*tout*' of archaic society, Mauss and Lévi-Strauss misrecognise it as a closed system, a totalisable whole that overlooks the ruptures and discontinuities characteristic of the social dynamic. They therefore miss the constitutive tension between the event of difference and the economic practices employed in its constraint.

This tension is also what gives rise to politics, which, though beginning with the differentiation of singularities on the plane of immanence, is moreover staged in the attempted actualisation of these singular relations, the organisation of pre-individuated differences into laws, habits, identities or economies, that curtail the intensity of the excessive, ungrounding event. Against the accusation that Deleuze and Guattari conflate the gift economy with the event, it becomes clear that a politics of the gift cannot be constricted to the regimes of archaic society. Its primary concern is rather to expand the field of the political to account for the conditions of possibility of politics: namely, the absence of a ground, for which politics compensates through the inscription of stabilising regimes of order. Understood as a response to the eternal return, to the repetition of difference, what Deleuze and Guattari call the micropolitics of becoming consists in taking flight from the gift economy, affirming the revolutionary potential of a gift that cannot be reduced to economic exchange. The line of flight is also a *vol*, requiring the affirmation of the theft of identity that coincides with the receipt of this gift. Deleuze writes in *Logic of Sense* that 'willing the event [*vouloir l'événement*]' is the primary question of ethics (LS, 164/168). That is not to say that all ethics and indeed all politics of the gift will be worthy of the event; that they would not be swept aside by the advent of the event in the eternal return, however. The question becomes one of how to recover when this happens, how to reconceive the gift without collapsing back into some form of restricted economy. Walter Benjamin's (and Lacan's) concerns over Bataille, in this respect, have already been noted in Chapter 1, while those of Miller regarding Deleuze and Guattari have been discussed above. From Bataille, to Lacan to Deleuze, in each of its incarnations, there has been a suggestion that the thinking of the gift can never achieve the aneconomy to which it aspires. There is a risk that the attempt to elaborate a politics of the eternal return, of the rejection of all grounding figures of essence and identity, is inevitably reterritorialised around a surreptitious return of a transcendent, foundational truth that becomes paradoxically totalitarian in its affirmation of difference, and which accordingly raises the stakes of its relation to the political. Nowhere is this more starkly illustrated than in the politics of the gift, the politics of repetition, of the one-time Nazi, Martin Heidegger. We shall see in the attempts to salvage the gift from his legacy that the question of the political – of what the political *is* and also how it relates to fascism – surges up as *das grösste Schwergewicht* of thinking politics in relation to the event.

3. Repeating the Political: Heidegger and Nancy on Technics and the Event

The Heidegger Affair has complicated matters: a great philosopher actually had to be reterritorialized on Nazism. [...] It had to be a philosopher, as if shame had to enter into philosophy itself.

(Gilles Deleuze and Félix Guattari)[1]

The rise of the human sciences was one of the conditions for a distinctly philosophical thinking of a politics of the gift – one of the conditions for thinking politics both in its relation to anthropology and in its relation to an event in excess of the human. But it was not the only one; and the nascent field of anthropology was not the only academic discipline to engage with the problematic. The brief mentions of Husserl and Jean-Luc Marion in the introductory chapter noted how phenomenology too was also and still is immersed in a language of the gift, of what *es gibt* in consciousness, distinct from the anthropological discourse of giving (Husserl 1960: 24/64). Writing from within this phenomenological tradition of 'givenness', Martin Heidegger was among the first to seek to wrest philosophy back from what he perceived as its restrictive framing by 'Anthropology'. He dismisses anthropology's 'lacking ontological foundations [*fehlende ontologische Fundament*]' as an obstacle to the fundamental ontology through which he could conceptualise giving as the essential characteristic of the event (BT, 75/67 [§10, 49]). Rather than welcome the emergence of the discipline, recognising it as a resource for philosophy, he condemns it as the apogee of a deleterious history of Western metaphysics, the culmination of an anthropomorphosis of being, in which the metaphysical essence of man is taken for granted: 'the *anthropological* mode of thinking, which, *no longer comprehending the essence of subjectivity*, prolongs modern metaphysics by vitiating it. "Anthropology" as metaphysics is the transition of meta-

---

1. WIP, 108/104.

physics into its final configuration: "Weltanschauung", or worldview'
(N, 441/179). In so far as it neglects, or suppresses, the fundamental
relation of beings (*Seiende*, the *Dasein* Heidegger substitutes for the
subject) to the event of being (*Sein*), the anthropological world view
is linked to 'the question concerning technology', the question – also
the title of one of Heidegger's most influential essays – of how man's
relationship to the event is mediated by the manipulation of the world
through technics. Heidegger understands modern technology as a technics for the immortalisation of the subject, a way of framing being so
as to conceal its excess over finite beings. This leads him to diagnose a
crisis of global technological nihilism, brought on by man's inability to
confront the imminence of death. In so far as similarly framed by the
technological-nihilistic attempt to evacuate death, the crisis is one to
which politics alone proves dramatically insufficient a response. The
critique of modern technology accordingly entails a rejection of politics, in its traditional (institutional) conception, and causes Heidegger
to seek beyond the technologically enframed institutions of the modern
state a philosophically purified, which is to say 'authentic', essential
and, crucially, 'pre-political [*vor-politisch*]' way of existing (HHI,
82/102). To this end, he returns to analyse the relationship between
being and technics in the Greek *polis* and argues for the ontological
superiority of ancient over modern technicity. The latter works by
subsuming being under the dominion of man, framing it in terms of a
conscious subjectivity that is constitutively unable to capture the event
of giving in its withdrawal, the experience of giving in excess of the
subject. The *technè* of Ancient Greece, by contrast, refers to a language
able to disclose the gift's withdrawal without betraying the event,
without substituting the being of beings for the impersonal *es gibt* of
being and time. Heidegger's commitment to the purity of language
underlies his faith in the prospect of a philosophy of repetition whose
political implications would exceed those of any revolution (Beistegui
2003: 60). Through language, he argues, it becomes possible to repeat,
to reground, a concept of being that has been lost since the onset of
Platonic (Christian) modernity, and with it, to receive the gift – the
giving of being – that would take us beyond nihilism. A Heideggerian
politics of the gift thus in some respects looks quite similar to that of
Bataille, Lacan and Deleuze and Guattari, who seek to free the gift from
the anthropological gift economy and to think it in terms of a singular,
inexchangeable excess that cannot be expressed through the traditional
concepts of political economy.

Heidegger's concept of the gift, which he significantly conceives in
terms of presencing in language, is for all that less radical than the

impossible, avowedly non-self identical one employed by Derrida and
Deleuze. The effect of this lesser radicality is discernible and moreover
decisive in its consequences for his relation to the political, the rhetoric
of which is worryingly replete with the centripetal themes of essence,
destiny and homecoming (*Heimischwerden*). Heidegger asserts the need
to 'think more Greek than the Greeks themselves' (HHI, 81/100), in
returning to the pre-political, *ontological* meaning of the Greek *polis*.
In so doing, however, his argument famously dovetails into an extreme
political conservatism and a dalliance with Nazism that for many necessitates the refusal to engage with his thought. After Heidegger, there
is accordingly a deep-seated suspicion, if not an outright rejection, of
the philosophical attempt to think the politics of an event that exceeds
the modern politics of the subject. Compounded by the concerns of
Lyotard, who fears that the problematic of the gift originates in the fetishisation of a pre- or non-capitalistic other (Lyotard 1993a: 106/130),
the project of a politics of the gift – of discerning a relationality to and of
the event that precedes the individuation of *homines economici* – risks
being fundamentally compromised, condemned by its dubious reliance
on conjectural, speculative history, to collapse back into an ambiguous
relation to the totalitarian or fascistic. At stake is an allegedly totalising
philosophical arrogation of the historical and political. We also saw
this in Miller's grievance over the relation of philosophy to anthropology in Deleuze and Guattari, his suspicion that they romanticise the
nomad as an anarchic site of aneconomy, prior to the (technological)
overcoding that coincides with the birth of the State. One is naturally
led to wonder how or whether this relates to Deleuze's insistence that
we 'must not refuse to take Heidegger seriously' (F, 91/118).

Deleuze rarely engages with Heidegger and phenomenology, but it
is still a constant, albeit implicit influence (see WIP, 46–7/48–9; and
the largely complimentary footnote on Heidegger in *Difference and
Repetition*, DR, 77/89–91n). The Deleuzian emphasis on repetition
and becoming is ostensibly a repetition of Nietzsche. But as a philosophy of repetition, it also stands in a relation of similarity to Heidegger,
and therefore risks contamination by the latter's injunction to repeat
the pre-political Greek *polis*. We see this in the possibility of reapplying
a critique of Heidegger elaborated by Jean-Luc Nancy to the Deleuzian
philosophy of immanence. But there is a crucial difference between
Deleuze and Guattari and Heidegger, which concerns the Deleuze and
Guattari's insistence on the intractability of the politics that Heidegger
seeks to circumscribe, notably their claim in *Mille plateaux* that 'politics precedes being' (TP, 203/249). With additional reference to their
description of Heidegger's Nazism as the entry of shame into philoso-

phy, one could and perhaps should argue that this crucial difference offers itself as a point of departure for the recovery and rehabilitation of a politics of the gift, creating the conditions of possibility for a new philosophical thinking of politics beyond the point of its destitution, where it encounters the impossibility of repetition, of restituting a lost origin, and gives up trying to make present that which precisely refuses presence. In other words, rather than getting caught up in and contaminated by 'one of the most compromised thinkers of our recent past' (Hallward 2006b: 55), Deleuze and Guattari facilitate an escape from the Heideggerian legacy through an account of the irreducibility of the *politics* of the gift.

This becomes more apparent by reading Deleuze and Guattari through the work of Nancy and his collaborator, Philippe Lacoue-Labarthe. As already suggested, a critique of Heidegger is only inter-mittently encountered in Deleuze: for instance, in his passing reference to the 'the deep ambiguity of his technical and political ontology', in *Foucault* (F, 113/121), and a short but damning parody reading him through the absurdist Alfred Jarry (Deleuze 1998: 91–8/115–25). A similar approach does, however, inform and find itself reflected in Lacoue-Labarthe and Nancy, whose efforts to politicise the event, to politicise the technicity of giving, anticipate and indirectly read as a detailed response to both points of Heidegger's 'deep ambigu-ity'. Working both collaboratively, through the *Centre de recherches philosophiques sur le politique* (*Centre for Philosophical Research into the Political*), and individually, subsequent to the centre's dissolution in 1984, Lacoue-Labarthe and Nancy seek to repeat Heidegger in full knowledge of his shame, precisely in order to uncover and thereby move beyond the impasse that sunders his thought. They do this by elaborat-ing a concept of the political, *le politique*, that cannot be reduced to the technologically enframed politics of institutions. Arguing that politics consists in precisely the absence of a ground, they advocate a 'retrait du politique', a withdrawal of politics from the philosophy that habitu-ally overdetermines it. Lacoue-Labarthe and Nancy can also thus be seen to qualify Deleuze and Guattari. There is none the less something deeply Deleuzian about their return to and differential repetition of the Heideggerian project of ontology. Despite being known primarily as a Heideggerian student of Derrida, and despite making almost no explicit reference to Deleuze, Nancy in particular, and particularly in his latter works, can and will be read as a thinker of the '*vol et don*' that for Deleuze characterises the politicity of the virtual.

With figures like Nancy in mind, the philosopher and historian of poststructuralism, Alan D. Schrift, has cautioned against trying to read recent French philosophy as a mere response to Heidegger, at the expense of other influences (Schrift 2004: 38). Like Deleuze, Nancy is formed by the French legacy of Nietzsche and can be seen to return to the problematic of how to ontologise the eternal return, how to think repetition and circulation in terms of an ontology of the political. Nancy follows Heidegger in locating repetition in technicity, but central to his work is the re-elaboration of an irreducibly political, pre-linguistic concept of technicity, which enables him to resist Heidegger's understanding of language as the site of pre-political, ontological privilege. In developing a critique of the dangerously aestheticised, or *poietic*, concept of *technè* employed by Heidegger (Lacoue-Labarthe 1990), Lacoue-Labarthe paves the way for Nancy to articulate the gift as *praxis*, rather than *poiesis*: the offering of an originary *political* technicity, expressed by what he calls *ecotechnics*, or the shared finitude of corporeal bodies (SW, 101/158; C, 89/77–9). This shared finitude gives rise to an ontology of singular plurality that, though subtly different, is strongly reminiscent of the Deleuzo-Guattarian metaphysics of virtual, singular multiplicities. It is also inseparable from a concept of *espacement* or 'spacing' movement of ungrounding that Nancy uses to rearticulate the Deleuzo-Guattarian concept of the nomad (EF, 145/187).

Far from eliciting complicity with fascism, this renewed thinking of the event entails a politics of the gift that is inherently opposed to it: a politics based on the ceaseless, ungrounding repetition of singularity, on the *flight/theft* and *gift* of Hermes rather than the Hestial *Heimischwerden* sought by Heidegger.

TECHNOLOGY AND THE FORECLOSURE OF THE EVENT

A brief discussion of Derrida's critique of Lacan, in Chapter 1, outlined how the former suspects the latter of idealising the phallus, foreclosing the play of the signifier by imposing a psychoanalytic interpretation on the literary text. The broader gist of Derrida's complaint is that Lacan presupposes the phallus as a transcendental structure, such that everywhere the psychoanalyst turns, the phallus is already there, awaiting detection (PC, 413/441). The term he later uses to capture the catch-all Lacanian strategy is *encadrer*, the act of *framing* the text within a restricted economy of interpretation (PC, 431/461). Derrida, of course, argues that the gift intrinsically exceeds any such confinement; this is reflected in his thinking of technology, which he insists must preserve the possibility of invention, the production of a novelty that overflows any attempt to frame (*encadrer*) it within an essence (Derrida 2007: 30/42). The latter position is more radical than the one laid out by the essentialist philosophy of Martin Heidegger, from whom Derrida inherits the concept of the frame. Unlike Derrida, Heidegger remains committed to a thinking of essence (*Wesen*), albeit one whose withdrawal from experience means essences do not readily lend themselves to representation. He opposes a technics of the event to a technics of framing, *Ge-stell*, that forecloses the giving of being. *Ge-stell*, he argues, 'means the way of revealing that holds sway in the essence of modern technology and that is itself nothing technological' (QT, 325/24). As the non-technological essence of technology, *Ge-stell* is the means by which man attempts to subordinate being to his own mastery, to incorporate it within the economy of subjectivity and presence. Here, technology figures as the extension of this economy, an extension that, like Hegel's master, seeks to exercise dominion over a world that will exist purely *for it* in the consciousness of a presence divested of the otherness of the event. Heidegger writes: 'Thus "technology" does not signify here the separate areas of the production and equipment of machines' (OM, 74/76). It refers, rather, to the ontico-metaphysical structure that privileges the being of beings (*Seienden*) over the being of being (*Sein*) and which determines the history of Western metaphysics as the forgetting of being. If, in Derrida, every act of foreclosure is an irreducibly violent attempt at essentialisation, in Heidegger technology is also dangerous: 'The destining of revealing [*das Geschick der Entbergung*] is in itself not just any danger, but *the* danger':

> enframing [*das Ge-stell*] does not just endanger man in his relationship to himself and to everything that is. As a destining, it banishes man into the kind of revealing that is an ordering [*das Entbergen von der Art Bestellens*]. Where this ordering holds sway, it drives out every other possibility of revealing. (QT, 331–2/30–1)

Enframing serves to impose upon being an ordering, a *logos*, that distorts it, misrepresents it, prevents being from being in the way that is 'proper', or essential, to it. Its ordering takes the form of dragging being into the orbit of a privileged subject, for whom it will provide a 'Bestand', a 'standing-reserve' of energy and economic resources to be deployed in its flight from death. In this respect, there is a clear parallel between Heidegger's thinking of technology and the theory of non-consumptive production of Georges Bataille. For Bataille, too, the world of manufactured objects, or things, is symptomatic of a retreat from the futurity of death. And death is indeed what is at stake here: standing-reserve is accumulated to minimise the possibility of the withdrawal of the subject's lifeworld; to minimise the risk of a future that violently ruptures the stability of the present. Heidegger uses the example of the commercial forestry industry, which orders the landscape so as to be able to stockpile timber for fuel and production. Enframing is a mechanism for the reconfiguration of time as an economy, that is, the subordination of time – above all, the future – to the present, or presence. It is an economy where the future is made to return to the place of identity, the *oikos* of subjectivity, through a deployment of technology that functions analogously to the Lacanian fantasy in its suppression of difference. Technology thus sustains the narcissistic, nihilistic fantasy of the ontologically privileged subject, by concealing what, in *Being and Time* (1927), Heidegger describes as the ontological reality of *Geworfenheit*, or 'thrownness', *Dasein*'s existence as being-thrown into the world (BT, 224/237 [§38, 179]).

Technology conceals the being that is ontologically prior to *Dasein* and whose being is presupposed by the operation of technology upon it. This is nothing less than the being of the event, or rather being as event: the *es gibt* of *Ereignis*. Heidegger's thinking of the relation between the event and the gift prefigures the work of Derrida and Deleuze on this point, although crucially he does not consider the being of temporality in terms of the non-presence to which Derrida and Deleuze would later attach so much importance – or at least not to the same extent. Both time and Being are given, in Heidegger: 'It gives Being, It gives Time [*Es gibt Zeit, Es gibt Sein*' (TB, 17–18/17), but, and in accordance with his phenomenological heritage, the gift is also always related to presence, making presence possible, even if giving cannot definitely be located in presence: 'Being proves to be destiny's gift of presence [*Gabe des Geschickes von Anwesenheit*], the gift granted by the giving of time. The gift of presence is the property of Appropriating [*Die Gabe von Anwesen ist Eigentum des Ereignens*]. Being vanishes in Appropriation' (TB, 22/22). Where Deleuze is critical of the thinking of past and future as dimensions of the present, Heidegger explicitly justifies this move, noting that 'absence, too, manifests itself as presence' (TB, 17/18). Even absence gives itself in presence. The past is that which is no longer present, the dimension that denies itself presence. The future is the present that has yet to become present and as such withholds itself from presence. These dimensions of presencing and the denial and withholding of presence are thus in excess of Dasein. They belong, or are rather *appropriated*, by a fourth dimension of time, the time of 'the giving that determines all [*das alles bestimmende Reichen*]' (TB, 15/16), which might equally be called the time of the event, *Ereignis*. Perhaps paradoxically, after Derrida's disarticulation of the gift from any form of appropriation, Heidegger describes *Ereignis* as appropriation that is also giving. As giving, it also withdraws in the very moment of its giving.

> To giving as sending there belongs keeping back [*Zum Geben als Schicken das Ansichhalten gehört*] – such that the denial of the present and the withholding of the present, play within the giving of what has been and what will be. [...] Keeping back, denial, withholding – shows something like a self-withdrawing, something we might call for short: withdrawal [*ein Sichentziehen, kurz gesagt: den Entzug*]. But inasmuch as the modes of giving that are determined by withdrawal – sending and extending [*das Sichen und das Reichen*] – lie in Appropriation, withdrawal must belong to what is peculiar to the Appropriation. (TB, 22/23)

If the present is that which is presently being-presenced and the past is the denial of presence – namely, that which is no longer present – what withdraws from being given immediately in presence is the future. Technology is deployed to overwrite the unpredictability of the future that the fact of its being withdrawn from presence makes possible. As 'ordering' ('das Entbergen von der Art Bestellens', QT, 332/31), it carries connotations of *logos* and hence chronology, the organisation of time into measurable instances of presence that pass homogeneously in succession.

To the extent that it grants the future its own mode of presencing as withdrawal, *Ereignis*, the event, stands over *Seienden* as the cause of their vulnerability, exposing them to the excess of the future over the present. That is not to say that *Sein* does not require *Seienden*, however. The later Heidegger does away with the ontological difference between being and beings, marked out in *Sein und Zeit* (BT, 29–35/12–20 [§3–4, 9–15]), in favour of a notion of *Ereignis* in which *Sein* cannot 'be' in accordance with its ownmost essence without the presence of *Seienden*. Whereas Derrida argues that the gift is necessarily annulled by the presence of a recipient, Heidegger sides with Mauss in writing of reciprocity. The event takes the form of an exchange between the giving of time and being and the beings who receive and thereby recognise this gift as having been given. This recognition, as we shall see, takes the form of naming being in language in a way that captures its essence. The event of *Ereignis* is as such fundamentally economic. It is by virtue of completing the circuit of exchange that being becomes being and man, whose being is defined in terms of language, becomes man, each returning to itself via the mediation of the other:

> Man: standing within the approach of presence, but in such a way that he receives as a gift the presencing that It gives [*Es gibt, als Gabe emfängt*] by perceiving what appears in letting-presence. If man were not the constant receiver of the gift given by the 'It gives presence' [*der stete Empfänger der Gabe aus dem 'Es gibt Anwesenheit'*], if that which is extended in the gift

[*der Gabe Gereichte*] did not reach man, then not only would Being remain
concealed in the absence of this gift, not only closed off, but man would
remain excluded from the scope of: It gives Being. Man would not be man.
(TB, 12/12–13)

The reciprocity of this exchange leads Heidegger to describe the event
of the gift as precisely *Fug*, meaning jointure, or harmony between the
event and the beings who will shepherd it in language (IM, 171/169
[123]). But the term again points to the difference between Heidegger
and Deleuze and Derrida, both of whom borrow from Shakespeare in
describing the gift as time 'out of joint', 'hors de ses gonds' – a phrase
that would, as Derrida notes in *Specters of Marx*, be rendered in
German as 'aus der Fuge' (DR, 111–12/119–20; SM, 25/49–50).

This emphasis on harmony means that, in place of the explicit anti-
humanism of Derrida and Deleuze, Heidegger's thinking of *Ereignis*
contains within it the prospect of reconciliation between time and
human subjectivity. In Heidegger's residual *humanitas*, the sovereignty
once accorded to the subject is shifted on to being, and *Dasein* recov-
ers some sense of being by existing to receive, or appropriate, the gift
of the event. Through language there exists the possibility of equilibrium, or justice, in so far as *Dasein* bears witness to the presencing of
the event, where being and beings give and receive in equal measure.
The presencing of the gift takes the form of a constant strife between
these two forces of propriation, between what, in his *Introduction to
Metaphysics*, Heidegger calls the *dikè* of being (*physis*) and the *technè*
of beings (IM, 169–71/168–70 [122–3]). As Fried has recently argued at
length, this striving, also called *polemos*, is at the heart of Heidegger's
'pre-political' thinking of politics (Fried 2000: 142–8); it also conveys
the difficulty inherent in *Dasein*'s attempt to coexist with the event.
Ansell-Pearson has criticised the contradiction of a humanism that
'turns the human into little more than an "instrument", a mere organ
of the time of technology, so that mankind is sacrificed on the altar
of self-withdrawing being' (Ansell-Pearson 1997a: 153). The default
position is not one of passive instrumentality, however, but rather of
an ultimately futile attempt to wrest away the sovereignty of the event.
Dasein creates a tension within the harmony, the *Fug*, of the event by
attempting, in an inauthentic concealment of its own mortality, to take
possession and thereby curb the prospective intensity of time.

THE GIFT OF THE *POLIS*

We saw in Chapter 1 how Bataille detects in the archaic societies of
the *potlatch* a sense of the sacred that has been missing since the emer-

gence of non-consumptive production. Heidegger, too, locates a purer form of experience in an age prior to the advent of metaphysics. Where Bataille writes of the lost '*intimacy* of the divine world' (TR, 44/308), the loss in modern man of the ability to achieve sacred communication with the general economy of life, Heidegger writes roughly contemporaneously of the forgetting of the meaning of being that coincides with the Platonic advent of modernity. In both thinkers, (non-consumptive) production and technology feature as respective techniques for the avoidance of death and are held responsible for the institution of an age of nihilism. The same nihilism leads Heidegger to yearn for 'non-political politics [*eine unpolitische Politik*]', an intervention that would escape the 'laborious business of preserving and asserting [particular] interests', the 'quarrelling, selfishness and conflict' that characterised the political scene of the Weimar Republic (Safranksi 1998: 230/271). Accordingly, just as he insists on non-technological *Ge-stell* as the essence of modern technology, so Heidegger looks for an essence of politics that would be *pre-* or *non*-political; that would escape the bureaucratism of political practice. His location of this essence in the Greek *polis* receives its first explicit formulation in the 1935 text, *Introduction to Metaphysics*, where Heidegger differentiates the *polis* from its habitual rendering as *Staat*. 'Rather, *polis* is the name for the site [*Stätte*], the Here, within which and as which *Da-sein* is historically. The *polis* is the site of history, the Here, *in* which, *out of* which and *for* which history happens' (IM, 162/161 [117]). This account is considerably nuanced by the time of the 1942 lecture series on Hölderlin's 'Der Ister', which is more deliberate in designating the *polis* as *pre*-political:

> The pre-political essence of the *polis* [*das Vor-politische ... Wesen der Polis*], the essence that first makes possible everything political in the originary and in the derivative sense, lies in its being the open site of that fitting destining [*die offene Stätte zu sein der Schickung*] from out of which all human relations toward beings – and that always means in the first instance the relations of beings as such to humans – are determined. The essence of the *polis* therefore always comes to light in accordance with the ways in which beings as such in general enter into unconcealing. (HHI, 82/102 [TM])

As in Deleuze and Guattari, the original question of the political (or in this case, the pre-political) refers to beings' relationship to the excess of the event. Heidegger's privileging of the *polis* has little or nothing to do with its status as the birthplace of democracy. What accounts for the privileging of the *polis* is the ancients' accommodation of a thinking of being in excess of the being of man. In line with the identification of politics with the inauthentic sphere of the 'ontic', Heidegger considers the *polis* philosophically rather than politically, and this entails that it be thought aside from any consideration of the 'calculative', quantitative enumerations associated with direct voting.

The importance of the passage cited above resides in the positing of a relation between the (non-political) essence of the political and the event of giving. The pre-political *polis* is the site of the presencing of the gift and it is this presencing of the gift in time that determines the relationality of beings to the event. Firstly, it is the place of the becoming, or unfurling, of History, *Geschichte*. (The word is chosen to resonate with *Geschick*, destiny, and thereby imply an affinity, or complicity, between the various modes of giving, which reveals itself in language.) Secondly, and in addition to this, the *polis* relates to time as the place where *Dasein* is opened on to its thrownness, exposed to the imminent facticity of its own death. The cause of this thrownness is the withdrawal of the future from giving itself immediately in presence; the future comes to denote anything that does not offer itself to experience in representation. To borrow a Deleuzian formula, this withdrawal brings *Dasein* to realise that time is not internal to *Dasein*. *Dasein* is rather abandoned to, and in, time.

The *polis* is thus ontologically significant because it exposes *Dasein* to an event in excess of its dominion, because it precedes the subordination of the event to the technical domination of the subject. Rather than an *oikos*, a place of comfort and security, it is a name for the site of *Dasein*'s abandonment, of the originary experience of time as the time of death, the withdrawal from presence that threatens the economy of self-identity. Another way of saying this, provisionally, is that, rather than a *Heim*, the *polis* is the site of an *unheimlich* excess that exposes *Dasein* to *Dasein*'s own homelessness, *Unheimischkeit* (HHI, 59–75/73–87).

However, it is crucial to Heidegger's argument that the Greek *polis* is not the site of technological nihilism. Rather than succumb to inauthenticity, the challenge, as Heidegger sees it, is for *Dasein* to accept the constitutive *Unheimischkeit* of the *polis*, and accordingly to affirm the mortality to which it is exposed. Another way of saying this is that, for Heidegger, *Unheimischkeit* is not simply originary. There is also the ontological prospect of a *Heimat* and a homecoming, *Heimischwerden*, to be revealed and reappropriated in the unconcealment of the essence of the *polis*. In other words, in spite of his critique of privileged subjectivity, Heidegger continues to affirm the possibility of recuperating the event as an ontological ground. What he rejects is not the idea of a ground *per se*, but the conflation of the ground with the Cartesian *cogito*. Being-as-one with the origin is achieved by surrendering the conceit of the sovereign subject in favour of becoming a shepherd to the sovereignty of the event.

Heidegger does not himself employ the term *oikos*, but he does consider *hestia*, which has the same connotations of hearth and home, as a site that exists in harmony and is moreover explicitly identified with the *polis*. Translating *hestia* by *der Herd*, he writes: 'The hearth is the site of being-homely [*Der Herd ist die Stätte des Heimisch-seins*]' (HHI, 105/130); *Stätte*, of course, is also the word he uses to translate *polis*. It is perhaps significant that Hestia, according to Greek mythology, is the daughter of Chronos, the god Deleuze explicitly identifies with the *economic* structure of time. Doubly significant is the traditional opposition of Hestia to Hermes. The latter god is characterised by the traits of flight and theft, the *vol* that Deleuze explicitly attaches to the *don* of repetition in the event. By positing a ground that is prior to the ungrounding, hence arguably *an*economic effect of the polis, Heidegger reinscribes being within a restricted and ultimately symbolic economy:

> Hearth is the word for being [...]. Being is not something that is actual, but that which determines what is actual in its potential for being, and determines especially the potential for human beings to be; that potentiality for being in which the being of humans is fulfilled: being unhomely in becoming homely [*das Unheimischsein im Heimischwerden*]. Such is our belonging to being itself. What essentially prevails as being is never beings or something actual and therefore always appears as a nothingness that can only be said in poetizing or thought in thinking [*wie das Nichts, das kann nur im Dichten gesagt oder im Denken gedacht werden*]. (HHI, 120/150 [TM])

Beistegui notes that 'the *polis* was also, and possibly more so than the domestic home, considered as providing one with a genuine sense of place: the homeland, the *Heimat*' (Beistegui 2003: 161). Indeed, more than just another name for the restricted domestic economy, *hestia* is given as a name for being as such. The same claim is reiterated throughout Heidegger's writings, including notably the 1947 text, *Letter on Humanism* (*Brief über den Humanismus*), where he writes: 'The homeland [*Heimat*] of this historical dwelling is nearness to being' (LH, 242/338). If (pre-Platonic) Ancient Greece is characterised by the harmonious coincidence of *polis* and *hestia*, the *Unheimischkeit* and *Heimatlosigkeit* of the technological epoch derive from the forgetting and abandonment of the *hestia*, which is to say, the forgetting of being as such: 'Homelessness so understood consists in the abandonment of Being by beings. Homelessness is the symptom of oblivion of Being. Because of it the truth of Being remains unthought' (LH, 242/339). The claim hints at a worrying circularity: if homelessness, as Heidegger suggests, is actually only the effect of the forgetting of being, rather than

what leads *Dasein* to seek to forget it, then what caused this forgetting? But it also indicates a problematic conception of the relationship
between philosophy and politics, in which the latter is seen to take
place only in the absence, or failure, of the former. In its technological
conception, politics is what lives on as the remainder of the forgetting
of being, a spectre that must also be forgotten, or exorcised, if man is
to recover the original experience of the *polis* as the site of the giving
of the event. Rather than condemn the *hestia* as a fantasy, Heidegger
designates it as quite the opposite: namely, the site of being to which
thinking must return if it is to escape the impasse of global technological nihilism.

THE RETURN OF THE GIFT OF SPEECH

Heidegger argues that the path to the essential reappropriation of
Heimischwerden is to be found in a return to the thinking of the essence
of technology. By this he does not simply mean *Ge-stell*, which is only
the essence of *modern* technology. What he seeks to return to is the
Greek concept of technology, the *technè* whose forgetting made *Ge-stell*
possible. In its original Greek sense, *technè* captures precisely what is
excluded from *Ge-stell*: 'There was a time when it was not technology
alone that bore the name *technè*. Once the revealing that brings forth
truth into the splendor of radiant appearance was also called *technè*'
(QT, 339/38). The modern technological process of forcibly reorganis-
ing being into standing-reserve stands in stark contrast to the revealing
as bringing forth and presencing of the type encountered in the Ancient
polis, namely unconcealing (*Unverborgen, aletheia*). Whereas *Ge-stell*
exists in tension with the event of *Ereignis*, whose forgetting it continually re-enacts, *technè* precedes this forgetting and can therefore depict
the giving of being and time in presence without committing violence
against the simultaneous giving and withdrawal of presencing.

This movement of making present, or presencing, Heidegger also
calls *poiesis*, translated by the German *Dichtung*, meaning poetry but
also, more broadly, creative invention. *Dichtung* names the originary
essence of the *technè* that reveals itself in language as the process of
unconcealing the forgotten essence of being:

> The essence of art is poetry [*Das Wesen der Kunst ist Dichtung*]. The essence
> of poetry, in turn, is the founding of truth [*die Stiftung der Wahrheit*]. We
> understand founding here in a triple sense: founding as bestowing, found-
> ing as grounding, and founding as beginning [*Stiften als Schenken, Stiften
> als Gründen und Stiften als Anfangen*]. [...] The setting-into-work of truth
> thrusts up the awesome and at the same time thrusts down the ordinary and

what we believe to be such. The truth that discloses itself in the work can never be proved or derived from what went before. What went before is refuted in its exclusive actuality by the work. What art founds can therefore never be compensated and made up for by what is already at hand and available. Founding is an overflow, a bestowal [*Die Stiftung ist ein Überfluß, eine Schenkung*]. (OWA, 199–200/63)

Whereas modern technology is rendered corrupt by its imposition of a frame around whatever it seeks to bring to presence (namely, the subject), *Dichtung* is the reinstatement of a *technè* prior to the corruption of its essence by metaphysics; the founding of truth that allows presencing to take place unconstrained by the imposition of any *Gestell*. Rather than forcefully reconfiguring the being that withdraws from representation as standing-reserve, it allows for the presencing of withdrawal and concealment. In other words, *Dichtung* is able to affirm the event of being as the double movement of the gift: the giving and withdrawal of presence as the strife that constitutes *Ereignis*; it thus becomes the site of conflict between presencing and withdrawal from presence. On account of its opening of beings on to the event, language is more than 'a kind of communication', a mechanism for 'verbal exchange and agreement' (OWA, 198/61). It serves ontologically to give expression to being beyond beings, the originary *polemos* between *physis* and *technè*, earth and world, concealment and the unconcealing of that which withdraws from presence. *Poiesis* in other words repeats the originary technical structure of the event, and is as such to be identified with the *polis*. There is a *polis* because there is language, because language opens the horizons for an encounter with the event. Repeating the earlier claim that modern technics is '*die* Gefahr', '*the* danger', Heidegger now affirms Hölderlin's description of language as '*das Gefährlichste*', the '*most dangerous*' of gifts (HHG, 61), the site of a repetition that harbours the potential for an encounter with the gift, and yet also, at the other extreme, facilitates its denial. If language creates the *polis*, it also makes possible the politics through which we lose sight of it.

Language is the originary repetition of a gift that does not precede but is rather inaugurated as repetition. For Heidegger, the concept of the gift is as closely linked to repetition as it is for the other post-Nietzschean thinkers of repetition and the work it does for him prefigures its role in the (post-)structuralisms of Lacan, Deleuze and Derrida. Despite this, Heidegger is one of, if not the only thinker under discussion explicitly to reject Nietzsche's eternal return. In both his Nietzsche lectures (1939) and another set of lectures dating from 1951–2, delivered and (posthumously) published under the title of *What Is Called*

Thinking (*Was heisst Denken?*), Heidegger dismisses the idea of eternal return as 'eine phantastiche Mystik', a fantastical mysticism, the ulti-mate and highest expression of Western technological metaphysics. The act of willing backwards, of affirming all that has come to pass as a condition of becoming who one is, discloses the highest sense in which *Dasein* has sought to become coextensive with being as such, subordinating the time of the event to the identity of an overarching subject: 'the essence of modern technology will come to light as the steadily rotating recurrence of the same [*Wiederkehr des Gleichen*]' (WCT, 109/112 [TM]). Where Nietzsche writes of repeating the same, Heidegger, anticipating Deleuze *et al.*, is only interested in a repetition of difference (even if he ultimately does not go far enough in repeating difference, collapsing back into the repetition of essential identity and the return of propriety). It is by means of differential repetition – the repetition of what falls outside the dominant history of metaphysics – that Heidegger thinks it possible to reintroduce novelty and thereby overturn the technologically exhausted paradigm of modernity. Crucial to note, in this respect, is that the repetition of the Greek origin requires us to go further than the Greeks themselves did, raising to the level of consciousness – of language – what was for them merely implicit. Like the theorisations of repetition that would follow, it is not so much a simple repetition of the past as a repetition from the future, a rupture that breaks with the chronological order of things: 'whenever there is a beginning – a thrust enters into history; history either begins or starts over again' (OWA, 201/64). *Dichtung* is the site of an excess, an overflowing, singular repetition that displaces the past in the giving, the *Schenken*, of itself. Heidegger's choice of the word *Stiften*, meaning (charitable) donation or bestowal, allows him to incorporate the three actions of giving, grounding and beginning in a single operation. The gift is not the disclosure of something that has always already been given, but rather what gives itself excessively each time anew, a rep-etition that grounds *itself* and in so doing clears away what has gone before. By repeating the *heimlich*, or *oikéotes*, structure of the event in a way that conveys the strife between giving and withdrawal, language emerges as the site of homecoming. 'Thus language is at once the house of Being [*Haus des Seins*] and the home of human beings' (LH, 262/561 [192]).

    Commenting on this, and in a formulation that closely recalls Lacan's 'gift of speech [*don de la parole*]', Lacoue-Labarthe succinctly notes how Heideggerian being 'gives itself originarily as the gift of language [*don de la langue*]' (Lacoue-Labarthe 1989: 194 [not included in the English edition]). This should not, however, be equated with the Lacanian

thinking of the same expression. Where Heidegger's gift of language
'brings Being *to* beings from *out* of their Being' (OWA, 202/63 [TM]),
for Lacan, 'the word is the murder of the Thing' (E, 261–2/318), which
sacrifices the real, replacing it with a performatively enacted fantasy of
reality. Repetition occurs not in the *füglich* presencing of language, but
in the *nachträglich* return of the real. There is thus an implicit critique
of Heidegger in Lacan, though it is perhaps not enough to defend Lacan
against criticisms that were also levelled against the former. We saw in
Chapter 2 how the Lacanian reworking of eternal return as a return of
the real to the same place, via the autarkic circulations of the libido,
leads to the accusation that Lacan excludes political, understood as a
form of relationality, by regrounding the subject in its suspension from
the self-identity of the drive. A similar problem is inherent in Heidegger,
albeit with more immediately devastating consequences.

NAZIONALSOZIALISMUS AND THE POLITICS OF REPETITION

This prospect of history beginning over, breaking free from its destitution by metaphysics, has led Beistegui to speak of a 'politics of repetition' in Heidegger, and more decisively to pose the question of whether
'beyond Heidegger's own political errancy [...] genuine repetition might
not be thought as a political alternative to revolution, whether the very
temporality of repetition is not such as to have from the start opened
onto another relation to praxis altogether' (Beistegui 2003: 60). The
reference to political errancy is to Heidegger's arguably short-lived but
immensely controversial Nazism, manifest in his appointment, in April
1933, to the rectorate of Freiburg University. Heidegger would hold
the position of *Rektor-Führer* for less than a year, resigning in protest
at Hitler in April 1934, but his commitment to the Nazi cause over this
period is borne out in a number of explicitly pro-Hitlerian speeches,
replete with the Nazi rhetoric of the *Volk* and *Führung*. This rhetoric
would also live on after the resignation. Written in 1935, *Introduction
to Metaphysics*, for example, describes the 'innere Wahrheit und Größe',
'the inner truth and greatness', of *Nazionalsozialismus*, '(namely the
encounter between planetary technics and contemporary man)' (IM,
213/208 [152]). The citation needs to be qualified: its context makes it
clear that Heidegger is differentiating the *inner, ontological* potential of
Nazism from its 'ontic' manifestation in an ideology of biological and
racial superiority of which he is unreservedly dismissive. The passage
could therefore be read as 'what was, in the circumstances, a daring
critique of many aspects of Nazism' (Young 1997: 2), but for the fact,

as Žižek notes, that 'Heidegger never speaks of the "inner greatness" of, say, liberal democracy' (Žižek 1999: 13). Elsewhere, the work of Alexander Garcia Düttmann on Heidegger's thinking of 'Germania' has shown how Heidegger believed the German *Volk* to occupy a histori-cally privileged and unique position for the receipt and repetition (the repetition in receipt) of the gift of the Greek sending (Düttmann 2002: 152–3, 170–2/154, 170–4).

The explicit references to Nazism disappear from Heidegger's work toward the end of the 1930s, though it has been argued that the shift is more a change in rhetorical register than a genuine renunciation of the ideas that led him toward National Socialism (Bambach 2003). Lacoue-Labarthe is in agreement with Bambach, observing that Heidegger's centripetal language of the *Heimat* and *Heimischwerden* remains highly significant in his later writings, even undergoing a 'certain accentua-tion' (RP, 63). Unlike some commentators, however, Lacoue-Labarthe does not regard Nazism as an inevitable culmination of Heidegger's philosophy, contaminating it to the extent that it 'loses all greatness' (Lyotard 1990: 53/90). He does not attempt what one critic calls a 'de-Nazification of Heidegger' (Young 1997: 1), nor does his interest in Heidegger stretch only to diagnosing the philosophical causes of Nazism (Fried 2000: 137–8). In spite of the furore caused by the so-called 'Heidegger affair', Lacoue-Labarthe – like Derrida, Deleuze and Guattari – is interested in what caused Heidegger to collapse back from radicality into a fundamental economism. He affirms that there are ele-ments of radicality, or aneconomy, in Heidegger's concept of repetition, but laments how their radical potential is compromised by the economy of what is to be repeated: namely, essence. The difficulty of this is captured succinctly by Lacoue-Labarthe's influential essay, 'Finite Transcendence Ends in Politics' ('La Transcendance finie/t dans la poli-tique'), which concludes with the assertion that there is 'a fundamental *mimetology* at work in Heidegger's thought' (Lacoue-Labarthe 1989: 297/170). In other words, Heidegger's personal and conceptual engage-ment with politics and the political is overdetermined by the question of identification and the search for an ontological ground. Another way of saying this is that the gift, Heidegger's event of *Ereignis*, remains inscribed within an *oikos*, torn asunder by its reluctance to bear the risk of thinking aneconomically (Beistegui 1998: 145).

REPEATING REPETITION

The prospect that Heidegger's Nazism stems from a residual econo-mism, an insufficient thinking of the gift as aneconomic, opens us on to the greatest weight of what is at stake in the decentring of the subject of politics and the unfurling, in its place, of the event. Indeed, if a politics of the gift is a politics of eternal return, of coming to terms with the ungrounding event of a giving that exceeds our ability to recognise it as such, we might ask whether the project of trying to think the political aneconomically is not inherently compromised, destined at every level to abandon the subject yet ultimately collapse back into another form of restricted economy, in which the privileged sovereignty of the subject returns under another name. Recalling Deleuze's analysis of *habitus* as a defence mechanism against the revolutionary power of difference, it is as if – and in this respect Heidegger recalls Hegel, who also saw the home as a place of respite from the brutality of the market (EPR, 222–5/343–5 [§185]) – a reactionary Heidegger clings to the *oikos* as a sanctuary from the uncertainty, the ungrounding effect of a technological future. Derrida has noted how Heidegger slips between the language of the ghost, the spectrality that haunts the *polis*, and the Romantic language of *Geist*, suggesting that the turn toward Nazism occurs in the shadow of an inability to escape the centripetal logic of the latter (Derrida 1989: 98–9/126–8). The problem, as Jean-François Lyotard has noted, is that: 'the *oikos* in the Greek tradition [...] is not, and I insist on this, the place of safety. The *oikos* is above all the place of tragedy. [...] Tragedy is not possible outside this ecologic or ecotragic framework' (Lyotard 1993b: 97). The *oikos* is tragic because it poses as a sanctuary from the greatest weight of an event that it cannot ultimately resist. To realise this, to accept the impossibility of appropriating identity through and as *Heimischwerden*, is to overcome tragedy, or at least to affirm its inevitability. A politics of the gift is not simply prescriptive in this respect. Rather than advocate the actualisation of a new order, it discloses the absence of any instantiable, superior reality in which identity could be grounded and politics thereby sublated, obviated by the advent of a transcendent, foundational truth. In spite of his attempts to re-engage with and repeat the age of tragedy, the ultimately *un*grounding effect of repetition is precisely what Heidegger failed to see. It is on account of this failure, and owing to his inability to repeat the classical tragic gesture of learning from his mistakes, that Lacoue-Labarthe insists Heidegger 'is precisely not tragic' (RP, 79).

The attempt to learn from Heidegger's mistakes, to reinstate tragedy into politics, could well be posed as a mission statement for the *Centre de recherches philosophiques sur le politique* (CRPP), a project founded, in 1980, by Philippe Lacoue-Labarthe and Jean-Luc Nancy in response to an essay published, in *Margins – Of Philosophy* (1972), by Jacques Derrida. The essay, entitled 'The Ends of Man' ('*Les Fins de l'homme*'), would serve as the point of departure for a 1980 conference of the same name, held at Cérisy-la-Salle. The subject of both essay and conference was the need for an end to the 'anthropologism' of the Western '*oikonomia*' of philosophy (M, 133–4/161), an economy in which, up to and including Heidegger, man has been construed teleologically, in terms of the appropriation of a metaphysically determined destiny. In light of the culmination of this in Nazism and Stalinism, Derrida calls not only for a decoupling of the subject from the teleological, but also for philosophy to awaken itself to the unavoidable fact that: 'Every philosophical colloquium necessarily has a political significance' (M, 111/131). Set up, in response to this, to explore this question of the relationality between politics and (the metaphysics of) the subject, the CRPP would also become the site of an attempt to repeat the Heideggerian repetition of the Greek *polis*, to surpass the hegemony of the *oikos* by tracing the impasse of thought to its abyssal, impossible limit. The repetition, it will be argued, is implicitly Deleuzian, both in its rejection of the politics of identity and in its emphasis on repetition as a process of ungrounding. *Contra* Bataille, Lévi-Strauss and Lacan, it is also Deleuzian on account of an 'insistence on the philosophical', its refusal to relinquish the priority of philosophy 'faced with the almost undivided domination of anthropology' (RP, 109; RJ, 14). Against the putative criticism that Heidegger's impasse results from his dismissal of the ontic – his dismissal of the anthropological and political sciences – and the instrumentality of his reworked humanism, Lacoue-Labarthe and Nancy argue the contrary: namely, that the problems actually stem from an excess of anthropology.

According to Lacoue-Labarthe and Nancy, it has become necessary to recognise what they refer to as: 'a certain completion of the political [*accomplissement du politique*], or to use another lexicon, [...] of the *closure of the political* [la clôture du politique]. What we mean by this is not unrelated [*n'est pas sans rapport*] to what Heidegger [...] attempted to think under the question of technology' (RP, 110; RJ, 15). The ambiguity of the double negative raises the question of just how much proximity this 'not unrelatedness' entails: all the more so given Heidegger's own reduction of politics to technology. Indeed, it is tempting to think that Heidegger's claim, made in the 1954 essay, 'Overcoming Metaphysics', that 'the world of completed metaphysics can stringently be called "technology"' (OM, 74/80), lies at the heart of Lacoue-Labarthe and Nancy's thinking of the political, and that it is in terms of this completion of metaphysics that politics and a supposed 'end' of politics must also initially be thought. When they say that politics has become exhausted, what they mean is that being has been enframed by the metaphysics of the modern subject to the point where every other possibility of revealing or interacting with the world has been foreclosed. Politics has entered into crisis because it is unable to think itself beyond 'what is deployed in the modern age as the qualification of the political by the subject (and of the subject by the political)' (RP, 110; RJ, 15). It is entrapped, that is to say, in the paradigm of subjectivity, unable to disarticulate itself from the ever implicit presupposition of a self-transparent *oikos* of sovereignty. The result is an impasse:

> What completes itself (and does not cease to complete itself) is the great 'enlightened', progressivist discourse of secular or profane eschatology, and that is to say the discourse of the re-appropriation of man in his humanity, the discourse of the actualisation of the genre of the human. (RP, 111; RJ, 16)

This is true even of Heidegger, who, they suggest, remains caught up in a thinking of the *oikos* and presence, despite his substitution of *Dasein* for the subject. We find in the '*closure of the political* [clôture du politique]' an apocalyptic vision of ideals that have become monstrous and totalitarian; History, philosophy, anthropology and politics – each one having become another name, a non-identical synonym, for what Heidegger means by metaphysics, or technology – play themselves out in such a way that they can do no more than repeat the gesture of their own end, their own 'completion'. In contrast to the idea of a repetition of difference that exceeds subjectivity, we are confronted in Heidegger by an eternal return stripped of its difference, where the present is haunted by a presence that refuses to acknowledge its own non-existence; where the future is foreclosed because it remains unable to escape – to exorcise – the fantasy of presence, tied in turn to an emancipatory politics of subjectivity in which man re-appropriates his alienated essence from whatever obstacles or resistances (capital, technology) stand in his way.

What Lacoue-Labarthe and Nancy see as having reached a point of exhaustion is not 'the political', *le politique*, but 'politics', *la politique*. The distinction is absolutely crucial; 'in speaking of *the political* [du politique] we fully intend not to designate politics [la *politique*].' The present is diagnosed as a time of 'the absolute reign or "total" domination of the political' (RP, 110; RJ, 15), a time in which the political has succumbed to total domination – a domination of the political *by politics*, which is to say the politics of the subject. The totalising philosophical discourse of modernity means that politics has become coextensive with the politics of the subject, to the extent that the political (*le politique*) is forgotten. The *la/le politique* distinction thus appears to map neatly on to Heidegger's account of the forgetting of being through the process of its technological enframing, the domination of the ontological by the ontic. Following on from Heidegger's project of repeating the *polis*, Lacoue-Labarthe and Nancy also seek to repeat the forgotten site of the event. The title of the CRPP's second volume, *The Retreat of the Political* (*Le Retrait du politique*), makes it clear that what has 'retreated' is also to be 're-treated', which is to say repeated (RP, 112; RJ, 18).

Several commentators have emphasised this apparent continuity of Lacoue-Labarthe and Nancy with Heidegger: for instance, Francis Guibal, who remarks that 'Nancy will be, for me, the "lieutenant" of Heidegger' (Guibal 2004: 90). Another, Simon Critchley, has followed this line to the point of reading *la politique* as denoting the empirical facticity of political institutions – what Heidegger would describe as their 'ontic' arrangement which, in so far as it fails ontologically to interrogate the essence of the political, is not itself 'worthy of question', in the Heideggerian sense of the term ('*fragwürdig*'). By extension, Critchley reads *le politique* as referring to the Heideggerian notion of the 'essence' of the political, a reworking of the non-political essence of the *polis*, concealed by the totalitarianism of politics, but none the less recuperable. There is thus a straightforward translation of the *la/le politique* distinction from Heidegger's distinction between the ontic aspect, or facticity, of technology and its (non-technological) ontological essence as *Ge-stell*. Just as for Heidegger it is the very dominance of technology that conditions the forgetting of, and the failure to reflect upon, *Ge-stell*, so the dominance of the facticity of politics leads us to neglect the ontological 'essence' of the political (Critchley 1999a: 201). Echoing concerns expressed by CRPP member Denis Kambouchner, who queries the separability of politics and the political (RJ, 150–6), Critchley goes on to express deep suspicions about the allegedly Heideggerian pursuit of an ontological essence of the political, pointing to a tension between ontological description and a project (the CRPP) that sees itself as a continuation of Derridean deconstruction. He thus highlights an important ambiguity, noting that the term 'essence' is 'apparently employed [by Lacoue-Labarthe and Nancy] with little deconstructive reticence' (1999a: 201; see also Critchley 1993: 74).

The extent to which Lacoue-Labarthe and Nancy intend their notion of the political to carry the metaphysical baggage of the early Heidegger's fundamental ontology is none the less open to a radically different interpretation. Not only does Critchley neglect Lacoue-Labarthe and Nancy's own vocal concerns about the totalisation of technology in Heidegger, by accusing them of uncritically reinstating the language of a discredited metaphysics, he also underplays what Ian James has recently emphasised as Nancy's deliberate strategy of redeploying traditional metaphysical concepts in order to bring about their ungrounding (James 2006a: 171). Critchley thus neglects the constitutive significance of their *retrait* of the political: namely, the repetition of difference, of singularity, through which they return to Heidegger in order to move beyond him, to unground him.

The implications of this *retrait* go far beyond a simple critique of Heidegger, in that it also enables Lacoue-Labarthe and Nancy to rectify what Fynsk has perceived as deconstruction's ' "allusive" treatment of the political' in the earlier works of Derrida, notably in relation to Marx and the possibility of a complicity between Marxism and deconstruction (RP, 96). Despite an acknowledged commitment to Marxism on the part of both Lacoue-Labarthe and Nancy (former members of *Socialisme et barbarie* and the Christian socialist *Confédération française démocratique du travail* respectively; RP, 179n3; RJ, 16), they argue that Marx too is implicated in the stagnant paradigm of subjectivity: 'socialism (in the sense of "real or actually existing socialism") is the complete and completing figure of philosophy's imposition' (RP, 110–11; RJ, 16), the last stage in the framing of politics by the subject. Lacoue-Labarthe and Nancy argue that Marx, too, continues to subordinate politics to the (distinctly economic) figure of the subject, with the idea of socialist revolution presupposing an essentialised humanity that exists to be emancipated.

This indictment of Marx is one that Lacoue-Labarthe and Nancy would subsequently come to regard as hasty, in need of qualification, however. Apparently frustrated by members' descent into an 'easily accepted consensus of opinion' regarding the end of Marxism, the CRPP's co-organisers suspended the centre's activities after just four years, in 1984 (RP, 145). In a letter, '*Chers amis …*', outlining the reasons for the suspension, they suggest that this consensus is an obstacle to future enquiry into the essence of the political (RP, 146). James has also detected a sense of irritation with respect to other participants' reluctance to endorse the broadly Heideggerian methodology of Lacoue-Labarthe and Nancy (James 2006a: 167). Accordingly, much as their subsequent individual projects are decisively orientated by the agenda of the CRPP, their later work reflects an attempt to come to terms with some of these criticisms, to elaborate, for example, on their relations to Heidegger, while simultaneously reasserting a critical distance from him. Coinciding with this period of re-elaboration, Nancy's implicit engagement with Deleuze might be read in terms of the search for a way out of this Marxist-Heideggerian impasse. Over the course of developing an ontology that borrows increasingly from the Deleuzian language of singularity, Nancy returns to questions surrounding the legacy of Marx, to the post-Heideggerian meaning of technology and a concept of community that survives the (then anticipated) collapse of communism.

While critical of Marx's ontology, Nancy anticipates the need for what Derrida, in *Specters of Marx* (1993), will call a certain *spirit* of Marxism, a commitment to the goal of overturning alienation, even if there is ultimately no essential, ontologically privileged subject to be emancipated: 'It isn't a question, therefore, of giving up the struggle, but of determining in what name [*au nom de quoi*] we carry it on, in what name we desire the continued existence of beings' (FT, 20/38). The 'au nom de', 'in the name of', repeats the title of the paper and question posed to Derrida by Lacoue-Labarthe at Cérisy: namely, 'in what name' the essence of man might continue to be thought (RP, 63). At stake, in other words, is the elaboration of an ontology that, without metaphysically privileging the human, does not simply abandon it. In response, and intended as an alternative to the anthropologism of affording ontological privilege to language, Nancy creates the concept of *ecotechnicity*: 'From now on, then, ecotechnics is the name of "political economy"' (BSP, 135/160). This concept of ecotechnicity designates a radicalised Marxian account of the world and also contains within it a substantial critique of Heidegger's questioning of technology, above all of the latter's construal of technology in terms of *poiesis*, and the relation of this essence to politics. According to Heidegger, we remember, *technè* is essentially a crafting or production that actualises the essence of being in the work of art. *Dichtung* repeats the *Heimat* through which *Dasein*, exposed to the excess of being over finitude, finds solace and a home beyond the *unheimliche Unheimischkeit*, or uncanny unhomeliness, of the *polis*. As a form of repetition, *technè* is thus still subordinate to *aletheia*, the unveiling of being in its essentiality. For Nancy and, in particular, Lacoue-Labarthe, this configuration of technology as *poiesis* amounts to an aestheticisation of politics. In his 1987 book, *Heidegger, Art and Politics: The Fiction of the Political*, the latter argues that it is this aestheticisation, with its underlying conception of a return to the *oikos*, that underlies Heidegger's turn to Nazism. In privileging technology as an aesthetics, rather than a politics:

> This makes an immense difference, in which no less than the essence of Nazism – and consequently of the political – plays out. 'Work [*le travail*]' has been supplanted by 'the work [*œuvre*]' and in the very same process, it seems to me, in the innermost 'political' recesses of that discourse, National Socialism has been supplanted by what I shall call a national-aestheticism.

There is a vast difference between the two, a difference in which nothing less than the essence of Nazism – and, as a consequence, the essence of politics – is in play. (Lacoue-Labarthe 1990: 53/83)

The weight of Lacoue-Labarthe's concern is reiterated by Nancy, for whom 'Technics seems to tend to resemble a *praxis* rather than a *poiesis*' (SW, 101/158 [TM]). Implicit in this subtle distinction is the idea that Heidegger instrumentalises technics, reducing *technè* to that which works to make presence in the service of being. It thus recalls Ansell-Pearson's criticism, quoted above, that Heidegger reduces *Dasein* to a mere cipher, existing for no other reason than technically to articulate the event. For Nancy, by contrast, to say that technology is a *praxis* and not a *poiesis* means to do away with the hierarchy that teleologises being and to affirm that technics describes nothing other than the way in which existence simply *is*. Nancy denies that technology is an abstract system of expropriation, distinct from and outside the subject. It cannot be understood as the means of supplementing or *completing* a deficient subjectivity with a force (*technè*) that is distinct from and transcendent over nature (*physis*). He thus disputes the distinction between *technè* and *physis*, the supposition that technics does something that being cannot:

> Technology [*la technique*] doesn't reform a Nature or a Being in some Grand Artifice. Rather, it is the 'artifice' (and the 'art') of the fact that there is no nature. [...] So much so, in fact, that it ultimately designates that there is neither immanence nor transcendence. And this is why there is no technology 'as such' [*il n'y a pas 'la' technique*], merely a multiplicity of technologies [*mais une multiplicité de techniques*]. (FT: 25/45)

In place of an essentialised, homogeneous concept of *technè*, there are only multiple technics. Technical objects are not the instruments of nature, but the expression of the very technicity of existence, exposing the distinction between *technè* and *physis* as a fallacy: 'The "nexus" of technologies is existing itself' (FT, 24/44). The term *écotechnie* gives expression to a state of pantechnicity in which the *oikos* is not a home or the place of the identity of subjects, but a world of '*technè* of bodies' in which not just tools and crafts, but the very bodies that employ them, have their basis in an originary technicity (C, 89/77). In place of the symbolic economy of language as the 'Haus des Seins', the Heideggerian house of being, Nancy turns his attention to the pre-symbolic forms of (aneconomic) exchange that characterise the inter-relationality of finite bodies. The ecotechnical interactions of bodies are inherently deconstructive, breaking down rather than reinforcing the impression of subjective integrity and identity:

> Ecotechnics [*l'écotechnie*] creates the world of bodies in two correlated
> modes: for the projections of linear histories and final *ends*, it substitutes
> the spacings [*espacements*] of time, with local differences and numerous
> bifurcations. Ecotechnics deconstructs the system of ends, rendering these
> ends non-systematisible, non-organic and even stochastic (*except* under the
> imposition of the end of political economy or capital, which in fact imposes
> itself today on all ecotechnics, re-linearising time and homogenising ends
> [sauf *sous l'imposition de la fin de l'économie politique ou du capital, qui
> s'impose en effet aujourd'hui à toute l'écotechnie, re-linéarisant le temps,
> homogénéisant les fins*]). (C, 89/78–9 [TM])

By distinguishing between the originary ecotechnicity of finite bodies
and the forces of capital that reorganise them as linear and homogeneous, Nancy signals both his residual Marxism and that his thinking of
the body departs from the presupposition of the rigorously individuated, atomised body traditionally ascribed to *homo economicus*. With
its emphasis on the individual, the latter is symptomatic of the totalising
discourse of the subject and the concomitant forgetting of the political.
Nancy's turn to ecotechnicity and the *technè* of bodies thus extends
the positive aspect of his retreatment, or repetition, of *le politique*.
The Deleuzianism of this repetition is conveyed by the reference to the
non-organic, or non-organ-ised. In suggesting, somewhat elliptically,
that capital constitutes the upper limit to ecotechnical deconstruction,
Nancy also reworks another originally Deleuzo-Guattarian thesis,
to which we shall return in the next chapter. Where Deleuze and
Guattari's metaphysics of force allow for a sophisticated reworking of
capital as a form of life, the Nancian emphasis on finitude disinclines
him from incorporating capital into his ontology. It would seem to
be distinct from ecotechnical bodies, able to limit and organise them,
without being irreducible to them. The result, as at least one commentator has noted (Wurzer 1997: 98–100), is that capital has something of
an ambiguous ontological status in Nancy's work. This persists in his
more recent and sustained work on capitalism, found in *The Creation of
the World, or Globalization* (2002), where Nancy describes 'a struggle
between the two infinities, between extortion and exposition' (CWG,
53/60). Capitalism, he suggests, is a 'bad infinity', strictly incompatible
with the 'infinite finitude' of mortal *Dasein*.

This difference between Nancy and Deleuze and Guattari is reflected
in Nancy's reproach of the latter for substituting a metaphysics of force
for ontology. One wonders whether this ambiguous thinking of capital
does not feed into Derrida's concerns that Nancy continues to idealise
the human by according undue privilege to ontology.

NANCY, DELEUZE AND THE *SENS* OF THE POLITICAL

There is no longer any *polis* because there is *oikos* everywhere [*il n'y a plus de* polis *lorsqu'il y a partout de l'*oikos]: the housekeeping of the world as a single household, with 'humanity' for a mother, 'law' for a father.

But it is clearly the case that this big family does not have a father or a mother, and that, in the end, it is no more *oikos* than *polis* [*n'est pour finir plus* oikos *que* polis].

(Jean-Luc Nancy)[2]

In their early collaborative period, Lacoue-Labarthe and Nancy assert the need 'to displace, re-elaborate and replay the concept of "political transcendence"' (RT, 193; RP, 130). The assertion is perhaps understandable in light of what they perceive as Heidegger's collapsing of politics into aesthetics, but would not immediately appear to lend itself to a complicity with the anti-essentialism of Deleuze. In the conclusion to an influential essay on Deleuze, the Italian philosopher Giorgio Agamben asserts the need to distinguish 'in modern philosophy – which is, in a new sense, a philosophy of life – between a line of immanence and a line of transcendence' (Agamben 1999: 238–9). The line of transcendence moves from Kant to Husserl, passing through Heidegger before culminating in Levinas and Derrida. The line of immanence begins with Spinoza, passing through Nietzsche and Heidegger, again, on the way to Bataille, Deleuze and Foucault. Nancy is not named in the diagram, nor in a subsequent essay by Smith that, while expounding on Agamben's comments, rightly cautions that 'immanence and transcendence are both highly overdetermined in the history of philosophy, and it is not immediately clear what it would mean to be a philosopher of either one' (Smith 2003: 46). Despite following up the reference to political transcendence with a corruscating critique of immanence, Nancy becomes a perfect illustration of the truth of Smith's observation. Although highly critical of the 'closed immanence' of self-identical essences, Hutchens has emphasised Nancy's status as a thinker of 'open immanence', of being as a shared plurality of differences that cannot be conceived in terms of presence (Hutchens 2005: 42–52). The invocation of transcendence, Lacoue-Labarthe and Nancy insist, should not be conflated with the desire for a metaphysical ground, in the traditional sense of transcendence. They write of 'the exigency of getting away from the metaphysical *ground* of the political, of the transcendent and transcendental ground, for example, of the subject', all the while expressing doubts about the possibility of avoiding such a grounding

2. BSP, 135/160.

gesture (RT, 196; RP, 132). To minimise the risk, they invoke the need
for 'a transformation of the very idea of transcendence' (RT, 193; RP,
130). The result of this is a reversal in the traditional configuration of
the relationship between transcendence, essence and ground. In place of
the Heideggerian conception of transcendence as *poiesis*, we encounter
transcendence as *praxis*. The latter pertains to a type of labour that,
rather than constructing and grounding in the manner of *poiesis*, works
by deconstructing and ungrounding the aestheticised myths of the
subject (and by extension the State) that reign over politics.

In his own sole-authored post-CRPP work on politics, Lacoue-
Labarthe radicalises the Heideggerian distinction between the ontic
and the ontological by arguing that transcendence 'ends' ('*finit*') in
politics not simply because politics conceals the ontological ground,
but precisely because it is the imposition of a ground. Lacoue-Labarthe
goes on to describe 'the problem of identification' – in other words, of
a being-in-common or a common ontological ground – as 'the essential
problem of the political [*le problème lui-même du politique*]' (Lacoue-
Labarthe 1989: 300/172–3). The practice of politics presupposes and is
made possible by the fictioning or figuration of a ground, a mythology
that unifies the body politic and conceals the underlying absence of
pre-given, appropriable meanings or values on which politics could be
grounded. For Nancy, too, it is this absence of a ground that is transcendent. In fact, he defines it as transcendent simply because it resists
the figuration of a ground. It is ' "transcendence" that no longer has
any "sacred" meaning, signifying precisely a resistance to immanence'
(IC, 35/88). The same claim is reiterated in the later *Experience of
Freedom*, where he describes transcendence in terms not of appropriable essence, but of 'being-exposed at, on, and as the limit [...] *in
this being-taken-to-the-edge resulting from what has no "essence" that
is enclosed and reserved in any immanence present to the interior of the
body* [bordure]' (EF, 29/36). Immanence is the name given to politics,
which is defined by the attempt to figure the privileged narrative of a
metaphysical origin. In stark contrast to Deleuze, for whom immanence
is precisely liberation from the tyranny of essence, Nancy aligns it with
the foreclosure of being in an essentialised ground from which it cannot
escape.

There is an implicit reference here to the work of Emmanuel Levinas
and to the concept of transcendence within the phenomenological tradition of Husserl, where the term serves to describe the transcendent
appearance of objects within consciousness and the transcendence of
consciousness over the world. Levinas aligns immanence with the prospect of an (impossible) and oppressive experience of identity, of being

denuded of alterity, collapsed and locked in on itself. This concept of identity without subject is of an '*il y a*' from which there can be no escape. The phrase *il y a* translates the German *es gibt*, but Levinas plays on the imprecision of the translation to argue that the experience of immanence cannot be equated with one of giving or the gift. He affirms that 'there is no generosity in the "there is" [*il n'y a pas de générosité dans l'il y a*] [...] And there is neither joy nor abundance: it is a noise that returns after all negation of this noise. Neither being nor nothingness. I sometimes employ the expression of the "excluded third [*tiers exclu*]"' (Levinas 1985: 48/38). Levinas thus departs from Heidegger's identification of giving with the impersonal event of existence, a kind of raw givenness that is concealed by the labours of the subject. Elsewhere, he will also identify the excluded third with politics, as if politics were defined by the absence and moreover the negation of a generosity that is strictly ethical, or human, in origin (TI, 300/334–5; see also Caygill 2002: 65). As 'transcendence', a 'breach of totality', it is the exclusively ethical figure of *Autrui*, the other person, whose generosity consists in breaking open the oppressive horror of the self-identical *il y a* (TI, 35/24). The most distilled expression of this gift is found in the Other's death, 'something that is wholly other', which is experienced as absolutely ungraspable by consciousness, creating a rupture that renders the present non-identical to itself (Levinas 1987: 74/74).

Nancy borrows the Levinasian thinking of the transcendence of the other over the immanence of pure identity, but significantly corrects what (following Deleuze and Guattari) could be regarded as Levinas's unsatisfactory assertion of the priority of ethics over politics. He thus rejects Levinas's restriction of aneconomic exchange to ethics, the 'irreducible relation' of the 'face to face' encounter with the other (TI, 79/78), in order to rework it as the description of a *political* community that cannot be reduced to the abstract identity of the Levinasian *tiers*. Like Levinas, however, Nancy identifies immanence with a misguided fantasy of identity, of the subject as an autarkic ground, which exists without need to refer to the other: 'figure of immanence: the absolutely detached for-itself, taken as origin and as certainty' (IC, 3/16). Broadly in line with Heidegger, he also equates the philosophy of immanence with modernity's inability to cope with death, which is manifest in its attempt to conceptualise existence in terms of discrete, self-identical essences. In the age of the exhaustive self-completion of the metaphysics of the subject, immanence becomes another name for what Nancy and Lacoue-Labarthe earlier called the totalitarianism of politics (*la politique*), construed throughout modernity as the discourse of the essence of man. The figuration of man's immanence-to-self becomes the 'general horizon of our time':

> Wherereupon economic ties, technological operations and political fusion (into a *body* or under a *leader*) necessarily and through themselves represent or rather present, expose, and make real [*réalisent*] this essence. Essence is made into a work [*mise en œuvre*]; through them, it becomes a work of labour in its own right [*devient son propre ouvrage*]. This is what we have called 'totalitarianism', but it might be better named 'immanentism', as long as we do not restrict the term to designating certain types of societies or regimes but rather see in it the general horizon of our time, encompassing both democracies and their fragile juridical parapets. (IC, 3/15–16)

The reference to technology in this passage, taken from *The Inoperative Community* (*La Communauté désœuvrée*, 1986), is to the early Heideggerian conception thereof, not to the more nuanced thought of ecotechnicity, which appears in Nancy's later writings. Immanence – no longer just humanism – signals the exhaustion of the metaphysical possibilities of man, the limit horizon of modernity. Given Deleuze's reliance on the term, is this to be read as an indictment of Deleuzian philosophy as the highest moment in the self-completion of immanence?

In addition to Heidegger, the principal recipient of Nancy's critique of immanence in *The Inoperative Community* is Georges Bataille, whom, in contrast to the less centripetal reading of Bataille by Blanchot, Nancy suspects of privileging intimacy and an inner experience of being that borders on the centripetal, totalitarian logic of homecoming. A slightly later text, *The Experience of Freedom* (1988), comes closer to an explicit indictment of Deleuze by criticising another, more explicitly Deleuzian, representative of Agamben's 'line of immanence'. Nancy parenthetically suggests a continuity between modern conceptions of (institutional) politics – 'the dynamic of powers' – and Michel Foucault's philosophy of forces:

> we will at least posit that the political does not primarily consist in the composition and dynamic of powers (with which it has been identified in the modern age to the point of slipping to a pure mechanics of forces that would be alien even to power as such, or to the point of a 'political technology', according to Foucault's expression), but in the opening of a space. (EF, 78/104)

The generally acknowledged proximity of Deleuze to Foucault means that the reference to a pure mechanics of force might be deemed equally applicable to Deleuze's ontology of virtual forces. It is none the less thrown into relief by what, elsewhere, Nancy will affirm as his considerable indebtedness to Deleuze.

Even if he never refers it explicitly to Deleuze, there is a sense in which Nancy's critique of immanence repeats the standard criticism that Deleuze and Guattari are overly idealistic, that the Deleuzian *Übermensch*, who throws off individuation to become coextensive with the *Body without Organs*, is just another privileged form of the subject.[3] But the criticism seeks to nuance rather than to reject Deleuze and does not, consequently, undermine the possibility of reading Nancy as an implicit, albeit in crucial respects qualified, Deleuzian. In one of his only two short works to date that focus specifically on Deleuze, a paper delivered in commemoration of the latter's death, Nancy writes that 'one cannot avoid not sharing with this thought, to a greater or lesser degree,' before going on to note 'the strange proximity that obliges me in spite of everything to take up a fold of his thought' (Nancy 1998: 115). The 'in spite of everything [*malgré tout*]' acknowledges the different 'directions' between Deleuze's emphasis on immanence and (the early) Nancy's preferred term of transcendence, but also indicates the latter's willingness to negotiate, to attenuate the heuristic distinction made by Agamben between transcendence and immanence. Nancy achieves this by reworking the concept of finitude within a Deleuzian philosophy whose critique of phenomenology means that it contains almost no reference to death, understood as the limit horizon of subjectivity.

Reflecting the broad difference between philosophies of transcendence and those of immanence, where Nancy differs from Deleuze is foremost over the ontological status of negativity: whether it is merely a fallacy attributable to the impossibility of representing being's excess, as is asserted in the univocity thesis of transcendental empiricism ('MONISM=PLURALISM'), or whether we can speak, like Lacan, of a (pre-)ontological cut, a rupture within being that renders immanence impossible. Alluding to his own emphasis on finitude, Nancy acknowledges that Deleuze and he 'do not have the same concept of the negative [*pas le même négatif*]' (Nancy 1998: 122) and, in *The Inoperative Community*, he affirms the existence of an ontological *déchirure*, a tear, on the basis of the claim that *absolute immanence* is logically impossible. Absolute immanence here means being that is autarkic, present-to-self, essentially 'without relation [*sans rapport*]' (IC, 4/18–19). Yet in order to be absolute, Nancy maintains, being would have to be in relation to something else, external to itself, against which its own interiority to itself could be measured. The necessity of an external

3. A recent and highly sophisticated version of this criticism of Deleuze and Guattari is outlined by Jacques Derrida, in *On Touching – Jean-Luc Nancy* (see T, 124–6/141–5). Derrida is also the first to recognise Nancy's Deleuzianism; his remarks on Deleuze and Guattari in this respect are not incidental, but importantly inform his critique of Nancy's 'absolute realism'.

measure immediately reinstates being in a relation that contradicts its supposed immanence. Paradoxically, 'the logic of the absolute *sets it in relation* [*le* met en rapport].' It is the relationality of existence that exposes and *ungrounds* the absence of relation as impossible: 'The relation (the community) is, if it *is*, nothing other than what undoes [*désœuvre*], in its very principle – and at its closure or on its limit – the autarky of absolute immanence' (IC, 4/19 [TM]). Relation undoes, or ecotechnically deconstructs, the notion of being as immanent to itself, a locus of pure identity uncontaminated by alterity and difference. At the origin of this relationality is the face-to-face encounter with the Other (*Autrui*), whose alterity, fully experienced only in their death, creates a rupture on the oppressive self-identity of the *il y a*, exposing us to our own subjective finitude (Levinas 1987: 46–8/46–8). Nancy borrows his key concept of *désœuvrement* from Blanchot, who, in *The Space of Literature* (1955), reworks the Levinasian thinking of death as an impersonal event that cannot be 'worked', or aestheticised as a constituent of identity. *Désœuvrement*, for Blanchot, describes the idea of being-toward-death as 'pure beginning', an inappropriable 'superabundance' 'that can never be realised in a work [*qui ne permet jamais d'arriver à l'œuvre*]' (Blanchot 1982: 46/48–9). For Nancy, *désœuvrement*, usually translated as 'unworking', or 'inoperativity', is characteristic of what precedes and undoes any political attempt to project aestheticised narratives of shared identity and teleological destiny (IC, 31–2/78–9). As in Deleuze, who also cites Blanchot's account of impersonal death (DR, 138–9/148–9), the activity of unworking the synthesis of identity pertains to a multiplicity, or community, of singularities, whose interrelations resist and countereffectuate any effort to subsume them under a totalising logic. As if in acknowledgement of a proximity to Deleuze, in his later works, Nancy even deploys the term 'transimmanence' to describe the coexistence of singularities, thus nuancing his earlier critique of immanence (SW, 17–18, 55/33–4, 91). Without wishing to dwell too much on this point here, the concept of transimmanence is what enables Nancy to think the existence of *sens*, the ungrounded circulation of meaning between bodies. This account of *sens*, given primarily in *The Sense of the World* (1993), would seem to come quite close to the account of *sens* given by Deleuze in *Logic of Sense* (1969). Like Deleuze, Nancy is keen to emphasise the role played by the unsymbolisable in the creation of meaning.

In spite of the apparent lexical gulf, Nancy's transcendent essence of the political, once understood in terms of his thinking of a community of singularities, arguably comes close to the plan(e) of immanence in Deleuze. As a name for the being of relationality that exceeds its own representability, '*the being-ecstatic of Being itself*' (IC, 6/23), community and ecotechnicity connote the virtuality of existence that cannot be figured as a unified ground. The Deleuzian framework of virtual and actual thus offers itself as a more convincing schema for understanding the *le/la politique* distinction than the Heideggerian onto-ontological binary in which Critchley fears that Lacoue-Labarthe and Nancy remain trapped. Nancy none the less perhaps suspects Deleuze of not going far enough in his thinking of ungrounding. If, as suggested in Chapter 1, the Lacanian concept of ungrounding veers toward the opening up of differences (the symbolic order) on to the pure identity of the real, Nancy will side with Deleuze in characterising the *sans fond* as the site of difference and singularity:

> It is a groundless 'ground' ['*fond*' *sans fond*], less in the sense that it opens up the gaping chasm of an abyss than that it is made up only of the network, the interweaving, and the sharing [*partage*] of singularities: *Ungrund* rather than *Abgrund*, but no less vertiginous. There is nothing *behind* singularity [*il n'y a rien* derrière *la singularité*] – but there is, outside it and in it, the immaterial *and* material space that distributes it and shares it out [*qui la partage*] as singularity, distributes and shares the confines of other singularities, or even more exactly distributes and shares the confines of singularity – which is to say of alterity – between it and itself. (IC, 27/70)

The language is reminiscent of Deleuze's description of a virtual *plan d'immanence* populated by flows and distributions of singularities, whose interactions give rise to Guattari's claim that being, or rather life, is inherently political: 'politics precedes being' (TP, 203/249). The claim anticipates Lacoue-Labarthe and Nancy's designation of the relationality, or *partage*, of singularities as the essence of the political: 'the so-called "question of the relation" remains in our eyes the major question; it is perhaps even, as such, the question of the essence of the political' (RT, 133; RP, 197). Elsewhere, in another rare footnote on Deleuze, Nancy affirms that his own use of the term singularity coincides considerably with the former's descriptions of singularity as an 'ideal event', 'essentially pre-individual, impersonal and a-conceptual' (EF, 190–1n12/78). This impersonal, pre-individual event of multiple, coexisting singularities is what Nancy will call community:

> Community means, consequently, that there is no singular being without another singular being [*qu'il n'y a pas d'être singulier sans un autre être singulier*], and that there is only, therefore, what might be called, in a rather inappropraite idiom, an originary or 'ontological' sociality that in its principle exceeds the theme of man as a social being (the *zoon politikon* is secondary to this community). (IC, 28/71 [TM])

Prior to the community of individuals, the originary political community is a community of singularities, moreover a 'community of bodies'

(C, 57/73). Nancy argues that singularities do not exist independently, autarkically, but only in multiplicities of ecotechnical inter-relation. There is community, the political, in the sense that singularities are shared, mutually implicated and determining of one another. Another way of saying this is that the relations between singularities are constitutive of the singular as such. To cite the title of another of Nancy's books, 'being singular' is already 'being singular plural'. Nancy employs the Latin expression *partes extra partes* to connote the absence of interiority ascribed to subjectivity (see, for example, IC, 29/73; C, 29/27). The community of bodies is composed of 'parts outside parts', not self-contained and complete individuals, but (Deleuzo-Guattarian) flows of, for example, blood and air. Above all, community is an event that, in excess of individual experience, only exists extrinsically, as shared: the event of, or rather *as*, exposure of/to the finitude of bodies. An emphasis on the shared plurality of finitude is central to Nancy's rereading of Heidegger, the core of which lies in his assertion that *Dasein* is always *Mitsein*; it is by virtue of his being-in-common with others that man is singular. In *Sein und Zeit, Dasein* is constituted by its ability to die and only accedes to the authenticity of its own essence by actively appropriating death as that which is most proper to it. For Nancy, however, death is the singularity that cannot be appropriated, that renders impossible any form of the immanence-to-self presupposed by subjectivity. Heidegger writes: 'by its very essence, death is in every case mine [*wesensmäßig je der meine*], insofar as it "is" at all' (BT, 284/319 [§47, 240]). Radically reinterpreting Heidegger's infamous claim, Nancy denies that the *Jemeinigkeit*, the 'mineness', of death resides in its immanence to the subject, as the highest possibility of *Dasein*. The *sens* of death resides in its extrinsicity, in the fact of its being shared, experienced as other to oneself. Rather than the instance of identity, *Jemeinigkeit* becomes the moment of rupture in which essence and immanence to being as such are voided, which 'implies the withdrawal of all substance, in which is hollowed out the infinity of the relation according to which "mineness" *identically means the nonidentity* of "yourness" and "his/her/its-ness"' (EF, 67/92).

Intended to convey the non-self-identity of any concept of propriety and self-ownership, the formulation is ambiguous to the point of leading Derrida to worry that Nancy remains caught up in a classical thinking of the subject. This risk is of 'saving, at least surreptitiously, the "I can" of my own freedom, of the freedom that is mine, of the freedom of the I-myself, indeed of the voluntary-conscious-intentional-deciding-I-myself, the "I can", let's just say, of classical freedom' (R, 45/70). One could argue along with Ian James here that Derrida wilfully ignores the subtlety of Nancy's deconstructive redeployment of the traditional language of ontology (James 2006a: 148). In another essay, 'Finite Thinking', written roughly contemporaneously with *The Experience of Freedom*, Nancy returns to the concept of *Jemeinigkeit* in a way that, irrespective of the Heideggerianism of his language, through its mention of pre-individuated singularities reiterates the suggestion of a proximity to Deleuze:

> Here 'singularity' isn't simply understood as the singularity of an individual (not simply as Heidegger's 'in each case mine [*Jemeinigkeit* – GM]', but as the singularity of punctuations, of encounters and events that are as much individual as they are preindividual or common, at every level of community). (FT, 12/23–4)

If Nancy still clings to Heideggerian terminology, it is therefore because the *je* of *Jemeinigkeit* enables him to refer to both the French *je*, meaning 'I', and to the German '*je*', the time of singularity, 'this time' or 'this time just this once [*cette fois, cette seule fois*]' (EF, 67/91). The translation recalls the 'repetition once and for all [*une fois pour toutes*]' of Deleuze and the 'repetition *and* first time' that Derrida uses to describe the eternal return of *différance* (DR, 154/165; SM, 10/31; M, 17/18–19). It is here that we also find Nancy's concept of repetition as a reworking of Nietzsche's eternal return. Significantly, his rereading of Nietzsche differs from that of Deleuze. Rather than articulate the eternal return in terms of exposure to the transcendental experience of the 'beyond' of the death of the subject, Nancy uses it to emphasise the irreducible facticity of finitude, the fact that there is no such beyond. There is only 'the repetition of the instant, NOTHING but this repetition, and as a result, NOTHING (since it is a matter of the repetition of what essentially does not return)' (BSP, 4/21–2). What circulates in this eternal return is not just bodily flows, but ultimately the *sens* from which the *I* emerges. The *I* is not a continuous, underlying substrate of identity, but is rather continually recreated through these circulations, only existing in the instant. *Contra* Lacan, the circulation is not of language but of bodies. *Sens* is not symbolic but pre-symbolic. Nancy's insistence on this point has caused at least one prominent Lacanian to lament the emergence of the 'metaphysics of finitude' as 'our (contemporary) great narrative', 'a new Master-Signifier' (Zupančič 2006: 190).[4] The retort misses the subtlety of Nancy's critique of Lacan (Lacoue-Labarthe and Nancy 1992: 109–13/113–15; Nancy 1979;

---

4. The comment, originally given at the conference 'Is There Still a Politics of Truth?' (Birkbeck College, University of London, 25–26 November 2005), was greeted with enthusiastic approval by Slavoj Žižek and Alain Badiou.

James 2002: 125–6), and also arguably fails to account for his recent return to the concepts of infinity, in the 'good' and 'bad' infinities of ecotechnicity and capitalism (see also SW, 29–33/51–6). None the less, it dovetails with the Derridean suspicion that Nancy is overly reliant on the concept of finitude. In so far as there is a Nancian real, it is not the paradoxically idealised, singular but self-identical life of the libido, but what Derrida, commenting on Nancy, describes as the 'absolute, irredentist, and post-deconstructive realism' of finite bodies (T, 46/60).

Being, in this respect, is precisely coextensive with beings, nothing more than a community of shared finitude, or relationality prior to any metaphysical essence:

> In this relation, 'man' is not given – but it is relation alone that can give him 'humanity' [*l''homme' n'est pas donné – mais c'est le rapport seul qui peut donner son 'humanité'*]. It is freedom that gives relation by withdrawing being. It is then freedom that gives humanity, and not the inverse. But the gift that freedom gives is perhaps never, insofar as it is a gift of *freedom*, a quality, or property, or essence in the order of '*humanitas*'. Even when freedom gives its gift under the form of a '*humanitas*', as it has done in modern times, it is in face a transcendence that freedom gives: a gift that, as gift, transcends the giving, that does not establish itself as a giving but above all gives *itself* as gift and as a gift of freedom that gives itself in the withdrawal of being [*c'est en fait une transcendance qu'elle donne: un don qui transcende, en tant que don, la donation, qui ne s'établit pas comme une donation, mais qui avant tout se donne en tant que don, et que don de la liberté qui essentiellement donne et se donne, dans le retrait de l'être*]. (EF, 73/99 [TM])

The passage returns us to the question of the gift in its relation to the political. Once again, no longer is it the Maussian concept of the imposition of debt and obligation. Nancy writes of the 'gift *of freedom* [*don de la liberté*]' – the gift of freedom both by and of itself, in excess of the representation of the human, which it ungrounds. Freedom is prior to subjectivity, opening up as the space created by the withdrawal of the immanence of being. As in Heidegger, the gift is inseparable from this countermovement of withdrawal, which conditions the giving of freedom as relationality. But whereas for Heidegger the gift opens on to the previously concealed pre-political being of the *Heimat*, Nancy's gift is political precisely because behind its withdrawal there is NOTHING, because it has no substantial, instantiable existence that could be realised through an arrogative intervention of philosophy in the sphere of politics. The withdrawal of the gift 'aban-dons us', or gives us up, to a spatio-temporality in which NOTHING is given for us to receive. In the absence of a ground, there are only singularities, exposed and abandoned to their shared finitude.

Where Heidegger affirms the goddess Hestia, Nancy affirms Hermes, the god of theft and flight to whom Heidegger opposes Hestia. We recall from Chapter 2 that these very characteristics of theft and flight, captured simultaneously in the French, *vol*, are ascribed by Deleuze to the repetition of the event *qua* aneconomic gift. Reiterating his rejection of the politics of *Heimischwerden* and the fixed hearth, Nancy borrows the concept of the aneconomic nomad from Deleuze and Guattari's *Mille plateaux* to describe a spatio-temporal 'spacing [*espacement*]' in which neither time nor space is pre-given, but is rather created through the excessive repetitions, or interactions, of singularities (EF, 145/187). In this *espacement*, meaning, or *sens*, is created from nothing through the repeated ungrounding of (political) narratives, whose attempts to reappropriate an ontological ground (for politics) are condemned to failure. The *je*, the I, comes into existence as that which tries to appropriate the *Je*, the *chaque fois* of singularity, through the act of naming itself as a subject. Yet it is repeatedly displaced by exposure to other bodies, which expose the impossibility of appropriating one's own finitude. The attempt at appropriation thus occurs in a space without guarantee. It is for this reason that Nancy becomes increasingly reluctant, in his works published after *The Inoperative Community*, to adopt the Derridean language of the gift wholesale. Where Derrida qualifies the gift with a 's'il y en a' to account for the double-bind of there being a gift that would be negated both by its receipt and its non-receipt (GT, 7/18), Nancy circumscribes the aporia by writing instead of offering and abandoning:

> What takes place is neither a coming-into-presence nor a gift. It is rather the one or the other, or the one and the other, but as abandoned, given up [*abandonnées*]. The offering is the giving up of the gift and of the present. Offering is not giving up – it is suspending or giving up the gift in the face of a freedom that can take it or leave it. It is a proposition and exposed as such [*L'offrande est l'abandon du don et du présent. Offrir n'est pas donner – c'est suspendre le don en face d'une liberté qui peut le prendre ou le laisser. C'est une proposition, et comme telle exposée*].
>   What is offered is offered up – addressed, destined, abandoned – to the eventual to-come of a presentation, but it is left to this coming and does not impose or determine it. (FT, 237–8/185–6 [TM])

Existence is not 'given', in the phenomenological sense, but is rather abandoned, awaiting, offering itself up to naming.

WIEDERKEHR DES GLEICHES

Heidegger, we saw, memorably criticises Nietzsche's affirmation of eternal return as the ultimate symptom of global technological nihilism. By contrast, in the opening pages of *Being Singular Plural*, in a passage that decisively reflects the importance Nietzsche acquires through the work of Deleuze, Nancy writes that 'the thinking of the eternal return is the inaugural thought of our contemporary history, a thinking we must repeat (even if it means calling it something else)' (BSP, 4/21–2). We are condemned, even abandoned, to the repetition of this thought, just as politics (*la politique*) is condemned to repeat the gesture of its own demise, the exhausted paradigm of the subject, stalled by capitalism in the final phase of its ecotechnical deconstruction. Deleuze and Guattari say something quite similar in *Anti-Oedipus*, where they argue that capital constitutes the end point of universal history – beyond which philosophy alone (or, at least, only an overtly philosophical, which is to say creative, experimental micropolitics) is able to bring about the repetition of difference. As Nancy himself labours to point out, it is by no means certain that a grounding gesture can be avoided; that the repetition of the political can escape the frame of the subject it seeks to supersede. There is 'nothing but this repetition' (BSP, 4/21), nothing but the repetition of eternal return, of Nancy's repetition of Heidegger's repetition of Greece (which, in its notion of *Anfang* is also a reprise of Nietzsche's thought, 'even if it means calling it something else'). Unsurprisingly, then, it is far from certain that Nancy succeeds where Heidegger fails. Derrida's suspicion that Nancy's work is shot through with a residual self-presence of the subject has already been noted, alongside James's defence of Nancy.

A return to Deleuze re-raises the question of whether Derrida has a point (even if he will ultimately also accuse Deleuze and Guattari of doing something very similar). At the heart of Derrida's reading lies a critique of Nancy's transformed essentialism which, despite being tied to the ungrounding gesture of *désœuvrement*, continues to speak in terms of touching the origin, suggesting in turn the possibility of an originary experience of the human body, prior to its mediation by representation:

> Touching is the very experience of 'origin' as 'singular plurality'. The plural singular, originarily, is what finds itself given to touch [*ce qui se trouve donné à toucher*]. The origin could be touched, or would have to be, as – and like – touching itself as self-touching [*le toucher même en tant que se toucher*]. (T, 115/132–3)

Derrida makes a similar criticism of Deleuze and Guattari in the same work (T, 123–6/141–5). Returning to the latter none the less proves useful for an understanding of Derrida's critique of Nancy. We saw in Chapter 2 how the body is caught up in a history of inscription. *Anti-Oedipus* gives a lengthy account of the history of writing the body and of the way that bodies are formed through the mnemotechnicities of inscription. In this account, technicity functions not only *between* finite bodies, but is prior to them, playing a constitutive role in determining what it is that gets counted as a body. In the archaic societies of the gift economy, it is the body of the earth on which the collective identity of the community is inscribed through the gift-economic institutions of the *potlatch* and the circulation of women as gifts. Human bodies are not individuated, but gathered together under the overarching identity of the community through a number of inscriptive practices, including tattooing and scarification. In *Corpus* (1992), Nancy writes of 'incised, ingraved, tattooed and scarred, "written bodies"' that 'ultimately this is not the modern body [...] *exscribed* in advance of all writing' (C, 11/13). The inference is that these practices serve merely as primitive forms of the mythopoiesis to which, in *The Inoperative Community*, he attributes the figuration of an ontological ground (IC, 53–4/134–6). Inscription is understood exclusively in terms of the production of signification, serving the purpose of rendering bodies decipherable to the community that appropriates them. We see this in his claim that inscription – writing – is in no way prior to the body, but rather that which runs counter to it, attempting to create interiority there where there is only the exteriority of parts.

Determined to disclose the priority of ecotechnical bodies to the symbolic order of signification, Nancy rejects any suggestion that the body can function as a 'place of writing' (C, 85/76). To inscription, he opposes the novel concept of 'exscription'; the two concepts are furthermore declared to be mutually exclusive, the one being the inverse side of the other. Once the space of bodies is understood as *partes extra partes*:

> the body is no longer anything like a surface of inscription – in the sense of a site for the recording of signification. [...] Without doubt, the body is [the fact] *that one writes* [c'est *qu'on écrit*] but it is absolutely not *where* one writes, and the body is no more that *which* one writes [ce *qu'on écrit*] – but always that which writing *exscribes* [ce que l'écriture excrit]'. (C, 87/76 [TM])

The body is not that which is written, which is to say itself the product of the '*technè* of bodies', but rather what makes writing possible as the spacing of *sens*.

There is much in this claim that once again reflects the influence of Deleuze and Guattari, not least the idea that writing, as a form of *habitus*, works by means of an economy that ultimately conceals the aneconomic event of singularity, eliminating the alterity of the community of multiple singularities. In this sense, Nancy and Deleuze are in agreement that the event, the eternal return of difference, constitutes an ungrounding or unworking of inscription. There is nevertheless a question of whether, in his understanding of the event purely in terms of finitude and the mutual exposure of finite bodies, Nancy goes far enough; of whether he does not ultimately fall short of Deleuze by privileging the ecotechnical body as something that is still prior to the various *habituses* of which the human body is always already a product. There is a question, in other words, of whether Nancy's thinking of the body as exteriority is not still marked by an interiorisation of bodily *praxis* against the *poiesis* of writing, and in turn of whether this interiorisation would not thereby re-poeticise ecotechnicity as an ontological ground. This absolute priority of corporeal *Dasein* is what Derrida is referring to when he writes of Nancy's 'absolute realism', 'a sort of absolute, irredentist, and post-deconstructive realism', though importantly one that supersedes all previous incarnations of realism in the philosophical tradition (T, 47/60). But it is also the point at which Derrida provocatively poses the question of whether Nancy succumbs to idealism, surreptitiously regrounding (or reterritorialising) the event in a shared finitude that continues to presuppose the integrity of the human body. The problem, of course, stems from a deliberate strategy on the part of Nancy, intended to bring about the supersession of Deleuze and Guattari's politics of abstract mechanical forces; intended, moreover, as a response to the alleged Platonism of the Deleuzian virtual, to the idea that Deleuze posits a life of immanence that is somehow (metaphysically) distinct from its actual instantiations. As Derrida points out to Nancy, in a dialogue where the latter is only too happy to accept and affirm the criticism, in emphasising the relationality of shared finitude Nancy risks privileging a distinctly *human* political (Derrida and Nancy 2004: 195–8).

CONCLUSION

The chapter began by posing the question of whether a politics of the gift is inherently compromised by a tendency toward an arrogative philosophical overdetermination of the political, a philosophical reconstruction that entails the elision of politics, or its sublation in philosophy. Heidegger attempts to inaugurate a politics of repetition through a return to the pre-political origin of the Greek *polis*. His project, however, is limited by both the fixity of his concept of repetition and, linked to this, a persistent subordination of the *polis* to an *oikos*, encapsulated in a thinking of *Heimischwerden* that ultimately domesticates the *Unheimlichkeit* of the gift. The site of this recuperated *oikos* is language, which according to Heidegger repeats the ontological structure of the event; it is in language, more precisely in the naming of the *Heimat* of being, that we make present and thereby receive the gift in its withdrawal. Beyond the ostensive, ontic, politics of institutions, Heidegger argues for a politics of the gift that is a (non-)politics of the name. In so doing, however, he reduces repetition to mimesis, to the disclosure of what is already there. In so far as the *Anfang* is defined by a gesture of grounding, Heidegger's repetition of Nietzsche's eternal return falls foul of the same problems he sees Nietzsche as committing, framed by an inability to escape the technological nihilism of the modernity he set out to criticise. Nancy, by contrast, locates a more originary technicity in the ecotechnical sharing of bodies. Rather than a hypostatised excess of being over beings, seemingly endowed with its own historical agency, he strips it of any vestiges of destiny, teleology and the sacred, reworking the event as nothing other than the community of finitude, of inappropriable *partes extra partes*. It is in respect of this, moreover, that the event is inherently political. In place of an aestheticised being beyond beings, existence comes simply to name the relationality between singular bodies; the eternal return describes the shifting configurations of *partes extra partes*, generating *sens* through the movement of *vol* and *don*, the expropriation of identity that results from the offering of existence. Yet there remain doubts about whether Nancy goes far enough in his decentring of the subject; whether his attempts to desacralize existence do not merely shift the sacred from language to the body in a way that continues to privilege the human. We shall see in the next chapter how the ensuing charge of idealism is reflected in a tendency amongst commentators to see Nancy's politics as idealistic, ill-equipped to engage substantially with the task of receiving the gift of eternal return. Much as Lacoue-Labarthe and Nancy, in particular, make considerable progress in redeeming a politics of the gift tainted by Heidegger, there is still more to be done if they are fully to escape the Heideggerian tendency toward overdetermination. For reasons that Nancy has begun to appreciate, the same will hold true for Deleuze and Guattari.

4. 'Pour en finir avec ...': *Democracy and Sacrifice*

'The "and" conjoins but never innocently or romantically. So much at stake' (Ansell-Pearson 1997b: 1). At stake, precisely, is nothing less than the future of philosophy *and* politics, an allegedly impossible future no longer bound by the strictures of a period, no longer subject to the categories and binary oppositions of modernity. In the introductory essay on 'Rhizome' in *A Thousand Plateaus*, Deleuze and Guattari assert the need to 'establish a logic of the AND' in order to 'overthrow ontology, do away with foundations, nullify endings and beginnings' (TP, 25/36–7). The deployment of the rhizomatic 'and ... and ... and' serves to desubstantialise the hegemonic, arboreal logic of the verb, emphasising the theft, the withdrawal of substance that coincides with the giving of the event. It thus also frees us to trace constellations between the supposedly incommensurable: to seek in democracy, for example, a lens on to the fate of sacrifice.

Expressed through the elegantly desubstantialising ' "without" without privation or negativity or lack' of Blanchot and Derrida (LO, 87/140), the so-called postmodern age of high capitalism might loosely be defined as a period *without* period, a time *without* time, whose nostalgia for the present coincides with its being beyond the End of History and the 'metanarratives' of modernity (Jameson 1991: 19–21; Lyotard 1986: xxiv/7). There is also therefore an ambiguity of the end, an interminable repetition of the end (Nancy 1986: 15), inseparable from what Badiou has called 'the end of the End of History [which] is cut from the same cloth as this End' (Badiou 1999: 31/11; Badiou 2008b: 9–10/64). The latter is also encapsulated in a thinking of *phantasm*, spectrality and a neg(oti)ation of ghosts that live on beyond their apparent demise. After *Specters of Marx* and the spectres of Mauss whose haunting predominates this work, we now turn to the spectres of Hegel-Kojève, who diagnosed the end of History, and whose ghosts live on in the apparent failure of this diagnosis. Given the relation of Kojève to Bataille and Lacan – given, moreover, the disjuncture between the idealism of modern philosophy and the experience of the twentieth century – the whole project of a politics of the gift might be seen to follow from this failure. Following Hegel – and to the chagrin of Bataille, who turned to Mauss to argue the contrary – Kojève predicted that 'the end of human Time or History' would entail the end of philosophy and the contraction of politics into bureaucracy (IRH, 159/435n). Both live on, but in what sense and to what extent? The modern subject, the one who, according to Nietzsche, 'is never "through" with anything' (GM, 39/308 [2§1; TM]), has supposedly been replaced by an *Übermensch* all too happy to announce that he or she is through with *everything*, fully able to let go of history and affirm the transitory being of the human. But this too, is symptomatic, Nancy suggests (BSP, 4/21–2, which nuances the earlier *Forgetting of Philosophy* [*Oubli de la philosophie*], 1986: 24). With the eternal return perhaps nothing other than a prolonged and inescapable meditation on the age of an end without end, without *Aufhebung*, can philosophy and politics amount to anything more than disquisitions on their own end, fundamentally unable to establish whether or not they have actually died? In a similar reworking of Kojève through Nietzsche, Deleuze and Guattari invoke the end of History to describe the life of capital as the upper limit of the eternal return, the point at which becoming succumbs to a historical impasse that is reinforced rather than teased open by democracy. Rather than sublated in the movement of a dialectic, institutions once thought essential, purported to bear a privileged relation to the event, now appear desubstantialised, exposed to and by an ungrounding they prove powerless to withstand. Democracy, in the words of Heidegger, but echoed by those of Deleuze and Guattari and, on occasion, Nancy, becomes simply 'incompatible' (*nicht zugeordnet*) with the new forms of life – capital, technics – that threaten to surpass the human (Heidegger 1993b: 104–5/206). Likewise sacrifice, which has supposedly disappeared, thrown into '*sacrificial crisis or crisis of differences*' by the collapse of the binary sacred-profane it was once charged with safeguarding (Girard 1977: 49/81 [TM]). Philosophy lives on regardless; one could be forgiven for thinking that, in its evocation of the event, it absorbs the role once accorded to sacrifice.

The task of the present chapter is to challenge the givenness of this diagnosis, to question whether – recalling the Derridean logic of spectrality – something can so simply be abandoned unto death without thereby reanimating it in the very act of abandonment. Drawing on the words of Miguel de Beistegui, who notes that sacrifice 'was never as

alive as when at the announced threshold of its demise, never as flourishing as when at its end' (Beistegui 1997: 159), it will be argued that
the same can be said of democracy, and moreover that the two need to
be thought together, reasserted in the context of a politics of the gift
that is irreducibly framed by capitalism. It is, in other words, possible
to think democracy aneconomically, as a singularity that exceeds the
framing of politics by representation. Rather than the site of the completion of metaphysics, the reappropriation of essence through which
privileged *homines economici* would arrive at their destiny, democracy
need not be thought intrinsically incompatible with the ungrounding
event of the gift. To see this, however, it is first necessary to transform
the way it is conceived in relation to a concept of sacrifice that has been
thought similarly restrictively in terms of appropriation.

   This is not to deny that both concepts are deeply problematic, not to
overlook how, for a certain strand of (post-)Hegelianism, democracy
has reductively been thought a sufficient condition of politics; how, for
anti-Hegelians, it testifies to much that is wrong with modernity, necessitating the equally problematic demand for a sacrificial reconnection
with the sacred immanence of being. The problem, it will be argued,
stems from philosophical overdeterminations of both democracy and
sacrifice, but moreover from a philosophical overdetermination of
politics. Found in Kojève and Fukuyama, but arguably also Deleuze
and Nancy, this overdetermination renders their apparently opposed
positions complicit in the propagation of a paradigmatically idealising
Hegelo-Heideggerianism. We see this in the thinking of both democracy
and sacrifice too restrictively in terms of mimesis: that is, as instances
of the negative, restricted repetition of identity that a politics of the gift
seeks to abandon. Deleuze and Guattari regard democracy as the 'abou-
tissement', the culmination or outcome, of the Hegelian State and the
Heideggerian *Heimat*, a reterritorialisation that exists to furnish identity, to make habitable the deterritorialised *oikos* of capitalism (WIP,
98/94). Although he recently and emphatically clarified his earlier criticisms of democracy, Nancy has been similarly critical of a State that
embodies sacrifice, of representative democracy that, as 'a kind of last
sacrifice' (SW, 90/142), overlaps with Lacan's sacrificial gift of what
one does not have. Based on readings of Hegel, Heidegger and Bataille,
Nancy reads sacrifice as inseparable from the attempt to 'transappropriate' an ontological ground. Recalling his concept of the political as
désœuvrement, unworking, there is thus a constitutively *chiasmic* relationship between sacrifice and politics, in which a politics of sacrifice
must always amount to a sacrifice of the political. The disclosure of the
ecotechnical event raises the question of whether being is not always

already sacrificed in being offered: 'Shouldn't the age of technology be understood as the age of the end of sacrifice?' (FT, 72/98).

By way of a return to Derrida, but with interventions from Badiou, it will be argued that the politics of the gift articulated by Nancy and Deleuze risks continuing philosophically to arrogate the political, because they have failed sufficiently to deconstruct their Hegelo-Heideggerian past; because, through these rejections of democracy and sacrifice, they go simultaneously too far and not far enough in seeking superficially to distance themselves from their respective Oedipal fathers, and in so doing collapse back into the logic they seek to escape. Writing on Hegel, in *Glas* (1974), Derrida suggests 'the gift can only be a sacrifice, that is the axiom of speculative reason' (Derrida 1986: 243a/270a). In slightly different ways, both Deleuze and Nancy corroborate this reading, but only at the cost of unnecessarily disavowing a more political concept of sacrifice. The effect of this is to risk collapsing the gift back into a Hegelian logic of theodicy that fails to differentiate between sacrifice and the gift; that overlooks the translation of virtual into actual, the fatal but moreover *sacrificial* strategies that govern the impossibility of the gift's receipt in actuality. We miss the possibility of reading sacrifice as unhinged from mimesis, an affirmation of the excess of the gift and therefore of the impossibility of its appropriation. Understood in these terms, the relation of sacrifice to the sacred is not simply one of the performative enactment and perpetuation of a fantasy, but rather a creative destruction that is *vital* to the political process, and which is moreover embodied in the ungrounded decision-making of democracy.

At the heart of the Deleuzo-Guattarian and perhaps also – in spite of itself – the Nancian position is the claim that politics is effectively over; that revolution, were it possible, would be philosophical or aesthetic rather than political. It is here that, in spite of the critique of democracy, we find the paradoxical problem of theodicy, which manifests itself in the injunction to submit – to sacrifice oneself – to eternal return, to adjust ourselves to an experience of '*a* life' of the event in excess of the subject. Implicit in this position is the idea that grace, the gift, is already there, but for our inability to recognise it (or rather recognise the impossibility of recognising it). We know from previous chapters that the gift and a politics thereof coincide with neither the archaic gift economy, nor with the type of pre-political, ontological regime envisaged by Heidegger. Could it therefore be that an experience of the gift already pervades the capitalist society described by Mauss as precisely *lacking* in the logic of the gift? Such an 'idealised' position is attributed to Deleuze by Badiou, for whom the politics of difference serves

to legitimate capitalism. For Deleuze, Badiou argues, ' "All" ' *is* grace
[*'Tout'* est *grâce*]', but 'to say that all is grace means precisely that we
are never ever accorded any grace' (Badiou 2000: 97/142–3). To say
that 'All' *is* grace is either to privilege sacrifice as a sublime movement
of (re-)appropriation, or to do away with it by declaring that everything is already given, that there is no need for a sacrificial offering as a
condition of the gift's receipt. Politics of the gift becomes synonymous
with the sacrifice of politics to a philosophy that, in asserting the possibility (albeit virtual) of having everything, serves only to legitimate the
prevailing order. Badiou's rejoinder that grace is still possible – that we
need not reconcile ourselves to the idea that it has already been given
– points to a refusal to see democracy and sacrifice as irrecoverably
enframed by capital, and thereby to his insistence that they continue to
play a role in the realisation of eternal return. Badiou thus opens up a
space between Deleuze and the Derridean thinking of the gift, revealing
his unexpected proximity to a deconstructive position of which he is
habitually deemed only critical.

In the elaboration of this point, the second half of the chapter returns
to the later political writings of Derrida to elicit a politics of sacrifice
that functions as a necessary counterpart to his politics of the gift.
Through reference to a range of Derrida's late texts, it will be argued
that Derrida, too, conceives politics in terms of sacrifice, above all in
terms of a sacrificial *decision* – a decision about what is to be named
in the giving of the gift, about what is to be recognised in a receipt
that serves to destroy, or more precisely to *sacrifice*, the gift it receives.
Nancy states that sacrifice is impossible because existence is already
sacrificed in being offered. Derrida's more complex claim is that it is
precisely this offering that condemns us to sacrifice. There is politics –
sacrifice – because we are abandoned, because the withdrawal of the
gift from experience compels us to make decisions about what exactly is
to be received, or named as being given; compels us to offer hospitality
toward an other whose alterity will be violated, sacrificed, by this very
act of hospitality. The experience of sacrifice is thus not one of immanence to being, but of the limit of experience, the interface between
virtual and actual, the event and the subject it ungrounds. To decide is
accordingly to confront the impossible. It is to experience the absence
of ground, but immediately to respond to this ungrounding through the
performative fictioning of new grounds. It is to reciprocate the gift of
the event with the sacrificial offering of 'the gift of what one does not
have' – and, ultimately, to do so knowing that one does not have it.

Derrida goes on to argue that the decision thus also sustains and
resacralizes the gift, and that it has the same effect on democracy,

understood as a democracy-to-come (*démocratie-à-venir*) that would be another name for the gift. Democracy thus conceals a *promise* that, unlike Deleuze, Derrida refuses to dismiss as irreparably contaminated by the imperfection of its actual instantiations; which is moreover sacred in spite of its legitimation of capitalism. The promise of democracy – like the promise of the gift – exceeds its framing by capital, exceeds the possibility of capture in any *habitus*. Its excess furthermore gives rise to a sacred horizon without sacrifice, a horizon in which the gift could be received without negation, which would be the condition of the (im)possibility of politics: a condition that causes politics to exist through the failure, the impossibility, of receiving the gift. But it is precisely not, for this reason, a sacrifice in which sacrifice is sublated, *aufgehoben*, in a final figure of receipt of recognition. Sacrifice takes place precisely in order that it not take place, for the possibility of sacrificing sacrifice (GD, 66, 70–1/96, 101; Keenan 2005: 135–59), but also in so far as it is condemned to failure, in so far as this final act of sacrifice could never actually occur.

However much framed by capital, it is here that we come closest to an experience of eternal return, to an aporetic experience of the gift as ungrounding. The eternal return, in other words, is condemned to do just that: to return eternally with neither beginning nor end, without prospect of completion.

DEMOCRACY IN THE AGE OF THE EVENT

A decisive question for me today is how can a political system accommodate itself [*zugeordnet werden*] to the technological age, and which system would that be? I have no answer to this question. I am not convinced that it is democracy.

(Martin Heidegger)

We are perhaps living the end of the political. For, if it is true that politics is a field opened through the existence of revolution, and if the question of revolution can no longer be posed in these terms, then politics risks disappearing.

(Michel Foucault)[1]

We saw in the last chapter how Lacoue-Labarthe and Nancy rediscover the political as a question that precedes all forms of identity and all determinations of politics as the 'dynamic of powers' (EF, 78/104), the brokering of power in the institutions of state (not to mention the interaction of abstract forces in philosophies of immanence). There is

---

1. Heidegger 1993b: 104/206; Foucault 1994: 267.

politics because there is freedom, because existence is not 'given', in the phenomenological sense, to and in sovereign agents, but rather offers itself in an abandonment from which we must subsequently attempt to appropriate and name the subject. The attempt always ultimately fails, in so far as the subject shifts, is displaced, deconstructed, in the circulations of *sens*. Nancy offers the name of ecotechnicity to that which lives on after deconstruction; indeed, it is ecotechnicity that deconstructs. Yet there remain questions over whether Nancy goes far enough in his reworking of Nietzsche's eternal return; whether the eternal return of *sens* does not continue to presuppose a metaphysical integrity of the corporeal subject.

In the Nancian – and Deleuzian – politics of the gift, the political occurs in excess of subjectivity, in a rupturing of subjectivity characterised by repetition without schematism. In the Bataillean terminology adopted by Nancy, this is, strictly speaking, the repetition of NOTHING (*rien*), where NOTHING refers to the withdrawal of being, the absence of metaphysical foundation, that resides in the destitution of immanence. The offering of the political is the repetition of nothingness, the finitude of singularity through which finite singular beings are thrown into relation with one another. The scene of the political is the non-self identical void of being created by the withdrawal of the gift. The result is the constant circulation, or repetition, of parts outside parts, of singularities differing from one another in the sharing of finitude. Nancy's condemnation of Heidegger's Nazism has not stopped him from repeating the former's doubts that this virtual sharing could be incorporable into actual institutions of democracy. Were we to achieve 'a liberation of the political itself [*une libération du politique lui-même*]' from the exhausted paradigm of politics, there would be a risk, though by no means certain, that 'it may no longer even be possible, in the future, to think in terms of "democracy"' (EF, 79/105; compare SW, 90/144). The ambivalence of the statement is clarified in a much later essay, where Nancy proposes ' "communism" as the truth of democracy: for nothing is more common than the common dust to which we are all destined' (TD, 30/55). Communism should be understood here as a community of shared finitude, a sharing (*partage*) of the incalculable and unshareable (*impartageable*) that 'exceeds politics [*excède la politique*]' and cannot be thought in terms of politics, ' – not democratic politics, at any rate' (TD, 17/33–4). At the same time, he argues, democracy remains an essential precondition of our ability to access the offering of existence. Although in practice infinitely susceptible to ochlocratic homogenisation and 'the domination of calculations of general equivalence [...] (which goes by the name "capitalism")'

(TD, 32/59), democracy is 'first of all a metaphysics and only then a politics' (34/62), an uncontaminable principle of openness to change prior to being a kind of institutional organisation. Were democracy to be superseded, its supersession would have to be philosophical rather than institutional, because its truth lies in its irreducibility to any institutional set-up.

The position marked out by Deleuze and Guattari is similarly sympathetic to Marxism in principle, again holding back from advocating the viability of revolution, while not fully endorsing democracy either. They maintain that the democratic state is inherently majoritarian, as much in the service of capitalism as Heidegger thought it in the service of modern technics: 'If there is no universal democratic State, despite German philosophy's dream of foundation, it is because the market is the only thing that is universal in capitalism' (TP, 106/101–2). In spite of Heidegger, in spite of the tainting of the gift by Nazism, this position of scepticism toward democracy, marked by a reluctance to confer on it any kind of privileged relation to the event, is one that many of the thinkers discussed over the course of the present work have in common. In an essay on the aftermath of 9/11, (the openly communist) Slavoj Žižek captures the dissident poststructuralist mood by eloquently dismissing a liberal democratic centre whose 'main function is to guarantee that nothing will ever really happen in politics: liberal democracy is the party of the non-Event' (Žižek 2002: 151). He has since reiterated this point, declaring that 'democracy is not a sacred word.'[2]

At the other end of the political spectrum, the neoconservative, neo-Kojevian, Francis Fukuyama employs an effective but philosophically crude psychological model, based on Plato's theory of *thymos* (spirit), to argue that democracy alone 'solved' or has the potential to solve man's desire for recognition (Fukuyama 1992: 333). The claim risks overstating the extent of our sovereignty, reinforcing the conceit that the event can be subjugated to the human, leaving us ill-prepared for the prospect of a future over which there could be no control. Is this not what is at stake in Heidegger's posthumously published lamentation, 'Only a God Can Save Us' (1976)? The import of the title is that the technologically exhausted institutions of politics need to be supplemented with some kind of understanding of the event. Badiou reads Heidegger as nostalgic for the sacred, for the resacralization of a world saturated by technological profanity (Badiou 1999: 51/58). The return of the gods, of some form of messianic ground, would thus be a precondition

2. Opening remarks at the conference, 'Is There Still a Politics of Truth?' (Birkbeck College, University of London, 25–26 November 2005).

of the possibility of perfectible government, a necessary supplement
to the democracy he infamously suspects of being unable to accommodate itself to the technological age (Heidegger 1993b: 104–5/206).
Heidegger's comments, in this respect, bear comparison to those of
Jean-Jacques Rousseau, who wrote memorably in *The Social Contract*
(1762) that 'Were there a people of gods, their government would be
democratic. So perfect a government is not for men' (Rousseau 1993:
240/97). Reading Rousseau through the Nancian emphasis on finitude
and what he has elsewhere called the withdrawal of god(s) (Nancy
2001: 7), the allusion to democracy's end coincides with a renunciation
of the grand narrative of sovereignty. The implication is that democracy
should be left to those who can meet its demands or, like the gods, live
on as a fantasy of the disenfranchised, offered as a consolation for those
excessively fearful of its absence. *Contra* Rousseau, the gods need not
lay exclusive claim to it to be the (impossible) supplement that makes
it possible; whose withdrawal, moreover, condemns us to a repetition
that constantly and necessarily courts the risk of collapsing back into
the tyranny it seeks to escape.

   Read crudely, Nancy's speculation on the end of democracy would
articulate the incompatibility of his concept of community with any
form of modern democratic politics. One critic to ascribe this position
to Nancy is Richard Wolin, who, in a recent highly charged attack,
accuses Nancy of following Bataille and Heidegger in elaborating an
aesthetic concept of community. According to Wolin, 'This community
would be subtended not by the values of social transparency but by the
anti-conventional mores of transgression' (Wolin 2004: 164). Wolin is
right to recognise Nancy's willingness to take on the shibboleths, the
'sacred transcendences' of Western culture, but none the less absolutely
wrong in his diagnosis, which fails to consider Nancy's own critique of
the aestheticised politics of violence. Above all, as we shall see, Wolin
fails to appreciate Nancy's critique of sacrifice, which, by explicitly
condemning the attempt to uncover an ontological ground through
sacrifice, effectively rules out the prospect of violently instantiating a
community that is by definition *always already there*.

   A more serious criticism comes from within a climate that is more
broadly receptive to deconstruction. Where Wolin attacks Nancy for
according an excessively privileged role to violence in politics, another
critic takes him to task for understating it, for refusing to abandon
a fantasy of political purity. Nancy Fraser has argued that Lacoue-
Labarthe and Nancy's concept of the political, *le politique*, implicitly still borders on a totalitarian philosophical overdetermination,
which excludes the material reality of politics. In Fraser's view, just as

Heidegger's notion of the *polis* could not readily accommodate existing political institutions, so Lacoue-Labarthe and Nancy loftily and even puritanically cling to the hope of 'a philosophical interrogation of the political which somehow ends up producing profound, new, politically relevant insights without dirtying any hands in political struggle' (Fraser 1984: 149). Like Heidegger, Lacoue-Labarthe and Nancy's insistence on 'purity' (Fraser's term) sees them 'maintain the rigorous exclusion of politics, and especially of empirical and normative considerations', from the political. This means that they ironically elide precisely what it means to be political: namely, immersion in the daily grind of empirical reality and the contestation of incommensurable values (Fraser 1984: 149). Her complaint is echoed by a later article from Simon Critchley, who reiterates his earlier suspicions of the CRPP founder-members' excessive Heideggerianism. For Critchley, the attempted isolation of an essence of the political from the empirical state of institutional politics amounts to '*an exclusion of politics itself*, if by the latter one understands an empirical and contingent field of antagonism, conflict and struggle, the space of *doxa*' (Critchley 1993: 84). For both critics, the result is an impasse; Lacoue-Labarthe and Nancy's critique is unable to effect any kind of intervention or translation into the operations of politics and political institutions, condemning their philosophical work to impotence and, worse, ideology. Despite their explicit aims to the contrary, the political is reduced to a spectre, an idealised *phantasm* that passes through without ever quite making contact with political *praxis*.

Some ten years later, Derrida will say much more on the politics of spectrality, and will do so moreover in the context of an engagement with Marxism. Writing in 1984, however, Fraser views the CRPP as exemplary of Derrida's failure *vis-à-vis* Marx, highlighting the lacuna to which he later responds. According to Fraser, Lacoue-Labarthe and Nancy's

> programme for rethinking the political from the standpoint of deconstruction [...] is a programme which, in its purity and rigor, is far more faithful to the spirit of Derrida's work than the latter's own comparatively simplistic leftist remarks at Cérisy. But it also – indeed, *therefore* – reveals all the more starkly the limitations of Derrideanism as an outlook seeking to confront the political. (1984: 142)

The remarks in question refer to comments made by Derrida during the aforementioned conference on 'The Ends of Man', at Cérisy-la-Salle, in 1980, where he justified his oft-criticised lack of engagement with Marxism by stating that he did not want his rejection of Marx's ontology to undermine the potential of Marxism as a force for political change (1984: 133). Fraser believes Derrida to be guilty of shirking confrontations, of using ontological undecidability as an excuse to sit on the fence and avoid an engagement with radical politics. If so, then Lacoue-Labarthe and Nancy rearticulate this tacit avoidance – or *retrait* – as the very meaning of politics. She calls on them to join the struggles that define contemporary politics: for instance, the feminist fight at the front between *polis* and *oikos*, waged in order to repoliticise the family by casting off the immunity of the private from the gaze of the public sphere. Such an engagement, however, is already implicit in their position, which does not so much avoid struggle as avoid subordinating it to a grounding figure of subjectivity. Derrida is more explicit on this point, drawing on 'at least one of the spirits of Marx or Marxism' to produce a ten-point manifesto for political action. At the heart of this manifesto, he advocates the creation of a 'new International' to fight, amongst other things, against the global arms trade, third-world debt, interethnic conflict and the protectionism of first-world governments (SM, 81–3/134–8). Again, however, Derrida stops short of advocating full-scale revolution. Like the gift, for which it is effectively another name, the new International is defined by the impossibility of its identification, as a futural promise whose existence is virtual, inconceivable in terms of the 'ontic' categories of politics:

> It is an untimely [*intempestif*] link, without status, without title, and without name, barely public even if it is not clandestine, '*out of joint*', without coordination, without party, without country, without national community (International before, across, and beyond any national determination), without co-citizenship, without common belonging to a class. (SM, 85/141–2)

Clearly eager to avert the (predictable) accusation that he promotes a hollow, stripped-down Marxism, Derrida appears deliberately to avoid the typically deconstructive formulation Terry Eagleton derisively calls 'Marxism without Marxism' (Eagleton 1999: 86). This has not stopped Žižek, amongst others, from hastily judging him to be complicit in the liberal democratic avoidance of the real, a 'politics without politics' that refuses revolution while clinging to a consolatory 'promise' of its virtual conceivability (Žižek 2003: 140–1; see also Ahmad 1999: 104–8).

A similar brand of arevolutionary Marxism pervades the work of Deleuze and Guattari, who find themselves faced with the same predicament of wanting to criticise democracy without advocating a revolutionary overthrow of capitalism. Even more so than Nancy, Deleuze has received vehement criticism for his 'profoundly aristocratic' privileging of the philosophical over the political (Badiou 2000:

12/22), 'his haughtiness, and his condescendence toward democracies and politics' (Mengue 2006: 183). The alleged haughtiness is borne out most vociferously in *What Is Philosophy?* (1991), where Deleuze and Guattari portray democracy as inherently inimical to the eternal return of the gift. 'Democracies are majorities, but a becoming is by its nature that which always eludes the majority' (WIP, 108/104). Conceived as a principle of representation, democracy is inherently majoritarian, constitutively predisposed toward the ochlocratic imposition of laws of identity on the aneconomic repetition of difference. In what might seem to suggest an affirmation of unconstrained capitalism, they argue that democracy constitutes a reterritorialisation of the identities that capital breaks down, by concealing the extent of the damage it inflicts: 'The immense relative deterritorialization of world capitalism needs to be reterritorialized on the modern nation-state, which finds an outcome in democracy' (WIP, 98/94). Commenting on these passages in *What Is Philosophy?*, Mengue notes with consternation that 'whenever Deleuze mentions democracy, it is always accompanied by a reductive qualifier – "democratic imperialism", "colonising democracy", and so on' (2006: 181).

The basic problem, Mengue thinks, is that Deleuze and Guattari conflate the philosophically 'totalising' critique of identity with political totalitarianism. Much as Lacoue-Labarthe and Nancy allegedly do, they thus repeat Heidegger's mistake of philosophically overdetermining politics. The suspicion of this has led Alain Badiou to question 'how it is that, for Deleuze, politics is not an autonomous form of thought, a singular cut in chaos, one that differs from art, science and philosophy? This point alone attests to our divergence, and everything follows from it' (Badiou 2006: 69 [TM]). Mengue reiterates this point, lamenting that Deleuze and Guattari's distinction between art (the creation of 'percepts' of the event), science (the description of actualities) and philosophy (the creation of concepts) 'seems to pass over that which constitutes the specificity of the political' (Mengue 2003: 159). Central to his argument is an insistence on the irreducibility of politics to philosophy, the incompatibility of politics (the 'macropolitics' of statehood) with what Deleuze and Guattari call the 'micropolitics' of experimentation, becoming and the inherent excess of the event. Speaking in defence of the 'micropolitical' events of May '68, they write: 'those who understood things in macropolitical terms understood nothing of the event because something unaccountable was escaping' (TP, 216/264). Yet politics, Mengue insists, is not about the deterritorialisation of identity, but rather the accommodation of different identities and opinions; not the affirmation of instability and futurity, but rather the contrary attempt to create stability and consensus in the present:

> The concern of the political is that of a *stable and common* world. And this world is to be positively constructed from bits of everything, for it will not be done spontaneously and by itself, on account of the *plurality of opinions* and interests, necessarily divergent and in conflict, that they represent. (Mengue 2003: 134–5)

This view need not entail the reassertion of an essentialised grounding subject. In an argument that serves as a counterpart to Mengue, Badiou condemns poststructuralist philosophies of difference as the highest moment, the final figure, in the history of *homo economicus*, whose affirmation of difference conceals a desire not to be subjected to universal, prescriptive laws (Badiou 2001: 24/42). Yet prescription, he insists, is precisely what politics should consist in: not simply the attempt to elicit the complex truths of an event that precludes essential subjectivity, but moreover the active creation of new subjects from out of the ungrounding exposure to the event. Politics is not about the affirmation of a difference that cannot be universalised, but rather the universalisation, the rendering consistent, of a singularity. 'I call *politics* that which establishes the consistency of the event in the regime of intervention,' that which propagates the singularity of the event by working to translate it into the public sphere of the political (Badiou 1985: 77). 'This propagation is never a repetition. It is a subject-effect [*un effet de sujet*], a consistency,' which can be achieved only at the cost of sacrificing other singularities, other possibilities of existing that avail themselves in the multiplicity of actuality (1985: 77). Politics is precisely *not* about the actualisation, the privileging, of every singularity, but rather about the selection of which singularities should be privileged as the organisational bases of new forms of political consciousness. By configuring institutionalised politics as the majoritarian site of identity, to be abandoned in favour of an affirmation of virtual differences, Deleuze and Guattari commit the mistake of overlooking the 'space of *doxa*' as a space of *actual* differences. They thus miss the sense in which politics is defined by the making of decisions in relation to these differences, which is to say in the absence of an ontologically grounded consensus. In other words, Deleuze and Guattari's privileging of a philosophy of virtual difference over a politics of actual difference risks another evacuation of politics – of what one could call the constitutively *sacrificial* dimension of the political.

Badiou does not thematise sacrifice, but his polemical critique of Deleuze is replete with its rhetoric: 'I maintain that the forms of the multiple are [...] always actual, that the virtual does not exist; I *sacrifice* the One' (Badiou 2000: 46/69 [emphasis added]). In order to arrive at an ontology suitable for the legitimate treatment of politics, he argues, it is necessary to 'sacrifice the Whole [*le Tout*], sacrifice Life, sacrifice the great cosmic animal whose surface Deleuze enchants' (Badiou 1998: 71/72 [TM]). By 'the Whole [*le Tout*]', here, Badiou is referring to the singular life of absolute immanence, to the idealised conferral of grace on everything (*'la grâce du Tout'*) he takes to result from the Platonism of Deleuze's univocity thesis. Deployed in the context of ontology, it is hard not to be struck by the theological and *political* quality of Badiou's language. The theological inflection comes in spite of his trenchant critique of the sacred, a (rare) affirmation of capital as 'the end of the *sacred* figures of the bond [...] the general dissolvant of sacralizing representations, which postulate the existence of intrinsic and essential relations' (Badiou 1999: 56/36). We shall see later that, by understating the role of sacrifice in *making sacred*, Badiou sacralizes precisely what he wants to sacrifice. His intention, however, is to deploy religious language to deliberately political and philosophical effect. He does this elsewhere, too: for example, when designating 'the event as supernumerary givenness [*donation surnuméraire*] and incalculable *grace*' (Badiou 2003: 65/69 [emphasis added]). In accordance with his claim that it is the actual and not the virtual that is multiple, that actuality is accordingly susceptible to many different names, Badiou wants to make the point that ontology – and, by implication, the designation of the sacred – is ultimately a question of political choice, the outcome of a decision about what is to be counted as existing. Alex Callinicos notes that there is an ambiguous line between 'politicizing ontology', of which 'Badiou can legitimately be accused' in his earlier writings, and the 'ontologizing politics' of his more recent work (Callinicos 2006: 107–8). Badiou would hardly dispute this. Indeed, as the language of sacrifice suggests, he affirms that his reading of Deleuze's 'Platonism of the virtual' is politically motivated, driven less by the accuracy of its textual exegesis than by a desire to elicit by means of caricature a potentially deleterious tendency inherent to Deleuze's project.[3] Rather than seeking 'to do justice' to Deleuze's text, his reading is avowedly 'prescriptive' (Hallward 2005: 172–6), designed to draw attention to the prospect that Deleuze is more concerned with the event than with the politics of actual differences, more preoccupied with becoming other than with deploying this becoming to transformative political effect.

---

3. On the serious and numerous problems with Badiou's reading of Derrida, see Ansell-Pearson 2002: 103–5; Beistegui 2004: 371n.50; Kacem 2004: 101–16.

His point is not merely political, however. By emphasising the undecidability of ontology, he also returns us to the constitutive impossibility of capturing a gift that withdraws from experience. Badiou argues that by identifying the gift with a singular life of immanence, a single event (as opposed to multiple events), Deleuze implicitly posits a virtual theodicy that forecloses the site of and hence the potential for political change: ' "All" *is* grace. For what is, is nothing other than the grace of the All' for Deleuze (Badiou 2000: 97/142). Deleuze's affirmation of the eternal return of difference, of the breakdown of identity, becomes indistinguishable from a theodical position that 'in the final instance, always gives reason to what is there [*donne en dernier ressort toujours raison à ce qu'il y a*]' (2000: 97/142 [TM]). Rather than call on politics to eliminate suffering, in other words, Deleuze effectively legitimates it, by stoically affirming that redemption lies in the transformative thought of becoming-other. Hallward summarises the complaint in the assertion that 'Deleuze's work is essentially indifferent to the politics of this world' (Hallward 2006a: 162), because he sees philosophy rather than politics as the means to redeem suffering; because he sees in thought's access to the (sacred) immanence of the event the prospect of leaving behind the world of actuality. Viewed from the privileged philosophical standpoint of the virtual plane of immanence, actuality becomes theodic.

The indictment resonates with criticisms of the CRPP by Fraser, whose grievance that Lacoue-Labarthe and Nancy fail to understand the dirtiness and contamination of politics might also be reformulated in terms of their elision of the *sacrificial* dimension of the political, the aspect of politics that requires some values to be sacrificed for the sake of preserving others, or which calls for the sacrifice of oneself for a particular cause – out of what Badiou would call 'fidelity' to an event (Badiou 2001: 41–3/62; Badiou 1985: 77). Bearing in mind Nancy's rejection of the 'sacred' concepts of community and transcendence (IC, 35/86–8), a contestation of this type takes us to the core of a project that is explicit in asserting an antinomy, a chiasmus, between politics and sacrifice. More surprisingly, in light of Fraser's willingness to reduce these concerns to symptoms of *derridisme*, it will eventually return us to the critical readings of Nancy proffered by Derrida, who insists that politics cannot be extricated from a constitutive risk of totalitarianism.

HEGEL, NANCY AND THE END(S) OF SACRIFICE

One might even say that the gods retreated because one no longer gives a present to their presence: no more sacrifice, no more oblation [*on ne fait plus de présent à leur présence: plus de sacrifice, plus d'oblation*], except by way of custom or imitation. One has other things to do: write, for example, calculate, do business, legislate. Deprived of presents, presence has retreated [*Privée de présents, la présence se retire*].

(Jean-Luc Nancy)[4]

In anthropology and sociology, modern accounts of sacrifice tend to begin with Mauss and Hubert (1898), for whom 'the procedure consists in establishing a means of communication between the sacred and profane worlds through the mediation of a victim, a thing destroyed in the course of the ceremony' (Hubert and Mauss 1981: 97/302 [TM]; criticised by Nancy, FT, 61/81). It is Hegel, however, who casts the longer shadow over the philosophical history of sacrifice. His idea that sacrifice repeats the sacred, bringing it into the world but also rendering it coextensive with the event, is challenged by Bataille, who accuses him of submitting to a restricted economy of dialectical *Aufhebung* in which the meaning of sacrifice is forgotten. As seen in Chapter 1, Bataille develops a concept of sacrifice as the privileged experience of the event in excess of any dialectic. *Pace* Nancy, Blanchot has denied that this entails the receipt of a 'communitarian fusion' with being. Rather than an experience of interiority, Bataille charts the breakdown, the limit, of experience. His gift is 'a gift of "pure" loss that cannot make sure of ever being received by the other' (Blanchot 1988: 12/25), the experience of the *absence* of any ontologically guaranteed receipt of one's gift. Against Blanchot, Nancy suggests that Bataille continues to think in terms of a Hegelian logic of immanence (IC, 22–4/60–4; FT, 63/87).

Throughout his work, Hegel identifies dialectical *Aufhebung* with the movement of sacrifice, the surrender of the particular for the sake of its sublation in the universal. Rather than a movement of loss, it is ultimately one of accession or reappropriation, wherein the experience of loss is *aufgehoben*, superseded through the opening of identity on to its underlying unity with the other: 'But that sacrifice [*die Ausopferung*] made by the unessential extreme was at the same time not a one-sided action, but contained within itself the action of the other' (PS, 137–8/176 [§230]). The dialectical *Aufhebung* thus describes the reward of sacrifice, the position to which one accedes in discovering the movement of the event underlying one's own actions. When the dialectic of History comes to an end in the modern (Napoleonic) State, it does so in a moment that discloses sacrifice as the highest moment of the sublime. Hegel is critical of sacrifice in its primitive religious context but, as Nancy notes, he seems only too happy to 'reclaim for the State the full

4. Nancy 2001: 7.

value of warlike sacrifice' (FT, 60/79 [TM]). As the final *Aufhebung* of *Geist*, or Spirit, the State is defined by sacrifice, which is expressed in the duty that citizens cede their individual lives for the preservation of its sublime totality: 'sacrifice for the individuality of the State is the substantial relation of everyone and therefore a *universal duty*' (EPR, 363/494 [§325]). The actualisation of the *Geist* at the end of History reveals itself as the sublime truth of sacrifice, which becomes a name for the event, to be thought coextensive with the gift of *Geist*. 'The gift can only be a sacrifice, that is the axiom of speculative reason' (Derrida 1986: 243a/270a).

This sacrificial sublation also marks the sublation of both philosophy and politics. Anticipating the Heideggerian idea of the *Heimat*, Hegel describes the State as a system of universal intimacy, which resolves the historical tension between the intimate, familial sphere of the *oikos* and the universal but brutal sphere of the market (EPR, 225/343–5 [§187]). With its universal recognition and consideration of basic rights, the political structure of the State ensures man's return from alienation in the other, bringing about the unity of subjective identity with objective (legal) recognition by others. Although not a democracy, it does not need to be. The State's existence as a self-identical, universal intimacy means that individuals are automatically incorporated through a system that expresses and privileges the rational, theodical sovereignty of the unfurled *Geist* (EPR, 238–9/359–60 [§207]). In Kojève's anthropologisation of Hegel, this amounts to the end of man's 'struggle for recognition', coinciding initially with what he describes as the 'communist' classless society of the United States (later revised to designate the 'post-historical' civilisation of Japan; IRH, 161n/436–7n). Hegel and Kojève identify the end of History not just with the end of substantial political change, but also with the end of philosophy. This is because, as Hegel states in the preface to *Elements of the Philosophy of Right* (1821), the task of philosophy is purely retrospective: 'As the *thought* of the world, it appears only at a time when actuality has gone through its formative process and attained its completed state' (EPR, 23/28). Philosophy, in other words, serves only to bear witness to the historical, dialectical, movement of the *Geist*, to accord recognition to the theodicy of reason, the self-identity of the world with the human consciousness embodied in the state. Kojève predicts the disappearance of philosophy and, with no more great decisions to be made, the dissolution of politics into bureaucratic administration:

> The end of human Time or History – that is, the definitive annihilation of Man properly so-called or of the free and historical Individual – means quite simply the cessation of Action in the strong sense of the term. Practically,

this means: the disappearance of wars and bloody revolutions. And also the disappearance of *Philosophy*; for since Man himself no longer changes essentially, there is no longer any reason to change the (true) principles that are at the basis of his understanding of the World and of himself. (IRH, 159n/435n [TM])

History, philosophy and politics thus become something we pass through between archaic, primitively religious sacrificial rituals and the sublation of sacrifice at the end of History.

The Hegelo-Kojevian position is thus broadly, even fundamentally, opposed to the one adopted by Deleuze and Guattari, whose philosophical and political stance(s), like those of so many of their postmodern and poststructuralist contemporaries, specifically seek to reverse the Hegelian thinking of History. Jean-François Lyotard in particular has expressed 'incredulity toward meta-narratives', the great historical narratives of modernity that govern the Hegelian system (Lyotard 1986: xxiv/7). In a similar vein, Jacques Derrida's *Specters of Marx* incorporates a scornful critique of Kojève and, in particular, 'the *idealist* logic of Fukuyama' (SM, 86/142). In a revealing move that should perhaps have raised the suspicions of both Lyotard and Derrida (who is already suspicious of Lyotard's version of the argument; Derrida 1999b: 228–9/36–7), Deleuze and Guattari reaffirm the Hegelian thesis of universal history, albeit with significant qualifications. Principal amongst these is that history, which comes to an end with capitalism, does not proceed dialectically and does not culminate in an *Aufhebung*. Rather, it appears as universal only retrospectively, once capitalism has disclosed itself as the upper limit of the eternal return that plays out in the (counter)historical repetition of difference:

> The answer – as we have seen – is that capitalism is indeed the limit of all societies, insofar as it brings about the decoding of the flows that the other social formations coded and overcoded. But it is the *relative* limit of every society; it effects *relative* breaks, because it substitutes for the codes an extremely rigorous axiomatic that maintains the energy of the flows in a bound state on the body of capital as a socius that is deterritorialized [...]. Schizophrenia, on the contrary, is indeed the *absolute* limit that causes the flows to travel in a free state on a desocialized body without organs. (AŒ, 267/292)

Recalling from Chapter 2 the first synthesis of time, or life, in Deleuze, the above citation reveals capital to constitute the minimum possible degree of *habitus*, a minimal degree of organisation, which shows itself continually able to adapt, to contract differences into identity without requiring fundamental changes to its organisational axiomatic.

Capital is defined by a subjectivity that is distinct from, irreducible

to, the subjectivity of humans, but it is not yet the life of immanence
(TP, 452–3/565). Deleuze and Guattari hold back from identifying
capitalism with a simulacral experience of the gift, an experience, that
is to say, in which the gift is encountered in its ungrounding withdrawal from presence. Under capitalism, every *de*territorialisation of
life is accompanied by a corresponding *re*territorialisation of identity.
'It axiomatizes with one hand what it decodes with the other' (AŒ,
267/292). Every exposure to the event triggers a repression culminating in the contraction of singularities into a law-governed *habitus*. The
reorganisation of identity is ultimately executed by capital itself: for
example, in its forced erosion of traditional (i.e. inefficient) working
practices, its demand that labour migrate to follow the relocations of
capital investment, attenuating the bases of some national and regional
identifications while simultaneously intensifying other expressions
of the same. In contrast to the eternal return of difference in the life
of the event, the eternal return of capital is the eternal return of the
same, the return to and of the profit in whose name lines of flight are
repeatedly reterritorialised by the market. However far deterritorialisation progresses, it will never escape the logic of capital. The general
economy of difference always collapses back into a reterritorialised,
restricted economy of identity.

The Deleuzo-Guattarian end of History is thus evolutionary rather
than ontological or explicitly theodical, the result of contingency rather
than destiny. Capitalism constitutes the end of history not by virtue of
some teleologically ordained destiny, but rather because it constitutes
the minimum possible degree of organisation. There is, as such, no
Aufhebung, no sublation of historical contradictions in a higher truth.
Nor does capitalism bring about the end of philosophy. On the contrary, where Kojève writes of 'the disappearance of *Philosophy*' (IRH,
159n/435n), Deleuze and Guattari describe how philosophy is precisely
that which lives on after the advent of capital, a revolution in thought
being the sole prospect of revolution after what may or may not constitute an end of politics. Where the Hegelian concept is retrospective,
formalising that which is already given in experience, the Deleuzian
concept appropriates the inappropriable futurity of an event that withdraws from experience. In other words, it traces the utopian horizon of
(im)possibility to which politics, in its strict macro-, institutional, sense
has no access:

> Philosophy takes the relative deterritorialization of capital to the absolute; it
> makes it pass over the plane of immanence as movement of the infinite and
> suppresses it as internal limit, *turns it back against itself so as to summon
> forth a new earth, a new people*. But in this way it arrives at the nonpropo-

sitional form of the concept in which communication, exchange, consensus
and opinion vanish entirely (WIP, 99/95)

On account of its thinking of eternal return, its ability to escape the
habitus of capital, philosophy lives on after the end of History, but
politics, perhaps, does not, or at least can do so only by changing,
becoming other. Rather than wither away, it becomes impotent, in
need of supplementation if it is to conceive possibilities of becoming
beyond the reterritorialising countertendencies of capitalism. By virtue
of the inherent ochlocracy of democracy, 'this people and earth will not
be found in our democracies' (WIP, 108/104), but rather in a philosophical 'experimentation' that Deleuze elsewhere identifies with politics:
'Politics is an active experimentation, since we do not know in advance
which way a line [of flight] is going to turn' (D, 137/165–6; see also
WIP, 111/106).

Could this injunction to experiment be construed in terms of a sacrificial sublimation (of the political), the attainment of an immanence
or a communion with the event in which the (political) assertion of
identity is obviated? Deleuze and Guattari obviously do not want to
repeat the Hegelian identification of sacrifice with the State. When, in
A Thousand Plateaus, they write of 'an entire politics of becoming-
animal, as well as a politics of sorcery' based on the *agencement*, or
assemblage, of minority groups and the oppressed (TP, 247/302),
they do so in deliberate opposition not just to the Hegelian logic of
statehood and sacrifice, but also and more explicitly to the Freudian
thinking of sacrifice. Writing in 1914, in *Totem and Taboo*, the latter
locates sacrifice in the 'duty to repeat the crime of parricide again and
again in the sacrifice of the totem animal' (Freud 2001a: 145/175), the
sacrificial killing of an animal that substitutes for the primal father, or
God. As in Hegel, Freudian sacrifice is identified with mimesis, rather
than creativity. The repetition of the foundational moment of society
and politics, it recalls the murder of a primal father whose monopoly
over women led his sons to rebel and divide power in accordance with
a social contract. Deleuze and Guattari employ the old French adjective
'anomal' (*anomalous*), designating 'the unequal, the coarse, the rough,
the cutting edge of deterritorialization' to contrast such mimesis with
the anomic, aneconomic repetition of difference in the micropolitics of
becoming (TP, 243–4/298), the implication being that sacrifice presupposes a negative understanding of difference; that it is therefore incompatible with an affirmation of positive difference in the event. Unlike
Bataille, Deleuze and Guattari do not formulate a new concept of sacrifice. In other respects, however, their work suggests a clear continuity

with what Lacan and Nancy take to be the Bataillean thinking thereof. Commenting on the treatment of sacrifice in the history of philosophy, Deleuze writes of a 'spirit of sacrifice' that 'will enable us to rediscover everything in the moment of sacrifice [...] even before the sacrifice is enacted' (CI, 116/164). At the risk of being disingenuous, Hallward takes the passage to express Deleuze's own position rather than a Deleuzian reading of the history of philosophy, and uses it to accuse Deleuze of perpetrating a negative theodical recovery of the 'whole of creation' (Hallward 2006a: 138). Deleuze, in other words, would thus be suggesting the act of sacrifice to bring about absolute immanence *to* and *of* the gift, the sublation of the gift in sacrifice.

The move is not entirely illegitimate. In a rare attempt to address the Deleuzian treatment of the sacred, the anthropological-cum-literary theorist, René Girard, makes a near-identical claim apropos of Deleuze and Guattari's privileging of delirium as an experience of absolute immanence, which paradoxically amounts, he argues, to a sublime 'nullification of differences' (Girard 1978: 96). Like Badiou, Girard argues that the philosophy of difference 'does not constitute a real rupture with the past' but is rather its final figure, unable to escape it on account of an inability to recognise the constitutive role of sacrifice in social organisation. This role is to maintain a necessary distinction between profane and sacred, 'between impure violence and purifying violence' (Girard 1977: 49/80–1), the effect of which is to 'quell violence within the community and to prevent conflicts from erupting' (1977: 14/30). *Anti-Oedipus* becomes symptomatic of what elsewhere Girard describes as a 'sacrificial crisis', a collapse in the binary oppositions of sacred and profane around which society is structured (1977: 49/80–1). Like Bataille, Deleuze and Guattari seek to transgress every transcendent binary, to achieve an impossible experience that exceeds these binaries, but they therefore remain fundamentally framed by a sublative logic of immanence. Their polemic amounts to 'an effort to monopolise whatever remains of the sacred, to appropriate the sacrificial virtue that seems to belong to the other' (Girard 1978: 116). In suggesting as much, Girard anticipates what, as we saw in Chapter 3, Nancy implies to be the excessive Batailleanism of Deleuze. He also thus anticipates Nancy's reading of the concept of sacrifice as deleteriously and irreducibly bound up with the totalitarianism of immanence. Nancy, however, affirms the end of sacrifice, whereas Girard laments it.

In 'The Unsacrificeable' ('*L'Insacrifiable*'), published in 1991, Nancy sets out to explain what he describes as 'the singular absence in us and for us of sacrifice' (FT, 51/66 [TM]). The absence, he suggests, must be traced via a rupture that causes the modern sense of sacrifice to differ fundamentally from its archaic predecessor. It is on account of this rupture that we can no longer find, nor even understand, archaic sacrificial practices. The *motif* of the latter none the less persists and is repeated at the heart of the former:

> the truth of sacrifice is brought to light in terms of its *mimesis*: 'ancient' sacrifice is an external and, by itself, futile figure of this truth in which the subject sacrifices itself in spirit, to spirit [*où le sujet se sacrifie lui-même en esprit, à l'esprit*]. Through spirit, it is to *truth itself* that sacrifice is offered up, in truth and as truth that it is accomplished [*Et par l'esprit, c'est à la vérité elle-même que le vrai sacrifice est offert*]. (FT, 58/76–7)

Nancy argues that modern (self-)sacrifice is a sacrifice of the subject undertaken for the very purpose of acceding to, or 'transappropriating' one's own subjectivity: 'Sacrifical transappropriation is the appropriation of the Subject who penetrates into negativity, who keeps itself there, enduring its own dismemberment, and who returns sovereign' (FT, 73/99 [TM]). It thus pertains to 'the fascination with an ecstasy turned toward an absolute Other or toward an absolute Outside, into which the subject is emptied better to be restored' (FT, 75/103). In sacrificing, the subject seeks to achieve some experience of participation (*methexis*) with, or immanence to, a transcendent ontological ground. Sacrifice, in other words, is the attempt to substantiate the event *in* the subject, by declaring the excess of the event to be something that can actually be brought into the world. We see this in Heidegger, who, though critical of Hegelian 'ontotheology', on account of its failure 'to confront the true meaning of loss, to face the full meaning of sacrifice without redemption' (Schmidt 1999: 100), adopts a markedly similar stance *vis-à-vis* sacrifice.

Heidegger refers eliptically, in 'The Origin of the Work of Art' (1936), to 'das wesentliche Opfer', essential sacrifice, as 'one essential way in which truth establishes itself in the beings it has opened up, deploys itself [and] is grounded' (OWA, 186–7/49 [50]). In the postscript to the second edition of *What is Metaphysics?* (1943), he qualifies this claim, citing beings' willingness to die for the sake of the event, in order to fulfil the destiny of a historical *Volk* reconciled with its *Heimat*. This amounts to a '*thanking*' of being:

> In sacrifice there occurs the concealed thanks that alone pays homage to the grace [*Im Opfer ereignet sich der verborgene Dank, der einzig die Huld würdigt*] that being has bestowed upon the human essence in thinking, so that human beings may, in their relation to being, assume the guardianship of being. (PWM, 236/310 [105])

Sacrifice thus offers the possibility of an authentic relationship with being, one that is moreover denied to the subject by global technological nihilism. In what can be read as asserting the incompatibility of this bestowal of thanks with the nihilistic, technical structure of democracy, the same passage asserts that such sacrifice cannot be fulfilled 'through working and achievement with respect to beings' (PWM, 236/310 [106]). Politics is merely ontic, but sacrifice is ontological. Ostensibly, the position is directly opposed to the one found in Deleuze and Nancy.

The underlying premise of transappropriation means that, for Nancy, 'sacrifice as self-sacrifice, universal sacrifice, the truth and sublation of sacrifice, is the very institution of the absolute economy of absolute subjectivity' (FT, 62/83). Sacrifice could never instantiate political community because sacrificial transappropriation presupposes the traditionally 'sacred' possibility of achieving communion with being, the existence of a substantial ontological ground to which and for the sake of which sacrifices would be made. The Nancian critique of sacrifice thus overlaps with his critique of immanence; following Girard, one could also see in it the potential for a critique of Deleuze, the suggestion that Deleuze, too, seeks to transappropriate sovereignty in becoming coextensive with the body without organs. Nancy, incidentally, has rejected this reading, using the occasion to reassert his affinity to Deleuze as an anti-sacrificial thinker: 'how could one sacrifice a subject that one does not think to exist?'[5] The remark leaves little space for the possibility that this sacrificial logic persists in spite of Deleuze's intentions.

Despite implying that Bataille, too, is guilty of transappropriation (FT, 67/87), the Bataillean equation of sovereignty with 'NOTHING' remains central to Nancy's critique of nostalgia for an ontological ground. The absence of ground exposes that there is 'NOTHING' to be transappropriated; sacrifice is destined to fail because sovereignty is not something that resides elsewhere, but is rather *nowhere* and *nothing*. Underlying the equation is a position broadly in line with the Deleuzo-Guattarian analysis of the experience of high capitalism. A key element of Nancy's critique of sacrifice derives from the way sacrifice is bound up with the history of capitalism and technology, his perception that the world has entered a phase of ecotechnical decomposition. If ecotechnicity exposes the end of the age of sacrifice, it is because technology no longer testifies to the sovereignty of the subject, but has rather become the originary technicity of bodies that ungrounds it: 'In a sense, then, ecotechnics is also pure *technè*, the pure *technè* of nonsovereignty' (BSP, 135/160). Moreover, it is what exposes the space once occupied by the subject as the empty space of spacing in 'a world where sovereignty is NOTHING' (BSP, 140/165). Writing

5. In conversation with the author, 6 May 2005, London.

in an essay on 'War, Right, Sovereignty – Technè', appended to Being Singular Plural (1996), Nancy suggests that the post-Cold War climate of conflict in Bosnia, Kuwait and the former USSR is governed not by a logic of the United States' hegemonic, unipolar sovereignty, but rather by the very absence of sovereignty: 'War – with ecotechnics – lets us see the henceforth empty space of sovereign Meaning' (BSP, 137/162 [TM]). Beneath the veneer of reterritorialising ethno-nationalisms, human rights violations and competition for scarce resources, war has become the ultimate expression of, or rather the attempt to stave off, the NOTHING of ecotechnicity, the ungrounding exposure to the event. The use of force serves only as a futile sacrificial gesture that, in attempting performatively to re-enact the hierarchy of symbolic order, protests and seeks to mask the retreat of sovereignty.

As Nancy argues in a slightly earlier work, The Sense of the World (1993), the same can be said of ' "democracy" ', which 'would thus not go beyond a kind of last sacrifice, the sacrifice of the truth or of the Cause itself, though without ceasing to adhere to sacrificial logic [une sorte de dernier sacrifice, celui de la vérité ou de la Cause elle-même, ne cessant donc pas d'adhérer à la logique sacrificielle]' (SW, 90/141–2 [TM]). The image is reinforced by the recent Truth of Democracy (2008), where he states that 'democracy has not yet clearly freed its "conceptions" from the presupposition of a subject that is master of its representations, volitions and decisions' (TD, 11/25). In other words, the practice of democracy sustains the fantasy of sovereign subjectivity. Like war, democracy lives on as an insubstantial remainder, the desubstantialised spectre of a sacrifice without cause, whose effective impotence exposes its lack of ontological privilege. Nancy's sole-authored works do not explicitly and thematically reprise the opposition between le and la politique, thus raising the prospect that he departs from the supposed 'Heideggerianism' of the collaborative period. But he does make a corresponding distinction between 'sacrificial politics [la politique sacrificielle]', or 'politics in truth, which is to say of the "theologico-political" ' (SW, 89/141 [TM]), and an underlying ontology of 'the political [le politique]' as 'the site of the in-common as such' in which sacrifice simply has no place (SW, 88/139). By repeatedly identifying sacrifice with the fictioning of an ontological ground, Nancy reduces it to a relic of metaphysics, denuded of positive potential. The ontology of finitude means that there is 'rien de sacrifiable', nothing sacrificeable, nothing whose sacrifice would open us on to a transcendent ground. 'If we have to say that existence is sacrificed, it is sacrificed by no one and to nothing. "Existence is offered" means the finitude of existence' (FT, 74/101). If sacrifice is to continue to exist, it can do so only in the bloodless context of ecotechnical abandonment, where henceforth it will not be active, governed by subjects, but rather passive, with sacrifice – offering – becoming another name for the event. Despite stating that 'nothing is more dissimilar' (FT, 74/101 [TM]), Nancy uses the two terms, sacrifice and offering, as if almost interchangeable. In treating them as such, he reiterates that the target of his critique is the Hegelian ontotheology that conflates sacrifice with the gift, rendering the event inherently sublime. One wonders, however, whether in saying this, ironically, Nancy's inversion does not effectively repeat the Hegelian identification.

What if the site of politics were the one opened up *between* being's being offered – the brute facticity of being abandoned to decision – and sacrifice *qua* impossible decision, the choice between possibilities that, in so far as ungrounded, are undecidable? In positing that there is ultimately 'nothing sacrificeable' (FT, 67/90) Nancy arguably fails to appreciate both the way that sacrifice is condemned to live on, in spite of its impossibility, and the prospect that it is indeed this very impossibility that sustains and politicises it. The fervour of his refusal to grant any relationality of politics to sacrifice becomes conspicuous, even political, as if his stated desire to abandon sacrifice leads him to miss that it is precisely here that the essence of the political (*'s'il y en a'*) would lie. This can perhaps only be seen, however, once sacrifice is denuded of ontological privilege, recognised as a (tacit) affirmation of ungrounding, rather than an attempt to recuperate lost sovereignty. If we have forgotten what it means to be political, it is on account of the forgetting of a sacrifice that, in the words of Beistegui, 'was never as alive as when at the announced threshold of its demise, never as flourishing as when at its end' (Beistegui 1997: 159). Nancy himself has recently shown a considerable willingness to renegotiate his stance, conceding that the conflation of sacrifice with a logic of *Aufhebung* does not adequately account for the role of sacrifice in the 'making and naming of the sacred'.[6] *The Truth of Democracy* similarly elaborates a more nuanced account of politics as the site of deciding how to translate incalculable, suprapolitical, infinite – one might say aneconomic – values once thought 'divine, sacred or inspired' into an institutional framework that works only in terms of equivalence (TD, 18, 24/35, 46). The ' "spirit" ' of democracy signals, in this context, the possibility of avoiding sacrifice, of conceding ways in which differences can be accommodated without necessitating the sacrifice of their singularity. As 'a kind of last sacrifice', democracy becomes a way of preserving the

6. Again, in conversation with the author.

truth or causes it seeks to incarnate – precisely by sacrificing them. This paradoxical formulation brings us back to Derrida.

DERRIDA, DEMOCRACY AND SACRIFICE

> I am responsible to the other as other, I answer to him and I answer for what I do before him. But of course, what binds me thus in my singularity to the absolute singularity of the other, immediately propels me into the space of risk of absolute sacrifice. [...] I cannot respond to the call, the request, the obligation, or even the love of another without sacrificing the other other, other others [*sans lui sacrifier l'autre autre, les autres autres*]. Paradox, scandal, and aporia are thus none other than sacrifice.
>
> (Jacques Derrida)

> What we need is this apparent oxymoron: a Nietzschean democracy.
>
> (Jean-Luc Nancy)[7]

Returning more recently to the question of the political, Simon Critchley has argued that politics 'articulates an interstitial distance' between the site of power and those subjected to it. He names the specific interstice between the State and the self-determination of the people as the site of political struggle in which there opens up the possibility of what he calls 'true democracy' (Critchley 2007: 92). We need not buy into the loaded terminology of the State to affirm the idea – also found in the 'zone between two deaths' of Lacan (SVII, 280/326) – that politics is an interstitial occurrence, which cannot be reduced to a mere affirmation of the event. Nancy, too, has lately evinced a similar position, rearticulating his earlier ideas of *désœuvrement* as 'the truth of democracy'. This truth, he suggests, is that democracy 'is not in the first instance a form of politics [*n'est-elle pas d'abord une forme politique*]' (TD, 32/59). As what he calls 'in principle an exceeding [*dépassement principiel*] of the political order' (TD, 29/53), it rather falls *between* philosophy and politics. A broadly similar stance is discernible in Deleuze and Guattari, who, rather than being indifferent to democracy, as Mengue suggests, regard it as the precondition for an engagement with the event. Much as they elaborate a concept of 'micropolitics', a politics of becoming and experimentation that risks ultimately indistinguishability from the creation of concepts, this is intended to *supplement* rather than to replace the conventional, institutional, politics of the state: 'everything is political, but every politics is simultaneously a *macropolitics* and a *micropolitics*' (TP, 213/260). Understood as both *micro* and *macro*, we begin to appreciate that politics occurs in the margins of institutions, not in their

7. GD, 68/97–8; TD, 22/43.

absence. Badiou's fear is that, despite Deleuze and Guattari's sustained critique of capital, they endorse it, by implying that concerted deter-ritorialisation will inevitably remain framed by the market imperative of the eternal return of the same: namely, profit. Badiou, however, is unwilling to cede to what amounts to a stripping from democracy of the capacity to open itself up to the new. Although he stands apart from the tradition of French Nietzscheanism, from the predominant pursuit of ontologising the eternal return in the repetition of difference, he concedes the possibility of using the return to describe an interminable process of philosophical evaluation. Nietzsche's thought experiment becomes a way of acting out fidelity to the event of democracy:

> the task of philosophy is to expose a politics to assessment. [...] Politics can be defined sequentially as that which attempts to establish [*créer*] the impos-sibility of non-egalitarian statements relative to a situation, and as what can be exposed through philosophy, and by means of the word 'democracy', to what I would call some kind of eternity. Let us say that it is by means of the word 'democracy' thus conceived, and through philosophy and philosophy alone, that a politics can be evaluated according to the criteria of eternal return. (Badiou 2005a: 94/107–8)

It is only in reference to philosophy, in other words, that we are in a position to evaluate the democraticity of a political system independ-ently of the circumstances of its existence. For all Badiou's general criti-cism of the so-called philosophies of difference (Badiou 2001: 24/42), he finds a considerable degree of agreement with Derrida on this point. The latter also provides the possibility of thinking democracy as sacri-fice, while crucially distancing himself from the suggestion that sacrifice is inherently inauthentic, a technique for the transappropriation of a privileged experience of sovereignty.

For Derrida, sacrifice is far more than just a technique for the dis-avowal of the event. As a strategy through which we engage with the possibility of the event's arrival, it also repeats the possibility of eternal return that Deleuze and Guattari deem to be *politically* impossible. Derrida agrees that there is a tension between the event of the gift and democracy, but differs from the latter by locating sacrifice at the heart of this tension, as that which not only forecloses, compromises, democ-racy's claims to democraticity, but also brings about its perfectibility and promise. Treated deconstructively, sacrifice ceases to be about a privileged relation of immanence to a ground and becomes a way of communicating the absence of a ground. In so doing, it preserves the possibility of a sacrifice of sacrifice in which democracy would be redeemed against its hitherto compromised status.

In a by now familiar strategy, Derrida differentiates between the economic *practice* of democracy and its aneconomic *promise*. Election is economic because it is all about the selection and conferral of an identity and the laws that govern this identity through the exclusion of other identities. If voting is about exercising the right to privilege and subsequently submit to particular identities (those of the victorious parties or candidates), then it is, to reprise the criticism levelled at Heidegger, a technique for submitting the *polis* to an *oikos*. The means of this submission is calculation, pertaining not just to the calculation of winning majorities, but to the demographic and geographic questions of who can vote:

> the question of democracy is [...] the question of calculation, of numerical calculation, of equality according to number. [...] How does one count? What should count as a unit of calculation? What is a voice or a vote? What is an indivisible and countable voice or vote? So many difficult questions – difficult and more open than ever. A question of *nomos* and thus of *nemein*, of distribution or of sharing [*de la distribution ou du partage*]. (R, 29/53)

In its practice, democracy thus constitutes itself as a set of laws premised upon a further set of laws or calculations determining to whom or what these laws apply. But calculation alone cannot provide a ground for the constitutively undecidable decisions about how democracy should be structured, how the participating *polis* should be delimited, and so on. By way of example, Derrida observes that:

> one will never actually be able to 'prove' [...] that there is more democracy in a straight majority vote as opposed to proportional voting; both forms of voting are democratic, and yet both also protect their democratic character through exclusion, through expulsion or dismissal [*renvoi*]. (R, 36/60)

Even where proportionality and representativity are sacrificed for the sake of more efficient government, this efficiency, too, could be the choice of the electorate.

The use of the word 'sacrifice' might seem somewhat casual here, but it is not incidental. Back in the seventeenth century, Thomas Hobbes defined the social contract as the agreement by which '*I Authorise and give up my Right of Governing my selfe, to this Man, or to this Assembly of men*' (Hobbes 1996: 120). In an essay, 'Declarations of Independence', published initially in *Otobiographies* (1984), Derrida uses the term 'fabulous retroactivity' to describe the performativity, the circularity involved in this legitimation process, which must presuppose its own authority in the very act of legitimating itself (Derrida 2002: 50/22). The logic is precisely that of the sacrifice we find in Lacan and Žižek, the sacrificial gift of love, 'le don de ce qu'on n'a pas' that works by performatively enacting the ground it presupposes, giving to the other in order that there be another to whom one might give. In voting, we surrender a sovereignty that was never ours to give away, in order to instantiate the big Other of representative government. With its capacity to change increasingly exposed as a fantasy, democracy becomes a perfect expression of the fantasmically constructed big Other, a sovereignty that does not exist, which is strictly speaking NOTHING, but to which we none the less continually sacrifice for the sake of concealing the event. It is thus the site of what Žižek calls 'politics without politics' (Žižek 2003: 96), an insubstantial spectre that sanitises the real, by concealing its eternal return.

Derrida recognises the Žižekian point but is not so pessimistic in his reading of democracy, not so willing to see it reduced to a fantasy that masks the traumatic real of capital. Nor is he seemingly prepared to draw a hard and fast distinction between the inauthentic repetition of identity and the repetition of difference in the event, the sacrifice that instantiates a ground and the one that, in traversing the fantasy, seeks to sacrifice sacrifice. However, like Lacan-Žižek, Derrida also differentiates between two types of sacrifice: namely. the economic sacrifice that recuperates a ground and the aneconomic sacrifice of sacrifice that affirms the futility of the former:

> absolute sacrifice that is not the sacrifice of irresponsibility on the altar of responsibility, but the sacrifice of the most imperative duty (that which binds me to the other as a singularity in general) in favour of another absolutely imperative duty binding me to the wholly other [*le sacrifice du devoir plus impératif au bénéfice d'un autre devoir absolument impératif qui nous lie au tout autre*]. (GD, 71/101)

The second, aneconomic, sacrifice refers to a sacrifice that does not seek, in Nancian terms, to transappropriate an ontological ground. Apropos of Derrida's reading of Bataille, we would do well to remember, however, that the very absence of a ground means that the 'sacrifice of (economical) sacrifice inevitably turns into the sacrifice of (aneconomical) sacrifice', collapsing back from general to restricted economy (Keenan 2005: 137; WD, 348–50/404–8).

It is by accepting the relation of sacrifice to the impossibility of (trans)appropriation that Derrida is able to articulate democracy as an inherently sacrificial practice or, more precisely, a sacrificial practice constituted by its relation to the promise of a politics *without* sacrifice. Derrida defines sacrifice broadly as 'a noncriminal putting to death [*une mise à mort non criminelle*]', a form of giving death that, on account of its relation to the sacred, falls short of the legal concept of murder (Derrida 1992b: 278/293). More revealingly, in his most sustained engagement with the concept, in *The Gift of Death* (1999), he specifies that 'sacrifice supposes the putting to death of the unique in terms of its being unique, irreplaceable and most precious. It also therefore refers to the impossibility of substitution, the unsubstitutable' (GD, 58/85). The demand to sacrifice can only be met by the sacrifice of that which it is impossible to sacrifice; by that whose loss would be singularly irreplaceable. If, traditionally, this demand is met through the sacrifice of God – through the killing of the primal father, in the Freudian terms of *Totem and Taboo* – henceforth it is fulfilled through the (reluctant but inevitable) sacrifice of the virtual, of the singularity that exceeds life's actual manifestations. What is sacrificed is not just the actual, but the virtuality that is foreclosed from actuality by the decision that names what we recognise as existing. Undecidability means that the act of making decisions is inherently sacrificial, necessarily entailing the loss of the singular and inexchangeable. Crucially, Derrida does not want to say that this sacrifice is definitive. On the contrary: if it were, then it would not be impossible. The logic of *différance*, which he understands explicitly in terms of 'repetition in the eternal return' (M, 17/18–19), means that whatever is killed refuses death, returning to haunt the site of the decision that condemned it. Sacrifice is thus intimately linked to eternal return, to 'das grösste Schwergewicht' of the impossible, undecidable. It is impossible because it calls for the surrendering of something so precious that the incomprehensibility of its loss would destroy the one making the sacrifice; hence Derrida's example of God commanding Abraham to sacrifice Isaac (GD, 58–80/94–114). But moreover it is impossible because it is condemned to failure. That which is sacrificed cannot be put to death and accordingly lives on in the form of the spectre, a virtual trace of the *à venir*.

As he writes in the later text, 'Faith and Knowledge' (1996), it is this spectral life – once the life of God, now the life of the event – that would have to be sacrificed for sacrifice to take place as a definitive consignment to death, for the gift of death to be irreversible. Rather than conceiving sacrifice as the material sacrifice of something living, or tangible, Derrida argues that 'true sacrifice ought to sacrifice not only "natural" life, called "animal" or "biological", but also that which is worth more than so-called natural life' (FK, 51/78). The life at stake in sacrifice, that is to say, is irreducible to the individuated life of a particular sacrificial offering. Reread through Derrida, Badiou's injunction to 'sacrifice Life' acquires a significance not intended by its author. For Badiou there is only actuality, and the promising of anything beyond this amounts to negative theology (Badiou 1998: 71/72). Derrida's point, though, is that sacrifice only makes sense when conceived in terms of a life that exceeds the actual life of the individual, when in sacrificing one gives death to virtual possibilities whose actualisation will henceforth be precluded. In so far as sacrifice communicates with the event, it communicates by sacrificing a life that refuses individuation – the life of capital, but beyond this, the virtual life of an other that has yet to be embodied in an actual existence. This excessive form of life is 'dead [...] and yet more than living, the spectral fantasy of the dead as the principal of life and of sur-vival' (FK, 50/78). Outlined more fully in the early essay, 'Living On' ('*Survivre*', 1979), and resurrected in *Specters of Marx*, the concept of *survivance* names an aneconomic force of life in excess of the mortal, economic life of individuated organ-isms and organ-ised subjects: 'beyond any *present* life, life as *my* life, [...] *beyond therefore the living present in general*' (SM, xx/16–17; LO, 88–9/152–3). Like the other ontologised reformulations of Nietzsche's eternal return discussed over the course of this work, the spectral is governed by the differantial structure of repetition: 'Repetition *and* first time: this is perhaps the question of the event as the question of the ghost' (SM, 10/31). That which is sacrificed escapes the mimetic logic that causes Nancy to preclude sacrifice from the political. By contrast, the Derridean deconstruction of sacrifice not only is compatible with, but also even extends, the project of a politics of repetition. In his later writings, Derrida explicitly identifies democracy with a name for the life of the event, a non-identical synonym for the gift. Anticipating what Critchley calls the 'interstitial distance', the internal spacing of differ-ence constitutive of true democracy (Critchley 2007: 117), the novelty of Derrida's contribution consists in identifying democracy, like the gift before it, with a temporal *différance* that causes it to exceed its own presence. Captured in the otherwise banal notion of a 'gap between fact and ideal essence' (SM, 64/110), it is this *différance* that opens democ-racy on to the aneconomic time of the gift, the *à-venir*:

> For democracy remains to be known; this is its essence insofar as it remains: not only will it remain indefinitely perfectible, hence always insufficient and future, but, belonging to the time of the promise, it will always remain, in each of its future times, to come: even when there is democracy, it never exists, is never present, it remains the theme of a non-presentable concept. (PF, 306/339)

Where Heidegger conceives democracy as inadequate to the ontological reappropriation of the subject (*Dasein*), the Derridean understanding of democracy as promise means that it is not democracy, but rather the subject that is inadequate to the democratic imperative of justice. By emphasising its exteriority to chronological time, Derrida evokes an impossible politics of spectrality, in which the space of *doxa* is expanded to consider the indivisible remainder, the ghosts that live on after their sacrifice. Tracing the horizons of a politics without sacrifice, a politics without politics, without the necessity of imposing decision on the incalculable and undecidable, this promised democracy already exists virtually beyond the horizons of the subject. The impossibility of instantiating this horizon means that we are condemned to be political, to sacrifice. Yet sacrifice takes place in order that it not take place, as a putative sacrifice of sacrifice.

The excessive nature of democracy, overflowing its own concept as a multiplicity of often mutually exclusive permutations, means that democracy is constituted by an ineliminable trace of sacrifice. What is sacrificed is not just the votes that are consciously and calculably marginalised in the preference of one ballot structure over another; nor simply the criminals, immigrants and other disenfranchised who are excluded by the demo- or geographic delimitation of a *polis*. These marginalised groups identified by Derrida coincide with what, in the book of the same name, Giorgio Agamben identifies as *homo sacer*, the subcategory of life without intrinsic value whose exclusion from the *polis* Agamben takes to constitute the originary structure of the political (Agamben 1998: 74). Agamben argues that the exclusion of *homo sacer* is not itself sacrificial, however, but rather the condition of the possibility of sacrifice. The central tenet of Agamben's thesis is that politics consists in the naming of the sacred, a naming that excludes the sacred from membership of the *polis*, condemning or rather abandoning it to an *oikos* on the margins of the political (Wall 2005: 41). The recipient of the name is *homo sacer*, a life that can be 'killed but not sacrificed', put to death without falling victim to homicide, but not as part of a sacrificial ritual. Politics begins with an act of sovereignty, the decision that determines what counts as *homo sacer* and excludes said *homines sacri* from protection by the laws that govern over the *polis*. The violence of this decision makes *homo sacer* sacred, but in exempting him from the dignity of the law simultaneously renders him unworthy of sacrifice, unworthy of inclusion in subsequent decisions affecting the *polis*. Recalling Girard, in a much earlier work, *Language and Death: The Place of Negativity* (1982), Agamben implies that sacrifice comes into existence only later, as a ritual that repeats the violence enacted by the sovereign decision: '*it is this* sacred *violence that sacrifice presupposes in order to repeat it and regulate it within its own structure*' (Agamben 1991: 105–6). After Derrida, could we not rather say that rituals of sacrifice merely retrospectively seek to ground, to legitimate, the decision that is inherently ungrounded, by submitting it to a stabilising logic of mimesis that conceals the precariousness of its self-justification? Should we not also say that what defines *homo sacer* is less *unworthiness* of sacrifice than the fact of always already having been sacrificed?

Agamben reverses the Heideggerian position outlined above. Where the latter would argue that sacrifice is pre-political, essential, the former argues that it presupposes the foundation of the *polis*. The subtlety of the distinction has led at least one commentator to doubt its useful-ness. According to Andrew Norris, 'Agamben complicates his account unnecessarily when he concludes that the killing of bare life does not constitute a sacrifice' (Norris 2005: 25). In saying this, Norris opens up a space for a more Derridean account, in which the decision is always sacrificial – and never sovereign. Derrida has also been critical of Agamben, casting doubts on the legitimacy of the deconstructive move by which he differentiates between *bios* and *zoé*, the life that can be qualified as political and the 'bare life' that is excluded from the *polis* (R, 24/46). In other words, Derrida is concerned that Agamben's taxon-omy of life may still be too restrictive adequately to grasp the complex-ity of sacrifice. In excess of what Agamben, following Foucault, calls biopolitics – in excess, even, of what one might call *zoepolitics*, which, however inclusive, still implies a material, organismal conception of life (see, for example, Braidotti 2006: 129–38) – there is moreover a politics of the spectre, of the life that never achieves actualisation. Prior to the designation of life that can be killed but not sacrificed, there is a sacri-fice that does not kill, one which moreover cannot kill, in our 'actual' understanding of the term, on account of there being a virtual life that refuses to die, and continually returns in the guise of the spectre.

Democracy does not require that the life of the individual be expend-able, but it is founded on the sacrifice of the supra-biological *sur-vie*. It also thus encapsulates a sacrificial logic of 'auto-immune suicide', in which at its limit it must sacrifice itself in order to survive. Likewise community, which, in what implies a critique of Nancy not dissimilar to that of Fraser, Derrida suggests is also created through sacrifice: 'no community that would not cultivate its own auto-immunity, a principle of sacrificial self-destruction ruining the principle of self-protection (that of maintaining its self-integrity intact), and this in view of some sort of invisible or spectral sur-vival' (FK, 51/79). The decisional sac-rifice is the very condition of possibility of democracy, community, yet it is the failure of this sacrifice that sustains them. The eternal return of the spectre, both as threat and as messianic promise, is what:

> keeps the auto-immune community alive, which is to say, open to something other and more than itself: the other, the future, death, freedom, the coming or the love of the other, the space and time of a spectralizing messianicity beyond all messianism. (FK, 51/79)

In this eternal return, life and death are traversed by the life-beyond-death that is in excess of both. The community is not distinct from the spectre that animates it, but rather continually escapes death through the repeated sacrifice of that which refuses to die.

This does not mean that we could or should do away with sacrifice, since it is through sacrifice that we preserve the sanctity of its promise; through sacrifice, moreover, that we assume the responsibility – that we reveal our *ability to respond* – to the impossible arrival of the other and acknowledge the impossibility of our *not* sacrificing it. Derrida equates the affirmation of impossible sacrifice with the eternal return, but also thereby to politics as such, to the decision that seeks precariously to name, to appropriate, the event. In light of this, Nancy's dismissal of sacrifice as an aesthetic phenomenon simply repeats the illegitimate move of essentialising the political, of treating the political as something separable from and uncontaminable by the totalitarian, aestheticising pursuit of an ontological ground. Derrida's argument is that politics not only is unable to defend itself against contamination, but that it is *about* and defined by this contamination, whose inevitability and irre-ducibility must paradoxically be affirmed if the promise of escaping it is to be preserved. The space of undecidability in which the decision is made cannot be foreclosed in the way that the outlawing of totalitar-ian systems would require: 'nothing could make us more irresponsible; nothing could be more totalitarian' (Derrida 1999a: 117/201).

Rather than legitimate totalitarianism, what this means, for Derrida, is that democracy cannot allow itself to be idealised, aestheticised as a fixed and determinate, inflexible structure, whose principal decisions are effectively presupposed as cast in stone. Like the gift, democracy exists not as an essence but as a promise, and one that moreover risks destruction if overidentified with a specific set of beliefs or institutional practices; it is necessarily ambiguous and, at its limit, unrecognisable. We find an illustration of this in *Manderlay*, the second instalment of Lars von Trier's *America* trilogy, a film in which the unbearable weight of democracy causes a group of emancipated slaves to engineer their re-enslavement; where democracy becomes another name for slavery. The sequel to *Dogville* discloses the dangers of hypostatising the various names of the promise yielded by the eternal return. We saw this already in *Dogville*, when, in the very moment of becoming-gift, in being raped, sacrificed and stripped of humanity by townsfolk purporting to welcome her, Grace is reterritorialised, explicitly identifying herself as a sovereign angel of death, charged with enforcing the morality of those she goes on to kill. A similar scenario plays itself out in *Manderlay*, where, identifying her gift all too readily with a democracy that quickly descends into ochlocratic chaos, Grace once again succumbs to the fatal idealism of conferring a fixed and recognisable identity on the promise. Unable to accept the collapse of the routines of slavery that their receipt of democracy entails, the slaves that Grace emancipates vote to refuse her gift in favour of a reinstatement of totalitarian order. As in the first film, Grace is made the sacrificial victim, her dream put to death by her (unwanted) election to the position of tyrannical mistress. And yet she cannot but acknowledge the democracy paradoxically underlying the return to tyranny. Unable to reconcile two conflicting concepts of democracy in a single body, Grace's integrity gives way and she once again takes flight.

Despite arguing that democracy is not reducible to a readily identifiable set of criteria, Derrida does not think it inherently arbitrary, which is to say unqualifiable, unrelated to ethics. On the contrary: 'it is necessary to deduce a politics and a law [*droit*] from ethics. This deduction is necessary in order to determine the "better" or "less bad", with all the requisite quotation marks this calls for: democracy is "better" than tyranny' (Derrida 1999a: 115/198). Derrida thus continues to think the political in relation to the 'ethical' figure of the other, above all in terms of responsibility to and for the other. The formulation draws consternation from Žižek and also Ernesto Laclau, both of whom suspect a literal regrounding of politics in the Levinasian *Autrui*, hence a refusal, on Derrida's part, to accept the impossibility of ontologically privileging democracy over any other form of government (Laclau 1996: 77–8; Butler, Laclau and Žižek 2000: 229). It is crucial to note that Derrida's other is not simply the other person, however. Nor is his understanding of responsibility reducible to the 'classical' idea of individualisable, calculable, appropriable causes. This *economic* conceptualisation of responsibility is 'an obscene presumption' (Derrida and Nancy 2004: 177):

> When it comes, when it happens, there must be impotence, vulnerability. It must be that whoever or whatever, man or animal, to whom it happens, has no control over it, even performatively. And thus, in this here place, it must be that no-one (no would-be 'I'-saying subject, no ipseity) can assume responsibility, in the classic sense of the term, for what happens [*il faut que personne (aucun soi-disant sujet disant 'je', aucune ipséité) ne puisse assumer la responsabilité, au sens classique du terme, de ce qui arrive*]. (2004: 178)

Reconstrued as *aneconomic*, responsibility refers to the ability to *respond to the other*, to 'countersign such and such an affirmation' of the other (PF, 231/258 [TM]), to adjust one's experiential horizons to conceive, for example, of a democracy that would not foreclose the alterity of the other. *Specters of Marx* speaks of a 'principle of some *responsibility*, beyond all living present, within that which disjoins the living present, before the ghosts of those who are not yet born or already dead' (SM, xix/16). The other is thus not human, but spectral. Elsewhere, it is also potentially bestial (Derrida 2004: 470–1) and even technological: 'if there is a to-come, it will happen indissociably with a transformation of the world by, through or within technology' (Derrida 2001b: 78).

Rather than reinscribe the sovereignty of the subject by asserting it as the cause of the event, responsibility requires an affirmation of ungrounding, the ability to recognise the undecidability that originates the decision. *Pace* Laclau and Žižek, this is not a (Heideggerian) awaiting for the return of a ground, for a gift or a democracy that, one day, we could recognise as such. On the contrary, it is to affirm the possibility of exposure to the absence of a ground, a gift so heterogeneous as to overwhelm and overturn the subject in the moment of its receipt. It is also, as such, to affirm that the decision, too – the sacrificial technique through which we mediate between actual and virtual, through which we respond to the virtual life of the event – is heterogeneous in origin.

If democracy holds out the promise of such an affirmation in practice as well as ideally, it is because the principle of election allows for its continual reinvention, the perpetual renegotiation of the *polis* through sacrifice. Electoral decisions are precisely those to which, Derrida insists, democracy cannot be reduced, the vote being only a very rudimentary way of enumerating the *polis*. Yet it preserves the promise of expansion, the possibility of extending the franchise in principle, even if this would still fall short of the demand to sacrifice sacrifice, completely to do away with the need to count, to make decisions about what does and does not count as partaking in the life of the *polis*. Politics is ultimately a question of the decision, but, on account of the undecidability of the event to which it responds, this decision does not resemble the calculus of opportunity cost traditionally ascribed to *homo economicus*, a predetermined choice between actualities, named candidates and ballot structures, for example. Derrida repeatedly describes it as 'the decision of the other in me', a decision in excess of the *habitus* of the subject. In a move that recalls Deleuze's description of the passive syntheses of time and/as desiring-production (see Chapter 2), it is furthermore declared to be passive: 'The passive decision, decision of the event, is always in me, structurally, another decision, a rending decision as the decision of the other' (PF, 68/87 [TM]). Exercised without guarantee, it has no criterion of success other than its ability to respond to the other, to create subjectivities that respond to the shock of the new. Its task is to adapt the *oikos* to the *polis* and not *vice versa*. The type of democracy that would (cor)respond to this politics of alterity is therefore very different from the one instantiated in Western parliamentary systems of representation. As suggested in the above-mentioned concept of the new International, its *polis* would be unrecognisable, even. In place of a politics of space and territory, 'the political must be deterritorialized,' thought 'beyond the 'borders' of the political' (Derrida and Stiegler 2002: 65/76), become above all a politics of time and eternal return.

To return, momentarily, to the earlier assertion of a complicity between Derrida and Deleuze and Guattari, Derrida's invocation of a bestial, technical life would seem to endorse the aforementioned idea of a life of capital. Like the former, Derrida argues that capital should not be conflated with the event, which it continues to presuppose, 'inscribed and exceeded by a promise of gift beyond exchange' (SM, 160/254). Following Deleuze and Guattari, one might therefore question the extent to which our ability to respond to the event is governed by capital and the extent to which the sacralization of democracy is itself the result of sacrificial decisions made by capital. Derrida affirms the undecidability of this question, while also preserving the possibility of a decision that would not be determined by capital. If sovereignty implies control and the capacity to appropriate responsibility, he argues, the decision takes place beyond sovereignty, at the point where the subject – be it capital or the human – unravels in the intensity of life stripped of its subjectivity, the greatest weight of the eternal return of the event. Beyond the grip of conscious appropriation and control, the moment of decision is one of what Derrida, following Kierkegaard, calls madness:

> 'the instant of the decision is madness', Kierkegaard says elsewhere. [...]
> Like the gift and the 'gift of death', it remains irreducible to presence or to presentation, it demands a temporality of the instant without ever constituting a present. It belongs to an atemporal temporality, to a duration that cannot be grasped. (GD, 65/94)

The decision and hence politics, he continues, takes place in the exposure to the event, to (and in) the time beyond presence, the non-chronological 'atemporal temporality' of the gift. The delirium of undecidability, of *différance*, becomes the moment of exposure to the gift, where one touches on and simultaneously pulls back from the experience of the gift as gift of death, the destitution of the supposedly sovereign subject. And yet it is a moment that, strictly, does not take place. The ungrounding instant of exposure is instantly met with a decision that recuperates the subject. It is at this moment that the aneconomic gift-without-debt is reinscribed and negated in an economy of debt, the anxiety of responsibility that comes from the sacrifice of the alterity of the event. Nancy is in agreement: 'We say all the time nowadays that responsibility is the freeing from all guilt. On the contrary, guilt is perhaps the beyond of all measurable responsibility' (Derrida and Nancy 2004: 183). If the subject comes into being as the site of an anxiety, guilt and corresponding sense of responsibility, it is as a result of this sacrificial foreclosure of the event. Insofar as the subject is a 'principle of calculability' (Derrida 1992b: 272/287), the first calculus pertains to an economy of guilt and its attempted expiation. This explains the ambiguity of how Derrida can say both that the gift is negated by the obligation to reciprocate and that we are none the less obliged to respond to it. It is only as subjects for whom the gift is sacrificed in its moment of receipt that the trace of this receipt echoes as a call to responsibility, an obligation to reciprocate the giving of the event. Sacrifice is not prior to the other, a means of its performative enactment, but rather the response to its originary, ungrounding excess.

Keenan has noted that Derrida uses the concepts of suppression and repression in his work on sacrifice, particularly in regard to the logic of the gift. He cites Derrida's reference to both a 'double suppression [refoulement]' and a 'double "suppression of the object [of the gift]"' (Keenan 2005: 156; GD, 112/153). The first suppression is of the gift's unconditionality, which is suppressed by the libidinal economy that seeks to derive pleasure in giving. Following this, 'one must proceed to *another* suppression: that of keeping in the gift only the giving' (GD, 12/153). The latter refers to the gift's withdrawal in the very act of giving, which is to say its destitution of the subject that would stand to recognise and thereby negate the gift. Reading Derrida through Deleuze suggests also a third repression, in which the subject emerges as a reaction to the gift's unbearable intensity, as a means of escaping the aneconomy of the event. Not only does the gift necessitate the ungrounding of the subject, it also effects the repression of which the subject is born, and which must be ungrounded. In its effectuation of the subject, the secret of a giving whose exposure would entail its destruction is thus preserved, but for the trace of repression or forgetting.

Far from instantiating theodicy, the gift will always be reterritorialised as a subject, the name imposed on a multiplicity. In arriving from the other, the decision names not simply the assumption of causal responsibility, but more significantly the *ability* to *respond* to the event through the creation of new subjectivities, new laws of identity that would enable it to sustain an encounter with the event. To do this is to become aware of the sacrifice that is at stake in the making of a decision, but also to become aware of the precariousness, the constitutive undecidability, of the decisions that have already been made. We can, of course, doubt that there could ever be a pure decision, a decision without *habitus* – without the outcome being effectively predetermined, for example, by the minimal *habitus* of capital. (If there were, it would presumably operate on an unadulterated plane of immanence, in relation to which there would ironically be no need for the sacrificial decision.) By extension, we might also doubt whether, in creating a new subjectivity, we could ever successfully throw off the old one.

The point, for Derrida, is less that our decisions are contaminated, which is inevitable, and more that they must therefore remain in constant circulation, never allowed to settle, lest they hypostatise and become poisonous, more poisonous than they already are. Unlike the Maori *hau*, the 'esprit des choses', or spirit of things given, that becomes poisonous if stalled on its circuitous journey home, the decision becomes poisonous when made in view of a homecoming, when the name of the gift is thought definitive. However unsurpassable capital may seem, its insuperability cannot be taken for granted, as if rooted definitively in ontology. Democracy is not irreducibly condemned to be framed by capital. The withdrawal of the gift from experience means that the decisions about what the *polis*, the community of the life of the political, consists in, must also be subject to the repetitions of eternal return. The eternal return *of* the decision is also an eternal return *to* the decision. The gift and its sacrifice must continue to communicate with one another, to exchange, aneconomically, in a 'commerce without commerce of ghosts' (SM, xviii/15).

CONCLUSION

Understood as a politics of the eternal return, of the ungrounding repetition of difference, the politics of the gift has, or rather *have*, seemingly always existed in a relation of tension to both sacrifice and democracy. Rejecting the theodicy of Hegel-Kojève's end of History, Bataille originally articulates sacrifice as the key figure in a politics of general economy that exceeds the restricted (political) economy of capitalism. The gesture engenders resistance both within and without the continental tradition, on account of the violence of his dismissal of the institutions of modernity. That Heidegger argues much the same has the effect of meaning that those who follow in their wake – primarily Derrida, Deleuze and Nancy – have been thought similarly contaminated, complicit in what at least one eminent critic has called a 'critique of reason that shows reckless disregard for its own foundations' in the project of modernity (Habermas 1987: 337/391). In spite of repeated complaints about the constitutive inability of representative democracy to accommodate the singularity of an event that refuses representation, these need not translate into an active call for institutional overthrow.

If anything, Nancy has sought to distance himself too much from the Batailleanism of this politics, marked out in terms of his refusal of the concept of sacrifice. Tainted on one hand by Hegelian connotations of theodicy and on the other by the aestheticised politics of fascism, the concept of sacrifice, he argues, is incompatible with the eternal return of an inappropriable gift, the ecotechnical offering through which we are abandoned to politics. Nancy identifies sacrifice as the site of totalitarian drift, but in circumscribing the sacrificial leaves himself open to the accusation of idealism, of extricating the political from any sense of its relation to a field of political practice he regards as inherently compromised.

Through readings of Badiou and Derrida, we begin to see that sacrifice is made a scapegoat, whose abandonment only brings us closer to the prospect that there is no essence of the political, no isolable meaning of politics, beyond that of the decision through which we receive the gift, submitting it to an economy, a law of identity, in the process. The decision is itself sacrificial, at the root of sacrifice, pertaining to the way the excess of the event is represented, translated into a naming of the sacred. As the performative process of naming the sacred, sacrifice becomes entangled in the fictioning of an ontological ground, yet cannot be reduced to this fictioning; cannot be reduced to the transappropriation of essence, the subsumption of the event under immanence. To sacrifice, or rather to recognise in sacrifice the possibility of breaking with mimesis, is above all to acknowledge a gift that exceeds experience, to attempt to receive this gift by naming it in an act of reciprocation that is condemned to fall short of the offering to which it responds. It is equally, implicitly, to acknowledge the impossibility of naming, to acknowledge the inadequacy of the counter-offering. Understood in terms of the politics of decision, sacrifice is not a name for the event, an inherently sublime gesture of transappropriation, but rather the price – we might even say the *(an)economy* – of our abandonment.

Rather than recklessly breaking with modernity, Derrida's reassertion of the irreducibility of sacrifice serves to reaffirm the modern heritage, by opening up a space for the reinvigoration, the resacralisation of democracy. Far from recklessly diminishing its significance, thinking democracy through sacrifice as something fragile and ungroundable that must repeatedly be resacrificed, rethought, offers the means of preserving its integrity, of emphasising its promise. In this respect, it is vital that it not be essentialised as something whose mere instantiation is enough to ward off and differentiate it from totalitarianism. Were there a distinction between totalitarianism and democracy, it would lie in the promise of the latter, in its willingness to become subject to renegotiation, to reinvent itself through exposure to the eternal return of the new, the different. In practice, democracy's openness to the future is a question of contingency rather than essence, of its willingness to leave undetermined the question of what it is that is to be sacrificed. The question of the end of History and of the end of this end becomes one of how much we are willing to take for granted, to see as having been essentially resolved by the passing of time. For Derrida – as for Bataille, perhaps, in his original response to Kojève – theodicy, too, must be renegotiated, suspended, its concept submitted to trial by eternal return.

It is no longer simply the case that politics takes place by default, only in the absence or failure of a philosophical thinking of the event. On the contrary, it is also politics that gives rise to philosophy. The sacrificial decisions in which politics consists give rise to the spectral excess of an event that philosophy is charged with thinking.

Conclusion: Variations on a Theme from Nietzsche

Perhaps we should see the first attempt at this uprooting of Anthropology – to which, no doubt, contemporary thought is dedicated – in the Nietzschean experience. [...] Nietzsche marks the threshold beyond which contemporary philosophy can begin thinking again. [...] If the discovery of the Return is indeed the end of the philosophy, then the end of man, for its part, is the return to the beginning of philosophy.

(Michel Foucault)[1]

Several attempts have been made to discern an underlying thread or unifying thematic of twentieth-century French philosophy. Apparently oblivious to the critique of *homo economicus* that recent philosophies of the event have entailed, Gary Gutting has located this thread in an overarching 'concern with individual freedom as a concrete lived reality' (Gutting 2001: 380), in relation to which 'poststructuralism is an interlude rather than a decisive turning point in the history of French philosophy' (2001: 389). Todd May rightly describes the convergence of thinkers around the problematic of difference, particularly in a critique of foundationalism, viewed as a privileging of identity that is not only false but also 'insidious' and 'totalitarian' (May 1997: 4). Moved by the deaths of Deleuze and Derrida amongst others, not to mention the then serious illness of Nancy, Badiou writes nostalgically of an 'exceptional [...] French philosophical moment', seeing himself as 'perhaps its last representative' (Badiou 2005b). Stretching broadly from Sartre to Deleuze, this moment is characterised by interrogations of the human subject and the legacy of nineteenth-century German philosophy, as well as science, psychoanalysis and a desire to 'situate philosophy directly within the political arena without taking a detour via political philosophy' (2005b [TM]). Mauss is included in this

---

1. OT, 342/353.

panorama, named amongst the prophets of what, according to Badiou, is only 'mistakenly termed structuralism', who were increasingly sceptical of modern philosophy's insistence on the transparency of human experience, and amongst the first to decouple experience from 'a decentred real that is neither grasped nor localized' (Badiou 2008b: 213n.42, 48/173n.1, 76; Hallward 2003: 401n.11). But to capture the full significance of the politics of the gift, which brings together the problematics of difference, politics, the emergence of new academic disciplines and the legacy of German phenomenology, one must go further, recognising the anthropologist's role in fomenting a crisis in philosophy and a corresponding reconfiguration of the boundaries between philosophy, anthropology and politics.

While acknowledging the multiplicity of origins, the start of the *moment philosophique français* should be moved back, *pace* Badiou, from Sartre to Bataille, if not Mauss himself, and defined in relation to Bataille's response to Kojève. By calling for the 'anthropologisation' of the abstract logic of Hegel's philosophy of *Geist*, Kojève occupies a decisive yet ambiguous moment in French philosophy's negotiation with the anthropological. The call is less a clinging to the fading *epistémè* of philosophy-as-Anthropology than an attempt to break free from it by replacing Hegel's abstract account of reason with a description of man's being-in-the-world. And yet, rather than open philosophy on to a beyond of Anthropology, rather than anticipate Foucault's 'death of man' in the ungrounding of the modern subject, Kojève identified anthropologisation with the end of History, through the obviation of both philosophy and politics. A new paradigm emerges around the gift, defined by the rejection of this Anthropo-Hegelianism and the exposure of the limitations of dialectical exchange. Philosophy would henceforth have to open itself up to a shifting intellectual landscape with which it had hitherto resisted dialogue. As Kaufman observes, with a 'precedent set by the College of Sociology', there follows a deterritorialisation of philosophy, which is taken beyond the formal institutions of academia and toward a new form of intellectual exchange in 'a delirium that signals the ecstatic breakdown of identity' (Kaufman 2001: 7). Taken up by Bataille, Klossowski and Lacan, amongst others, Maussian anthropology becomes an other of the type whose spectres, Derrida argues, 'threaten the interiority of the home', by haunting the institutional *oikos* of philosophy through their compulsion of hospitality (Derrida and Dufourmantelle 2007: 53/51).

In terms of the legacy to which this gives rise, the effect is roughly discernible in two tendencies, which contrast with Agamben's distinction between trajectories of immanence and transcendence in French philosophy (Agamben 1999: 238–9). One might consider a pattern based on thinkers' hospitality toward anthropology and the newly emergent human sciences; on the extent to which they affirm an encounter with the (anthropological) other as a condition of reconceptualising the relationship between philosophy and anthropology. The alternative tendency is to see the human sciences as a legacy of philosophically sclerotic Anthropology and conceive politics from within a more narrowly, exclusively, philosophical discourse. A first group comprising Mauss, Lévi-Strauss, Bataille, Klossowski and Lacan is characterised by an ostensibly 'anti-philosophical' treatment of philosophy, by a willingness to move beyond the conventionally philosophical, into anthropology, heterology and psychoanalysis. Another group, comprising Heidegger and Nancy, perhaps also Jean-Luc Marion, distance themselves from philosophy-as-Anthropology, from the modern philosophy of privileged subjectivity, while continuing to insist on the priority of philosophical (phenomenological, ontological) discourse. The two tendencies need not be mutually exclusive, however. Alain Badiou has argued that 'philosophy should always think as closely as possible to antiphilosophy' (Badiou and Hallward 1998: 124), and Deleuze and Derrida exemplify this claim. Both deem phenomenology and ontology insufficient for an understanding of politics, which both precedes and exceeds the horizons of subjectivity. Rather than give up on philosophy, they conceive it as necessarily defined by the encounter with an other that cannot be subsumed under the logical categories of transcendental consciousness; the field of philosophy is even precisely that which survives this encounter.

Nancy has recently evoked the 'parallel differences' of 'the two Ds' who are ultimately incommensurable ('*sans partage*'), 'for whom 'there is no common measure.' The relationship between Deleuze and Derrida is defined by 'the impossibility of furnishing a common rule for two systems of writing [*régimes de phrases*], two language games. But', he continues, 'philosophy *itself* presents itself to us as the regime of the non-given rule' (2005: 10), as a kind of (aneconomic) exchange that never quite takes place, because it escapes any totalising identification; because it operates, not through fixed terms, but through unstable concepts that cannot be translated into one another without remainder. Similar comparisons might be applied to the relations, consisting in often deliberate misreadings of one another and near-imperceptible variations on the same concepts, between any of the thinkers discussed over the course of the present work, in a way that complicates the (arguably reductive, essentialist) attempt to articulate poststructuralism – and poststructuralist politics in particular – as coalescing around a paradigm of the gift. Regarding the two Ds, Nancy prefers to speak of a 'sharing' or parallelism of thought, or of a community, albeit one paradoxically defined by the 'absence of community'. A community *without* community, as Derrida would say, recalling Blanchot recalling Bataille, for whom 'the community of which I speak is one that will exist virtually from the fact of the existence of Nietzsche' (Blanchot 1988: 22/41; PF, 47/56–7n). A community of the eternal return that comes into existence only through the impossibility of thinking the ways in which this return plays out across thought and history.

The virtual community, or what Foucault has called the *epistémè*, of eternal return, is also a community – a *polis* – of the gift, in which the differences of its constituents coexist without being subordinate to any totalising figure of a ground. Much as Bataille, Klossowski, Lacan, Deleuze and Guattari, Derrida and Nancy share in the thinking of a gift that withdraws from subjectivity, it is also this withdrawal that keeps them apart, entailing an eternal return to the impossibility of naming what it is that is given in the event. We see this already in the multiple repetitions that play out in Mauss's legacy. Bataille repeats Mauss by turning to Nietzsche, invoking a general economy of life and death to take Mauss beyond the restricted Lévi-Straussian thinking of exchange purely in terms of culture. Lacan's account of a real that returns eternally to the same place further nuances the relation between the symbolic order of nature and its interruption by life (the undead life-beyond-death of the libido), and thus anticipates the Derridean thinking of spectrality. Derrida also follows Bataille in castigating Lévi-Strauss for his omission of Nietzsche. So too do Deleuze and Guattari, whose return to Nietzsche enables them to emancipate spectres of Mauss from their framing by the total social fact of structuralism. The problems of Heidegger stem from his attempt to surpass Nietzsche, to replace Nietzsche's 'metaphysics' with ontology, because in so doing he aestheticises the eternal return, restricting repetition to *poiesis*. But this is overturned by another return to Nietzsche, reincarnated in the constant, ungrounding circulations of Nancy's ecotechnical bodies. If Deleuze and Derrida are parallel, Nancy suggests, it is as repetitions of Nietzsche, repetitions of 'difference itself, the sameness of difference', where ' "eternal return" = not a flight out of time, but continuously discontinuous time, cutting short its completion, all results and all resolution' (2005: 11).

Poststructuralism's community of the gift never gives itself as a homogeneous present, never resolves the differences that can be traced to its origins in anthropology, phenomenology and a certain crisis in philosophy. The community created through the receipt of Nietzsche's legacy is also the (anti-)philosophical community of Mauss's *héritiers*, though it cannot be confined to either designation. *Le moment philosophique français* offers itself up to numerous names ('poststructuralism' included), but the very process of naming it entails the sacrifice of its multiplicity, the collapse of its aneconomy into an economy of representation. Derrida avoids ontologisation for just this reason, qualifying the gift with a '*s'il y en a*' that avoids committing it to some kind of presence. One might none the less point to a post-Maussian consensus over a gift that cannot be conflated with a thing or even with a present, which is resistant to any kind of identity-politics: a gift that would come from the future to disrupt the present, whose politics would pertain to a singular excess that escapes institutional organisation. Mauss rejected the paradigm of *homo economicus*, the utility-maximising individual driven to work by a combination of lack, the scarcity of resources and the desire to actualise his or her essence in labour. Derrida, Lacan, Deleuze and Nancy, amongst others, extend this critique by showing the *excess* of the gift to precede and unground any concept of essence, revealing politics and economics as responses to the absence of foundational, metaphysical structures. They furthermore argue that politics must come to affirm ungrounding, to do away with the desire for a founding gesture, rather than seek to conceal the effects of our abandonment. To this extent, the revolution the gift inaugurates is less institutional than philosophical. Its principal endeavour is less to foment revolution than to account for its failure, by reformulating politics as something prior to, and which does not simply supervene on, ontology; something that moreover renders ontology –the *logos* of being present – impossible. In this sense, a politics of the gift is both more and less than revolutionary: more, in that it breaks free from the circle, the economy of a founding figure of truth that would see revolution return to its point of origin; and simultaneously less, in that it discloses the impossibility of beginning again, of refounding the political on the primordial truth of an essential subject or ground.

Understood in these terms, there is politics because there can be no revolution. The site of the political is that of the gap between eternal return and its completion, of the minimal difference that ungrounds the law of the *oikos*, preventing the closure of the circuit of identity. This impossibility is what condemns politics to sacrifice, but equally forces philosophy to think the gift that is sacrificed in the moment of its receipt. The respective sites of philosophy and politics are perhaps the same after all, kept apart only perspectivally, by the minimal difference between virtual and actual, aneconomy and economy, the gift and its sacrifice. Whether by denying it or actively affirming it, politics deals with the eternal return that philosophy would have us envisage. Likewise, philosophy takes up the task of thinking 'das grösste Schwergewicht', the greatest weight, of the impossible futures to which politics attempts to respond. The one does not simply take place by default, through the failure of the other, but rather exists as its inverse face.

In decentring the political, in shifting the site of politics from the subject to the event, there is a risk that we will lose sight of the politics of scarcity and human need. Thinkers of a gift that cannot be conflated with recognition, hence with charity, have faced the inevitable accusation of privileging an aristocratic affirmation of the deficiency of human experience, a nihilistic preference for that which exceeds it, rather than an active engagement with the politics of this world. The privileging of the singularity and difference of the event means that the politics of the *anthropos* – of basic human equality and the potential forms of political subjectivity – is neglected. A newer generation of French philosophers are beginning to build a consensus over this point, criticising the excess of poststructuralism for making politics contingent on a philosophical thinking of difference that cannot be translated into practice. Badiou's concerns that Deleuze aristocratically recuperates suffering through a beatific, theodic thinking of the event are mirrored by Jacques Rancière, who has recently redrawn attention to the overtly theocratic language of Derrida's work on politics. According to Rancière, Derrida's 'political concepts are theological concepts that have hardly been secularized', and which, in the absence of any notion of the political subject, effectively just shift sovereignty away from God and on to the event (gift, democracy-to-come ...) (Rancière 2009: 279). What with his language of sacrifice and key concept of grace, the same criticism might be levelled at Badiou. But rather than work toward a politics freed from the restricted economy of Anthropology, a politics that begins with the abandonment of the subject, Rancière has joined with Badiou in emphasising that politics has a distinct logic of its own, which is that of the creation of political subjectivity (Rancière 2001/2004: 225–6). A similar focus is attributable to Bernard Stiegler, the philosopher of technology and desire, for whom 'politics is above all the motivation and organisation of a process of psychic and collective individuation': that is, the creation of individual and collective subjectivities, through the construction of symbolic exchange (Stiegler 2004: 36). Suspicious of the poststructuralist tendency to idealise and romanticise the event, Stiegler has sought to elaborate a politics that reinforces the symbolic order of subjectivity against its erosion by capitalist marketing technologies, which – recalling what Žižek describes as the eternal return of the 'real of capital' – he argues short-circuit the sublimation of libidinal drives into desiring subjectivity. Testifying to the anthropologist's enduring influence, he turns to Mauss's gift economy to develop the bases of an aneconomic 'economy of contribution' (Stiegler 2004: 35; Stiegler 2005: 55, 66).

The work of this new generation is by no means a regression to Anthropology, but a continuation of the movement away from the uncritical acceptance of the metaphysics of the subject. By shifting emphasis away from a philosophisation of the event and back on to the potential for political action, they remain faithful to the project of bringing an end to the philosophical overdetermination of the political. The shift also points to a renewal of revolutionary impetus and a reluctance to see Marxism reduced to what is perceived as the hollowed-out, impotent spectres of Derrida, or the idealism of Deleuze and Guattari. An appreciation of these new directions need not, however, entail fully conceding to the claims of antihumanism and insufficient radicality directed against Deleuze, Derrida *et al.* One might argue that to disclose the absence of ontological privilege is already to disclose the fragility, the contingency of the human, and thereby to reassert the need for its renewal, by reconceiving its relation to a capitalism that cannot be surpassed. This is by no means simply to become an apologist for capitalism . . .

*   *   *

On one of his final visits to the English-speaking world, during August 1999, local journalists in Sydney pressed Jacques Derrida to become involved in the debates surrounding the 'stolen generation' of Aborigines, the fate of the once predominant indigenous tribes of Australia. The request, to which the philosopher responded only hesitatingly, brought him head-to-head with the legacy of one of the cultures of the archaic gift economy from which the modern anthropological problematic of the gift originates. Asked whether the Australian government should offer an apology for its part in the historical persecution of the island's autochthonous peoples, for the politics that saw Aborigine and mixed-race children removed from their parents and effectively bastardised, orphaned, resettled away from the influences of native culture, Derrida gives the following comment (in English):

> If you insist, I will say yes, the government should apologise on behalf of the Australian people ... it is not a matter of forgiveness, we cannot ask forgiveness from a people who are dead or not here, but we know that an apology

is also a promise for the future, a promise to change the situation. (Derrida 2001b: 47)

If an apology is desirable, it is not because it stands as the condition of possibility of forgiveness, Derrida argues. He rejects the presupposition that forgiveness should be offered only as an expiative countergift, in response to a previous offering. Nor is it desirable as an assumption of fault, an admission of guilt, since this too would be to commit to distinctly economic concepts of repayable debt and individualisable responsibility. Nor, by implication, does it entail becoming complicit in the maintenance and perpetuation of a certain order, since on the contrary, an apology creates a rupture with the past. Conceived *aneconomically*, to apologise is rather to assume the responsibility of opening oneself to a future not governed by the awaiting of a messiah, the return of a ground or destiny. It is thus to recognise that there is no big Other, no sublimely redemptive gift or Messiah, no pure inheritance from which to derive a definitive response to the political; no higher agency that could supersede political struggle. This is less to legitimate what is than to offer hospitality to its illegitimacy, to affirm that, abandoned to politics, we are all orphans, bastards, shot through with an indiscernible, undecidable alterity whose precise delimitations can never be given.

Understood as the event of existence in all its multiplicity and unpredictability, the gift keeps on giving in excess of our ability to recognise it. To receive it we must sacrifice the subject in a paradoxical gesture that will also inevitably sacrifice the event, the gift itself, by resubmitting it to representation and, in so doing, reinscribing it in an economy of subjectivity. The gift accordingly remains impossible, with this impossibility serving as the condition of possibility of, the cause of our abandonment to, the political. Rather than Bismarck's famous art of the possible (*die Kunst des Möglichen*), politics occurs as the site and praxis of the impossible, to which we are eternally called upon to return, compelled to respond without simply giving up. We cannot be, and yet are condemned to be, subjects, subject to tension between the economic and the aneconomic. The politics of the gift, of the *à-venir* in which what is at stake dissolves and is reborn, otherwise, opens up in the space of this double bind.

Bibliography

Agamben, Giorgio (1991) *Language and Death: The Place of Negativity*, trans. Karen E. Pinkus and Michael Hardt. Minneapolis, MN: Minnesota University Press.

—, (1998) *Homo Sacer: Sovereign Power and Bare Life*, trans. Daniel Heller-Roazen. Stanford, CA: Stanford University Press.

—, (1999) *Potentialities: Collected Essays in Philosophy*, ed. and trans. Daniel Heller-Roazen. Stanford, CA: Stanford University Press.

Ahmad, Aijaz (1999) 'Reconciling Derrida: *Specters of Marx* and Deconstructive Politics', in Michael Sprinker, ed., *Ghostly Demarcations: A Symposium on Jacques Derrida's* Spectres of Marx. London: Verso.

Alliez, Éric (1998) *Gilles Deleuze: une vie philosophique*. Le Plessis–Robinson: Institut Sythélabo.

Ansell-Pearson, Keith (1999) *Germinal Life: The Difference and Repetition of Deleuze*. London: Routledge.

—, (1997a) 'Deleuze Outside/Outside Deleuze: On the Difference Engineer', editor's introduction, in Ansell-Pearson, ed., *Deleuze and Philosophy: The Difference Engineer*. London: Routledge.

—, (1997b) *Viroid Life: The Difference and Repetition of Deleuze*. London: Routledge.

—, (2002) *Philosophy and the Adventure of the Virtual Bergson and the Time of Life*. London: Routledge.

—, (2004) 'Demanding Deleuze', *Radical Philosophy*, 126, pp. 33–8.

Badiou, Alain (1985) *Peut-on penser la politique?* Paris: Seuil.

—, (1998) *Briefings on Existence: A Short Treatise on Transitory Ontology*, trans. Norman Madarasz. Albany, NY: SUNY; *Court Traité d'ontologie transitoire* (Paris: Seuil, 1998).

—, (1999) *Manifesto for Philosophy*, ed. and trans. Norman Madarasz. Albany, NY: SUNY; *Manifeste pour la philosophie* (Paris: Seuil, 1989).

—, (2000) *Deleuze: The Clamor of Being*, trans. Louise Burchill. Minneapolis, MN: Minnesota University Press; *Deleuze, la clameur de l'être* (Paris: Hachette, 1997).

—, (2001) *Ethics: An Essay on the Understanding of Evil*, trans. Peter

Hallward. London: Verso; *L'Éthique: essai sur la conscience du mal* (Caen: Nous, 2003).

—, (2003) *Saint Paul: The Foundation of Universalism*, trans. Ray Brassier. Stanford, CA: Stanford University Press; *Saint Paul: La Fondation de l'universalisme* (Paris: Presses Universitaires de France, 1997).

—, (2005a) *Metapolitics*, trans. Jason Barker. London: Verso; *Abrégé de métapolitique* (Paris: Seuil, 1998).

—, (2005b) 'The Adventures of French Philosophy', trans. Peter Hallward, *New Left Review*, 35, September–October. www.newleftreview.org/?view=2580; 'Panorama de la philosophie française contemporaine', in *Multitudes* (2004). http://multitudes.samizdat.net/Panorama-de-la-philosophie.htm, accessed 14 March 2007.

—, (2006) *Theoretical Writings*, trans. Ray Brassier and Alberto Toscano. London: Continuum; 'Un, multiple, multiplicité(s)', in *Multitudes* (2000). http://multitudes.samizdat.net/un-multiple-multiplicite-s.html, accessed 21 December 2006.

—, (2008a) *Conditions*, trans. Steven Corcoran. London: Continuum; *Conditions* (Paris: Seuil, 1992).

—, (2008b) *The Century*, trans. Alberto Toscano. Cambridge: Polity; *Le Siècle* (Paris: Seuil, 2005).

Badiou, Alain and Peter Hallward (1998) 'Politics and Philosophy', *Angelaki*, 3:3, pp. 113–33.

Bambach, Charles (2003) *Heidegger's Roots: Nietzsche, National Socialism and the Greeks*. Ithaca, NY: Cornell University Press.

Bataille, Georges (1976) *œuvres complètes*, 12 vols. Paris: Gallimard.

—, (1985) *Visions of Excess: Selected Writings 1927–1939*, ed. Alan Stoekl, trans. Alan Stoekl, Carl R. Lovitt and Donald M. Leslie, Jr. Minneapolis, MN: University of Minnesota Press.

—, (1988) *Inner Experience*, trans. Leslie Anne Boldt. Albany, NY: SUNY Press.

—, (1989a) *The Accursed Share: An Essay on General Economy, vol. 1: Consumption*, trans. Robert Hurley. New York: Zone.

—, (1989b) *Theory of Religion*, trans. Robert Hurley. New York: Zone.

—, (1991) *The Accursed Share: An Essay on General Economy, vols 2 and 3: The History of Eroticism and Sovereignty*, trans. Robert Hurley. New York: Zone.

Baudrillard, Jean (1993) *Symbolic Exchange and Death*, trans. Mike Gane. London: Sage; *L'Échange symbolique et la mort* (Paris: Gallimard, 1976).

Baugh, Bruce (2003) *French Hegel: From Surrealism to Postmodernism*. London: Routledge.

Bearn, Gordon F. C. (2003) 'Differentiating Derrida and Deleuze', in Christopher Norris and David Roden, eds, *Jacques Derrida*, vol. 1. London: Sage.

Beistegui, Miguel de (1998) *Heidegger and the Political: Dystopias*. London: Routledge.

—, (1997) 'Sacrifice Revisited', in Darren Sheppard, Simon Sparks and Colin Thomas, eds, *On Jean-Luc Nancy: The Sense of Philosophy*. London: Routledge.

—, (2003) *Thinking with Heidegger: Displacements*. Bloomington, IN: Indiana University Press.

—, (2004) *Truth and Genesis: Philosophy as Differential Ontology*. Bloomington, IN: Indiana University Press.

Benveniste, Émile (1969) *Le Vocabulaire des institutions indo-européennes*. Paris: Minuit.

Bernold, André and Richard Pinhas (2005) *Deleuze épars: approches et portraits*. Paris: Harmann.

Blanchot, Maurice (1982) *The Space of Literature*, trans. Ann Smock. Lincoln, NB: University of Nebraska Press; *L'Espace littéraire* (Paris: Gallimard, 1955).

—, (1988) *The Unavowable Community*, trans. Pierre Joris. Barrytown, NY: Station Hill; *La Communauté inavouable* (Paris: Minuit, 1983).

Boothby, Richard (2001) *Freud as Philosopher: Metapsychology After Lacan*. London: Routledge.

Borch-Jacobsen, Mikkel (1991) *Lacan: The Absolute Master*, trans. Douglas Brick. Stanford, CA: Stanford University Press; *Lacan: Le Maître absolu* (Paris: Flammarion, 2003).

Botting, Fred and Scott Wilson (2001) *Bataille*. Basingstoke: Palgrave.

Boundas, Constantin V. (2001) 'Exchange, Gift, and Theft', in *Angelaki*, 6.2, pp. 101–12.

—, ed. (2006) *Deleuze and Philosophy*. Edinburgh: Edinburgh University Press.

Boundas, Constantin V. and Dorothea Olkowski, eds (1994) *Gilles Deleuze and the Theatre of Philosophy*. London: Routledge.

Bourdieu, Pierre (1990) *The Logic of Practice*, trans. Richard Nice. Stanford, CA: Stanford University Press; *Le Sens pratique* (Paris: Minuit, 1980).

—, (1998) *Practical Reason*. Stanford, CA: Stanford University Press; *Raisons pratiques: Sur la théorie de l'action* (Paris: Seuil, 1994).

Bourg, Julian (1997) *After the Deluge: New Perspectives on the Intellectual and Cultural History of Postwar France*. Lanham, MD: Lexington.

Braidotti, Rosi (2006) *Transpositions: On Nomadic Ethics*. Cambridge: Polity.

Butler, Judith (1999) *Subjects of Desire: Hegelian Reflections on Twentieth Century France* (expanded 2nd edn). New York: Columbia University Press.

—, (2000) *Antigone's Claim: Kinship Between Life and Death*. New York: Columbia University Press.

Butler, Judith, Ernest Laclau and Slavoj Žižek (2000) *Contingency, Hegemony, Universality: Contemporary Dialogues on the Left*. London: Verso.

Callinicos, Alex (2006) *The Resources of Critique*. Cambridge: Polity.

Campbell, David and Michael Dillon, eds (1993) *The Political Subject of Violence*. Manchester: Manchester University Press.

Caputo, John D. and Michael J. Scanlon (1999) *God, the Gift, and Postmodernism.* Bloomington, IN: Indiana University Press.

Caygill, Howard (2002) *Levinas and the Political.* London: Routledge.

Cheah, Pheng and Suzanne Guerlac, eds (2009) *Derrida and the Time of the Political.* Durham, NC: Duke University Press.

Cixous, Hélène (1996) 'Sorties', in Hélène Cixous and Cathérine Clément, *The Newly Born Woman*, trans. Betsy Wing. London: I. B. Tauris; *Le Rire de la Méduse et autres ironies* (Paris: Galilée, 2010).

Colebrook, Claire (2002) *Understanding Gilles Deleuze.* Crows Nest: Allen & Unwin.

—, (2006) *Deleuze: A Guide for the Perplexed.* London: Continuum.

Colombat, Pierre-André (1996) 'November 4, 1995: Deleuze's Death as an Event', *Man and World*, 29, pp. 234–49.

Comay, Rebecca and John McCumber, eds (1999) *Endings: Questions of Memory in Hegel and Heidegger.* Evanston, IL: Northwestern University Press.

Critchley, Simon (1993) 'Re-tracing the political: politics and community in the work of Philippe Lacoue-Labarthe and Jean-Luc Nancy', in David Campbell and Michael Dillon, eds, *The Political Subject of Violence.* Manchester: Manchester University Press.

—, (1999a) *The Ethics of Deconstruction: Levinas and Derrida* (2nd edn). Edinburgh: Edinburgh University Press.

—, (1999b) *Ethics-Politics-Subjectivity: Essays on Derrida, Levinas and Contemporary French Thought.* London: Verso.

—, (2007) *Infinitely Demanding: Ethics of Commitment, Politics of Resistance.* London: Verso.

Dean, Carolyn J. (1986) 'Law and Sacrifice: Bataille, Lacan and the Critique of the Subject', *Representations*, 13, pp. 42–62.

—, (1992) *The Self and its Pleasures: Bataille, Lacan and the History of the Decentred Subject.* Ithaca, NY: Cornell University Press.

DeLanda, Manuel (2002) *Intensive Science and Virtual Philosophy.* London: Continuum.

—, (2006) *A New Philosophy of Society: Assemblage Theory and Social Complexity.* London: Continuum.

Deleuze, Gilles (1986) *Cinema I: The Movement–Image,* trans. Hugh Tomlinson and Barbara Habberjam. Minneapolis, MN: University of Minnesota Press; *Cinéma I: L'Image–mouvement* (Paris: Minuit, 1983).

—, (1990) *The Logic of Sense*, ed. Constantin V. Boundas, trans. Mark Lester and Charles Stivale. London: Continuum; *Logique du sens* (Paris: Minuit, 1969).

—, (1995) *Negotiations, 1972–1990,* trans. Martin Joughin. New York: Columbia University Press; *Pourparlers, 1972–1990* (Paris: Minuit, 1990).

—, (1998) *Essays Critical and Clinical,* trans. Daniel W. Smith and Michael A. Greco. London: Verso; *Critique et clinique* (Paris: Minuit, 1993).

—, (1999) *Foucault*, trans. and ed. Seán Hand. London: Athlone; *Foucault* (Paris: Minuit, 1986).

—, (2003) *Nietzsche and Philosophy*, trans. Hugh Tomlinson. London: Continuum; *Nietzsche et la philosophie* (Paris: Presses Universitaires de France/Quadrige, 1962).

—, (2004) *Difference and Repetition*, trans. Paul Patton. London: Continuum; *Différence et répétition* (Paris: Presses Universitaires de France, 1968).

—, (2007) *Two Regimes of Madness: Texts and Interviews (1975–95)* (revised edn), trans. Ames Hodges and Mike Taormina. New York: Semiotext(e)/ Foreign Agents; *Deux régimes de fous et autres textes (1975–95)*, ed. David Lapoujade (Paris: Minuit, 2007).

Deleuze, Gilles and Félix Guattari (1971) 'La Synthèse disjonctive', *L'Arc*, 43: *Klossowski*, pp. 54–62.

—, (1988) *A Thousand Plateaus: Capitalism and Schizophrenia*, trans. Brian Massumi. London: Athlone; *Mille Plateaux: Capitalisme et schizophrénie II* (Paris: Minuit, 1980).

—, (1993) *What is Philosophy?*, trans. Graham Burchell and Hugh Tomlinson. London: Verso; *Qu'est-ce que la philosophie?* (Paris: Minuit, 1991).

—, (2004) *Anti-Oedipus: Capitalism and Schizophrenia*, trans. Robert Hurley, Mark Seem and Helen R. Lane. London: Continuum; *L'Anti-œdipe: Capitalisme et schizophrénie I* (Paris: Minuit, 1972).

Deleuze, Gilles and Claire Parnet (2007) *Dialogues II*, trans. Barbara Haberjam and Hugh Tomlinson. New York: Columbia University Press; *Dialogues* (Paris: Flammarion, 1977/1999).

Derrida, Jacques (1978) *Writing and Difference*, trans. Alan Bass. London: Routledge; *L'écriture et la différence* (Paris: Seuil, 1967).

—, (1979) 'Living On/Border Lines', trans. James Hulbert, in Harold Bloom *et al.*, *Deconstruction and Criticism*. London: Continuum; 'Survivre', in *Parages* (Paris: Galilée, 1986).

—, (1982) *Margins of Philosophy*, trans. Alan Bass. Chicago, IL: Chicago University Press; *Marges – de la philosophie* (Paris: Minuit, 1972).

—, (1986) *Glas*, trans. John P. Leavey, Jr and Richard Rand; *Glas* (Paris: Denoël/Gonthier, 1981).

—, (1987) *The Post-Card: From Socrates to Freud and Beyond*, trans. Alan Bass. Chicago, IL: University of Chicago Press; *La Carte postale: de Socrate à Freud et au-delà* (Paris: Flammarion, 1980).

—, (1988) *Limited Inc.*, trans. Alan Bass, Jeffrey Mehlman and Samuel Weber. Evanston, IL: Northwestern University Press; *Limited Inc.* (Paris: Galilée, 1990).

—, (1989) *Of Spirit: Heidegger and the Question*, trans. Geoffrey Bennington and Rachel Bowlby. Chicago, IL: Chicago University Press; *De l'Esprit: Heidegger et la question* (Paris: Galilée, 1987).

—, (1992a) *Given Time: Counterfeit Money*, trans. Peggy Kamuf. Chicago, IL: University of Chicago Press; *Donner le temps: la fausse monnaie* (Paris: Galilée, 1991).

—, (1992b) *Points . . . Interviews, 1974–1994*, ed. Elisabeth Weber, trans. Peggy Kamuf *et al.* Stanford, CA: Stanford University Press; *Points de suspension: Entretiens*, ed. Elisabeth Weber (Paris: Galilée, 1992).

—, (1994) *Specters of Marx: The State of Debt, the Work of Mourning and the New International*, trans. Peggy Kamuf. London: Routledge; *Spectres de Marx* (Paris: Galilée, 1993).

—, (1995) *The Gift of Death*, trans. David Wills. Chicago, IL: University of Chicago Press; *Donner la mort* (Paris: Galilée, 1999).

—, (1997) *Politics of Friendship*, trans. George Collins. London: Verso; *Politiques de l'amitié*, suivi de 'L'Oreille de Heidegger' (Paris: Galilée, 1994).

—, (1998) 'Faith and Knowledge: the Two Sources of "Religion" at the Limits of Reason Alone', trans. Samuel Weber, in *Religion*, ed. Jacques Derrida and Gianni Vattimo. Stanford, CA: Stanford University Press; *Foi et savoir*, suivi de 'Le Siècle et le pardon' (Paris: Seuil, 2000).

—, (1999a) *Adieu to Emmanuel Levinas*, trans. Pascale-Anne Brault and Michael Naas. Stanford, CA: Stanford University Press; *Adieu à Emmanuel Levinas* (Paris: Galilée).

—, (1999b) 'Marx and Sons', in Michael Sprinker, ed., *Ghostly Demarcations: A Symposium on Jacques Derrida's Specters of Marx*. London: Verso; *Marx and Sons*. Paris: Presses Universitaires de France/Galilée.

—, (2001a) 'I'm going to have to wander all alone now', trans. Leonard Lawler, in *The Work of Mourning*, ed. Pascale-Anne Brault and Michael Naas. Chicago, IL: Chicago University Press; 'Il me faudra errer tout seul', in *Chaque fois unique, la fin du monde*, ed. Pascale-Anne Brault et Michel Naas (Paris: Galilée).

—, (2001b) *Deconstruction Engaged: The Sydney Seminars*, ed. Paul Patton and Terry Smith. Sydney: Power Institute.

—, (2002) 'Declarations of Independence', in *Negotiations: Interviews and Interventions, 1971–2001*, ed. and trans. Elizabeth Rottenberg. Stanford, CA: Stanford University Press; 'Déclarations d'indépendance', in *Otobiographies: L'Enseignement de Nietzsche et la politique du nom propre* (Paris: Galilée, 1984).

—, (2004) 'La Bête et le souverain', in Marie-Louise Mallet, ed., *La Démocratie-à-venir: Autour de Jacques Derrida*. Paris: Galilée.

—, (2005a) *On Touching – Jean-Luc Nancy*, trans. Christine Irizarry. Stanford, CA: Stanford University Press; *Le Toucher, Jean-Luc Nancy* (Paris: Galilée, 2000).

—, (2005b) *Rogues: Two Essays on Reason*, trans. Pascale-Anne Brault and Michael Naas. Stanford, CA: Stanford University Press; *Voyous* (Paris: Galilée, 2003).

—, (2007) *Psyche: Inventions of the Other*, ed. and trans. Peggy Kamuf and Elizabeth Rottenberg. Stanford, CA: Stanford University Press; *Psychè: Inventions de l'autre* (Paris: Galilée, 1987).

Derrida, Jacques and Anne Dufourmantelle (2000) *Of Hospitality*, trans.

Rachel Bowlby. Stanford, CA: Stanford University Press; *De L'Hospitalité* (Paris: Calmann-Lévy, 1997).

Derrida, Jacques and Jean-Luc Marion (1999) 'On the Gift: A Discussion between Jacques Derrida and Jean-Luc Marion', in John D. Caputo and Michael J. Scanlon, eds. *God, the Gift, and Postmodernism*. Bloomington, IN: Indiana University Press.

Derrida, Jacques and Jean-Luc Nancy (2004) 'Responsabilité – du sens à venir', in Francis Guibal and Jean-Clet Martin, eds. *Sens en tous sens: Autour des travaux de Jean-Luc Nancy*. Paris: Galilée.

Derrida, Jacques, Alexis Nouss and Gad Soussana (2001) *Dire l'événement, est-ce possible?* Paris: L'Harmattan.

Derrida, Jacques and Elisabeth Roudinesco (2004) *For What Tomorrow . . .*, trans. Jeff Fort. Stanford, CA: Stanford University Press; *De quoi demain . . .* (Paris: Galilée, 2000).

Derrida, Jacques and Bernard Stiegler (2002) *Echographies of Television: Filmed Interviews*, trans Jennifer Bajorek. Cambridge: Polity; *Échographies de la télévision* (Paris: Galilée/Institut de l'audiovisuel, 2002).

Derrida, Jacques and Gianni Vattimo, eds (1998) *Religion*. Stanford, CA: Stanford University Press.

Didi-Huberman, Georges (2006) *Ex-voto: Image, organe, temps*. Paris: Fayard.

Diprose, Rosalyn (2002) *Corporeal Generosity: On Giving with Nietzsche, Merleau-Ponty and Levinas*. New York: SUNY Press.

Dosse, François (1997) *The History of Structuralism, vol. 1: The Rising Sign*, trans. Deborah Glassman. Minneapolis, MN: University of Minnesota Press; *Histoire du structuralisme, tome 1: Le Champ du signe, 1945–1966* (Paris: La Découverte, 1991).

Düttmann, Alexander Garcia (2002) *The Memory of Thought: An Essay on Heidegger and Adorno*. London: Continuum; *Das Gedächtnis des Denkens: Versuch über Heidegger und Adorno* (Frankfurt: Suhrkamp, 1991).

Eagleton, Terry (1999) 'Marxism without Marxism', in Michael Sprinker, ed., *Ghostly Demarcations: A Symposium on Jacques Derrida's* Specters of Marx. London: Verso.

Farias, Victor (1987) *Heidegger et le nazisme*, Lagrasse: Verdier.

Ferris, David S. (1996) *Walter Benjamin: Theoretical Questions*. Stanford, CA: Stanford University Press.

Firth, R. (1959) *Economics of the New Zealand Maoris*. Wellington: R. E. Owen.

Forrester, John (1990) *The Seductions of Psychoanalysis: Freud, Lacan and Derrida*. Cambridge: Cambridge University Press.

—, (1997) *Truth Games: Lies, Money and Psychoanalysis*. Cambridge, MA: Harvard University Press.

Foucault, Michel (1970) *The Order of Things: An Archaeology of the Human Sciences*, trans. Alan Sheridan. New York: Pantheon; *Les Mots et les choses* (Paris: Gallimard, 1966).

—, (1994) 'Non au sexe roi', in *Dits et écrits 1954–1988, vol. III: 1976–1979*. Paris: Gallimard.

Fournier, Marcel (1990) 'Marcel Mauss et Heidegger: une lettre inédite de Marcel Mauss à Roger Caillois du 22 juin 1938', *Actes de la recherche en sciences sociales*, 84, p. 87.

—, (2006) *Marcel Mauss: A Biography*, trans. Jane Marie Todd. Princeton, NJ: Princeton University Press; *Marcel Mauss* (Paris: Fayard, 1994).

Fraser, Nancy (1984) 'The French Derrideans: Politicizing Deconstruction or Deconstructing Politics?', *New German Critique*, 33, pp. 127–54.

Freud, Sigmund (2001a) *The Standard Edition of the Complete Psychological Works of Sigmund Freud, vol. XIII (1913–1914) Totem and Taboo and Other Works*, ed. and trans. James Strachey (London: Vintage-Hogarth, 2001); *Gesammelte Werke, Neunter Band: Totem und Tabu* (London: Imago, 1940).

—, (2001b) 'On Transformations of Instinct as Exemplified in Anal Erotism', in *The Standard Edition of the Complete Psychological Works of Sigmund Freud, vol. XVII (1917–1919) An Infantile Neurosis and Other Works*, ed. and trans. James Strachey (London: Vintage-Hogarth, 2001); 'Über Triebumsetzung ins besondere der Analerotik', in *Gesammelte Werke Zehnter Band: Werke aus den Jahren 1913–17* (London: Imago, 1946).

Fried, Gregory (2000) *Heidegger's Polemos: From Being to Politics*. London: Yale University Press.

Fukuyama, Francis (1992) *The End of History and the Last Man*. Harmondsworth: Penguin.

Gasché, Rodolphe (1997) 'Heliocentric exchange', in Alan D. Schrift, ed., *The Logic of the Gift: Toward an Ethic of Generosity*. New York: Routledge, pp. 100–17; 'L'Échange héliocentrique', *L'Arc*, 42: *Marcel Mauss* (1972), pp. 70–84.

Gill, Carolyn Bailey, ed. (1995) *Bataille: Writing the Sacred*. London: Routledge.

Girard, René (1977) *Violence and the Sacred*, trans. Patrick Gregor. Baltimore, MD: Johns Hopkins University Press; *La Violence et le sacré* (Paris: Grasset, 1972).

—, (1978) 'Delirium as System', in *'To double business bound': Essays on Literature, Mimesis and Anthropology*. Baltimore, MD: Johns Hopkins University Press.

Godbout, Jacques and Alain Caillé (1998) *The World of the Gift*, trans. Donald Winkler. Montreal: McGill-Queen's University Press; *L'Esprit du don*. Paris: La Découverte, 1992.

Godelier, Maurice (1999) *The Enigma of the Gift*, trans. Nora Scott. Cambridge: Polity; *L'Énigme du don* (Paris: Flammarion, 1996).

Guenther, Lisa (2006) *The Gift of the Other: Levinas and the Politics of Reproduction*. New York: SUNY Press.

Guibal, Francis (2004) 'Sans retour et sans recours', in Francis Guibal and

Jean-Clet Martin, eds. *Sens en tous sens: Autour des travaux de Jean-Luc Nancy*. Paris: Galilée.

Guibal, Francis and Jean-Clet Martin (2004) *Sens en tous sens: Autour des travaux de Jean-Luc Nancy*. Paris: Galilée.

Gutting, Gary (2001) *French Philosophy in the Twentieth Century*. Cambridge: Cambridge University Press.

Habermas, Jürgen (1987) *The Philosophical Discourse of Modernity*, trans. Frederick Lawrence. Cambridge: Polity; *Der philosophische Diskurs der Moderne: Zwölfe Vorlesungen* (Frankfurt: Suhrkamp: 1985).

Hallward, Peter (2003) *Badiou: A Subject to Truth*. Minneapolis, MN: University of Minnesota Press.

—, (2005) 'The Politics of Prescription', *South Atlantic Quarterly*, 104.4, pp. 771–91.

—, (2006a) *Out of this World: Deleuze and the Philosophy of Creation*. London: Verso.

—, (2006b) 'Retreatment', *Radical Philosophy*, 139, pp. 53–5.

Hanisch, Carol (1969) 'The Personal is Political', available online at: http://www.carolhanisch.org/CHwritings/PIP.html, accessed 2 August 2010.

Hayek, Friedrich A. von (1944) *The Road to Serfdom*. London: Routledge.

—, (1949) 'Individualism: True and False', in *Individualism* and *Economic Order*. London: Routledge & Kegan Paul.

Hegel, G. W. F. (1969–86) *Werke in Zwanzig Bänden*. Frankfurt: Suhrkamp.

—, (1975) *Lectures on the Philosophy of World History: Introduction*, trans. H. B. Nisbet. Cambridge: Cambridge University Press.

—, (1977) *The Phenomenology of Spirit*, trans. A. V. Miller. Oxford: Oxford University Press.

—, (1991) *Elements of the Philosophy of Right*, ed. Allen W. Wood, trans. H. B. Nisbet. Cambridge: Cambridge University Press.

—, (1998) *The Hegel Reader*, ed. Stephen Houlgate. Oxford: Blackwell.

Heidegger, Martin (1954) *Vorträge und aufsätze*. Pfullingen: Neske.

—, (1962) *Being and Time*, trans. John Macquarie and Edward Robinson. Oxford: Blackwell.

—, (1968) *What is Called Thinking*, trans. Fred. D. Wieck and J. Glenn Gray. New York: Harper & Row.

—, (1975–) *Gesamtausgabe*, 102 vols. Frankfurt: Vittorio Klostermann.

—, (1982) *Nietzsche, vols III and IV: The Will to Power as Metaphysics and as Freedom, Nihilism*, ed. David Farrell Krell, trans. David Farrell Krell, Joan Stambaugh and Frank A. Capuzzi. San Francisco, CA: Harper Collins.

—, (1993a) 'Overcoming Metaphysics', in Richard Wolin, ed., *The Heidegger Controversy: A Critical Reader*, trans. Joan Stambaugh. Cambridge, MA: MIT Press.

—, (1993b) ' "Only a God Can Save Us": *Der Spiegel*'s Interview with Martin Heidegger', in Richard Wolin, ed., *The Heidegger Controversy: A Critical Reader*. Cambridge, MA: MIT Press; 'Nur noch ein Gott kann uns retten', *Der Spiegel*, 30(23), 1976, pp. 193–219.

—, (1993c) *Basic Writings* (revised and expanded edn), ed. David Farrell Krell. London: Routledge.

—, (1996) *Hölderlin's Hymn 'The Ister'*, trans. Will McNeill and Julia Davis. Bloomington, IN: Indiana University Press.

—, (1998) 'Postscript to *What is Metaphysics?*', in *Pathmarks*, trans. and ed. William McNeill. Cambridge: Cambridge University Press.

—, (2000) *Introduction to Metaphysics*, trans. Gregory Fried and Richard Polt. New Haven, CT: Yale University Press.

—, (2002) *On Time and Being*, trans. Joan Stambaugh. Chicago, IL: Chicago University Press; *Zur Sache des Denkens* (Tübingen: Niemeyer, 1969).

Hénaff, Marcel (2002) *Le Prix de la vérité: le don, l'argent, la philosophie*. Paris: Seuil.

—, (2009) 'The Aporia of Pure Giving and the Aim of Reciprocity: On Derrida's *Given Time*', trans. Jean-Louis Morhange, in *Derrida and the Time of the Political*, ed. Pheng Cheah and Suzanne Guerlac. Durham, NC: Duke University Press, pp. 215–34.

Hill, Leslie (2001) *Bataille, Blanchot, Klossowski: Writing at the Limit*. Oxford: Oxford University Press.

Hobbes, Thomas (1996) *Leviathan* (revised student edn), ed. Richard Tuck. Cambridge: Cambridge University Press.

Hollier, Denis, ed. (1988) *The College of Sociology (1937–39)*, trans. Betsy Wing; *Le Collège de sociologie* (Paris: Gallimard, 1976).

Hubert, Henri and Marcel Mauss (1981) *Sacrifice: Its Nature and Function*, trans. W. D. Halls. Chicago, IL: University of Chicago Press; 'Essai sur la nature et la fonction du sacrifice', in *Marcel Mauss, œuvres, vol. 1: Les Fonctions sociales du sacré* (Paris: Minuit, 1968).

Hume, David (1975) *Enquiries Concerning Human Understanding and Concerning The Principles of Morals*. Oxford: Oxford University Press.

Husserl, Edmund (1960) *Cartesian Meditations: An Introduction to Phenomenology*, trans. Dorion Cairns. The Hague: Martinus Nijhoff; *Gesammelte Werke, vol. 1: Cartesianische Meditationen und Päriser Vorträge* (The Hague: Martinus Nijhoff, 1963).

Hussey, Andrew, ed. (2006) *The Beast at Heaven's Gate: Georges Bataille and the Art of Transgression*. Amsterdam: Rodopi.

Hutchens, B. C. (2005) *Jean-Luc Nancy and the Future of Philosophy*. Chesham: Acumen.

Hyde, Lewis (1983) *The Gift: Imagination and the Erotic Life of Property*. New York: Random House.

Irigaray, Luce (1985) *This Sex Which Is Not One*, trans. Catherine Porter. Ithaca, NY: Cornell University Press; *Ce sexe qui n'est pas un* (Paris: Minuit, 1977).

Jakobson, Roman (1971) 'Signe zéro', in *Selected Writings II: Word and Language*. The Hague: Mouton.

James, Ian (2000) *Pierre Klossowski: The Persistence of a Name*. Oxford: Legenda.

—, (2002) 'The Persistence of the Subject: Jean-Luc Nancy', *Paragraph*, 25.1, pp. 125–41.

—, (2006a) *The Fragmentary Demand: An Introduction to the Philosophy of Jean-Luc Nancy*. Stanford, CA: Stanford University Press.

—, (2006b) 'From Recuperation to Simulacrum: Klossowski's Readings of Georges Bataille', Andrew Hussey, ed., *The Beast at Heaven's Gate: Georges Bataille and the Art of Transgression*. Amsterdam: Rodopi.

Jameson, Fredric (1991) *Postmodernism: Or, The Cultural Logic of Late Capitalism*. London: Verso.

—, (2006) 'Lacan and the Dialectic: A Fragment', in Slavoj Žižek, ed., *Lacan: The Silent Partners*. London: Verso.

Jarvis, Simon (1998) *Adorno: A Critical Introduction*. Cambridge: Polity.

—, (1999) 'The Gift in Theory', *Dionysus*, 17, pp. 201–22.

Johnson, Barbara (1988) 'The Frame of Reference: Poe, Lacan, Derrida', in John Muller and William Richardson, eds, *The Purloined Poe*. Baltimore, MD: Johns Hopkins University Press.

Johnson, Christopher (1993) *System and Writing in the Philosophy of Jacques Derrida*. Cambridge: Cambridge University Press.

—, (1996) 'Mauss's Gift: The Persistence of a Paradigm', *Modern and Contemporary France*, 4.3, pp. 307–17.

—, (2003) *Claude Lévi-Strauss: The Formative Years*. Cambridge: Cambridge University Press.

Joseph, Keith (1975) *Reversing the Trend: A Critical Reappraisal of Conservative Economic and Social Policies*. London: Barry Rose.

Kacem, Mehdi Belhaj (2004) *événement et répétition*. Auch: Tristram.

Kaufman, Eleanor (2001) *The Delirium of Praise: Bataille, Blanchot, Deleuze, Foucault, Klossowski*. Baltimore, MD: Johns Hopkins University Press.

Kay, Sarah (2003) *Žižek: A Critical Introduction*. Cambridge: Polity.

Keenan, Dennis King (2005) *The Question of Sacrifice*. Bloomington, IN: Indiana University Press.

Klossowski, Pierre (1963) *Un si funeste désir*. Paris: Gallimard.

—, (1965) *Les Lois de l'hospitalité*. Paris: Gallimard.

—, (1973) 'Circulus Vitiosus', in *Nietzsche aujourd'hui?*, vol. 1. Paris: UGE 10/18.

—, (1997) *La Monnaie vivante*. Paris: Rivages.

—, (2005) *Nietzsche and the Vicious Circle*, trans. Danile W. Smith. London: Continuum; *Nietzsche et le cercle vicieux* (Paris: Mercure de France, 1969).

Kojève, Alexandre (1969) *Introduction to the Reading of Hegel*, ed. Allan Bloom, trans. James H. Nichols, Jr. New York: Basic; *Introduction à la lecture de Hegel* (Paris: Gallimard, 1947).

Kurzweil, Edith (1996) *The Age of Structuralism* (2nd edn). New York: Columbia University Press.

Lacan, Jacques (1977) *The Four Fundamental Concepts of Psychoanalysis*, trans. Alan Sheridan. London: Karnac; *Le Séminaire, livre XI: Les Quatre*

Concepts fondamentaux de la psychanalyse (1963–4), ed. Jacques-Alain Miller (Paris: Seuil, 1990).

—, (1997) *The Seminar of Jacques Lacan, book III: The Psychoses*, trans. Russell Grigg. New York: W. W. Norton; *Le Séminaire, livre III: Les Psychoses (1955–6)*, ed. Jacques-Alain Miller (Paris: Seuil, 1981).

—, (1984) *Les Complexes familiaux dans la formation de l'individu*, Paris: Navarin.

—, (1994) *Le Séminaire, livre IV: La Relation d'objet (1956–7)*, ed. Jacques-Alain Miller. Paris: Seuil.

—, (1997) *The Seminar of Jacques Lacan, book VII: The Ethics of Psychoanalysis 1959–1960*, trans. Dennis Porter. New York: W. W. Norton; *Le Séminaire, livre VII: L'éthique de la psychanalyse (1959–60)*, ed. Jacques-Alain Miller (Paris: Seuil, 1986).

—, (2000) *The Seminar of Jacques Lacan, book XX: On Feminine Sexuality, the Limits of Love and Knowledge*, trans. Bruce Fink. New York: W. W. Norton; *Le Séminaire, livre XX: Encore! (1972–3)*, ed. Jacques-Alain Miller (Paris: Seuil, 1999).

—, (2001) *Le Séminaire, livre VIII: Le Transfert (1960–1)*, ed. Jacques-Alain Miller. Paris: Seuil.

—, (2004) *Le Séminaire, livre X: L'Angoisse (1962–3)*, ed. Jacques-Alain Miller (Paris: Seuil).

—, (2006) *écrits: The First Complete Edition in English*, trans. Bruce Fink, Héloïse Fink and Russell Grigg. New York: W. W. Norton; *écrits*, ed. Jacques-Alain Miller (Paris: Seuil, 1966).

—, (2007) *The Seminar of Jacques Lacan, book XVII: The Other Side of Psychoanalysis*, trans. Russell Grigg. New York: W. W. Norton; *Le Séminaire, livre XVII: L'Envers de la psychanalyse (1969–70)*, ed. Jacques-Alain Miller (Paris: Seuil, 1991).

Laclau, Ernesto (1996) *Emancipation(s)*, London: Verso.

Lacoue-Labarthe, Philippe (1989) *Typography: Mimesis, Philosophy, Politics*, ed. and trans. Christopher Fynsk. Stanford, CA: Stanford University Press; *L'Imitation des modernes* (Paris: Galilée, 1986).

—, (1990) *Heidegger, Art and Politics: The Fiction of the Political*, trans. Chris Turner. Oxford: Blackwell; *La Fiction du politique: Heidegger, l'art et la politique* (Paris: Christian Bourgeois, 1987).

Lacoue-Labarthe, Philippe and Jean-Luc Nancy (1981) *Rejouer le politique*. Paris: Galilée.

—, (1983) *Le Retrait du politique*. Paris: Galilée.

—, (1992) *The Title of the Letter: A Reading of Lacan*, trans. François Raffoul and David Pettigrew. Albany, NY: SUNY Press; *Le Titre de la lettre (Une lecture de Lacan)* (Paris: Galilée, 1973).

—, (1997) *Retreating the Political*, ed. Simon Sparks. London: Routledge.

Lefort, Claude (1978) *Les Formes de l'histoire: Essais d'anthropologie politique*. Paris: Gallimard.

Le Rider, Jacques (1999) *Nietzsche en France: De la fin du XIXe siècle au temps présent*. Paris: Presses Universitaires de France.

Levinas, Emmanuel (1985) *Ethics and Infinity: Conversations with Philippe Nemo*, trans. Richard A. Cohen. Pittsburgh, PA: Duquesne University Press; *éthique et infini* (Paris: Fayard, 1982).

—, (1987) *Time and the Other (and additional essays)*, trans. Richard A. Cohen. Pittsburgh, PA: Duquesne University Press; *Le Temps et l'autre* (Paris: Presses Universitaires de France/Quadrige, 1979).

—, (1991) *Totality and Infinity: An Essay on Exteriority*, trans. Alphonso Lingis. Paris: Kluwer Academic; *Totalité et infini: Essai sur l'extériorité* (Paris: Kluwer Academic, 1971).

Lévi-Strauss, Claude (1963) *Structural Anthropology*, trans. Claire Jacobsen and Brooke Grundfest Schoepf. New York: Basic; *Anthropologie structurale, tome 2* (Paris: Plon, 1974).

—, (1966) *The Savage Mind*, trans. George Weidenfeld. Chicago, IL: Chicago University Press; *La Pensée sauvage* (Paris: Plon, 1962).

—, (1969) *The Elementary Structures of Kinship* (revised edn), trans. James Harle Bell and John Richard von Sturmer, ed. Rodney Needham. London: Eyre & Spottiswoode; *Les Structures élémentaires de la parenté* (Paris: Mouton, 1967).

—, (1987) *Introduction to the Work of Marcel Mauss*, trans. Felicity Baker. London: Routledge & Kegan Paul; 'Introduction à l'œuvre de Marcel Mauss', in Marcel Mauss, *Sociologie et anthropologie* (Paris: Presses Universitaires de France, 2004).

Lewis, Michael (2005) *Heidegger and the Place of Ethics*. London: Continuum.

Lingis, Alphonso (1994) 'The Society of Dismembered Body Parts', in *Gilles Deleuze and the Theatre of Philosophy*, ed. Constantin V. Boundas and Dorothea Olkowski. London: Routledge.

Lorraine, Tamsin (2003) 'Living Time Out of Joint', in Paul Patton and John Protevi, eds, *Between Deleuze and Derrida*. London: Continuum.

Lyotard, Jean-François (1986) *The Postmodern Condition: A Report on Knowledge*, trans. Geoff Bennington and Brian Massumi. Manchester: Manchester University Press; *La Condition postmoderne: rapport sur le savoir* (Paris: Minuit, 1979).

—, (1990) *Heidegger and the 'Jews'*, trans. Andreas Michel and Mark Roberts (Minneapolis, MN: University of Minnesota Press); *Heidegger et 'les juifs'* (Paris: Galilée, 1988).

—, (1993a) *Libidinal Economy*, trans. Iain Hamilton Grant. London: Continuum; *Économie libidinale* (Paris: Minuit, 1974).

—, (1993b) 'Oikos', in *Political Writings*, trans. Bill Readings and Kevin Paul Geiman. London: University College London Press; originally published in *Oekologie im Endspiel*. Fink: Munich.

Macey, David (1988) *Lacan in Contexts*. London: Verso.

Major, Réné (2001) *Lacan avec Derrida: Analyse désistentielle*. Paris: Flammarion.

Mallet, Marie-Louise, ed. (2004) *La Démocratie à venir: Autour de Jacques Derrida*. Paris: Galilée.

Mandeville, Bernard (1997) *The Fable of the Bees and Other Writings*. Indianapolis, IN: Hackett.

Marion, Jean-Luc (2002) *Being Given: Toward a Phenomenology of Givenness*, trans. Jeffrey L. Kosky. Stanford, CA: Stanford University Press; *étant donné: Essai d'une phénomenologie de la donation* (Paris: Presses Universitaires de France, 1997).

Marx, Karl (2000) 'Preface to *A Critique of Political Economy*', in *Karl Marx: Selected Writings*, ed. David McLellan. Oxford: Oxford University Press; 'Zur Kritik der politischen Ökonomie', in *Werke*, vol. 13, pp. 7–9.

Mauss, Marcel (1950) *Sociologie et anthropologie*. Paris: Presses Universitaires de France.

—, (1979) *Sociology and Psychology: Essays*, trans. Ben Brewster. London: Routledge & Kegan Paul; *Sociologie et anthropologie* (Paris: Presses Universitaires de France, 1950).

—, (1990) *The Gift: The Form and Reason for Exchange in Archaic Societies*, trans. W. D. Halls. London: Routledge; *Sociologie et anthropologie* (Paris: Presses Universitaires de France, 2004).

—, (1997) '*Gift, Gift*', in Alan D. Schrift, ed., *The Logic of the Gift: Toward an Ethic of Generosity*. New York: Routledge, 28–32; 'Gift, gift', in *Mélanges offerts à Charles Adler par ses amis et ses élèves* (Strasbourg: Publications de la Faculté des Lettres de l'Université de Strasbourg, 1924).

May, Todd (1997) *Reconsidering Difference: Nancy, Derrida, Levinas and Deleuze*. University Park, PA: Pennsylvania State University Press.

Mengue, Philippe (2003) *Deleuze et la question de la démocratie*. Paris: L'Harmattan.

—, (2006) 'The Problem of the Birth of Philosophy in Greece in the Thought of Gilles Deleuze', in Constantin Boundas, ed., *Deleuze and Philosophy*. Edinburgh: Edinburgh University Press.

Merleau-Ponty, Maurice (1964) *Signs*, trans. Richard C. McCleary. Chicago, IL: Northwestern University Press; *Signes* (Paris: Gallimard, 1960).

Miller, Christopher L. (1993) 'The Postidentitarian Predicament in the Footnotes of *A Thousand Plateaus*: Nomadology, Anthropology, and Authority', *Diacritics* 23.3, pp. 6–35.

Miller, Jacques-Alain (1994) '*Extimité*', in Mark Bracher, Marshall W. Alcorn, Jr, Ronald J. Carthell and Françoise Messardier-Kenney, eds, *Lacanian Theory of Discourse: Subject, Structure and Society*. London: New York University Press.

—, (2003) 'Lacan's Later Teaching', *lacanian ink XXI*, http://www.lacan.com/frameXXI2.htm, accessed 10 August 2006.

Moore, Gerald (2007) 'Corpus diei', *Oxford Literary Review*, 27. London: Central Books, pp. 181–6.

Mouffe, Chantal (2005) *On the Political*. London: Routledge.

Muller, John and William Richardson (1988) *The Purloined Poe*. Baltimore, MD: Johns Hopkins University Press.

Nancy, Jean-Luc (1979) *Ego sum*. Paris: Flammarion.

—, (1986) *L'Oubli de la philosophie*. Paris: Galilée.

—, (1991) *The Inoperative Community*, ed. Peter Connor, trans. Peter Connor, Lisa Garbus, Michael Holland and Simona Sawhney. Minneapolis, MN: Minnesota University Press; *La Communauté désœuvrée* (Paris: Christian Bourgeois, 1986).

—, (1993) *The Experience of Freedom*, trans. Bridget McDonald. Stanford, CA: Stanford University Press; *L'Expérience de la liberté* (Paris: Galilée, 1988).

—, (1997) *The Sense of the World*, trans. Jeffrey S. Librett. Minneapolis, MN: Minnesota University Press; *Le Sens du monde* (Paris: Galilée, 1993).

—, (1998) 'Pli deleuzien de la pensée', in Éric Alliez, ed., *Gilles Deleuze: une vie philosophique*. Le Plessis–Robinson: Institut Sythélabo, pp. 115–23.

—, (2000) *Being Singular Plural*, trans. Robert D. Richardson and Anne E. O'Byrne. Stanford, CA: Stanford University Press; *être singulier pluriel* (Paris: Galilée, 1996).

—, (2001) 'Between Story and Truth', *The Little Magazine*, trans. Franson Manjali. http://www.littlemag.com/jul-augo1/nancy.html, accessed 20 June 2008; *Un jour, les dieux se retirent . . .* (Bordeaux: William Blake, 2001).

—, (2003) *A Finite Thinking*, ed. Simon Sparks. Stanford, CA: Stanford University Press; *Une Pensée finie* (Paris: Gallimard, 1991).

—, (2005) 'Les Différences parallèles. Deleuze et Derrida', in André Bernold and Richard Pinhas, eds, *Deleuze épars: approches et portraits*. Paris: Hermann.

—, (2007) *The Creation of the World, or Globalization*, trans. François Raffoul and David Pettigrew. Albany, NY: SUNY Press; *La Création du monde ou la mondialisation* (Paris: Galilée, 2002).

—, (2008) *Corpus*, trans. Richard A. Rand. New York: Fordham University Press; *Corpus* (Paris: A. M. Métaillé, 1992).

—, (2010) *The Truth of Democracy*, trans. Pascale-Anne Brault and Michael Naas. New York: Fordham University Press; *La Vérité de la démocratie* (Paris: Galilée, 2008).

Nietzsche, Friedrich (1968—) *Nietzsche Werke Kritisch Gesamtausgabe*, ed. Giorgio Colli and Mazzino Montinari. Berlin: Walter de Gruyter.

—, (1969) *Thus Spoke Zarathustra*, trans. R. J. Hollingdale. London: Penguin.

—, (1974) *The Gay Science*, trans. Walter Kauffman. New York: Vintage.

—, (1994) *On the Genealogy of Morality*, ed. Keith Ansell-Pearson, trans. Carol Diethe. Cambridge: Cambridge University Press.

Nobus, Dany (2007) 'The Politics of Gift-Giving and the Provocation of Lars von Trier's *Dogville*', *Film-Philosophy*, 11(3), pp. 27–37. http:/www.film-philosophy.com/2007v11n3/nobus.pdf, accessed 23 August 2010.

Norris, Andrew, ed. (2005) *Politics, Metaphysics, and Death: Essays on Giorgio Agamben's* Homo sacer. Durham, NC: Duke University Press.

Osteen, Mark, ed. (2002) *The Question of the Gift: Essays Across Disciplines*. New York: Routledge.

Patton, Paul (2000) *Deleuze and the Political*. London: Routledge.

Patton, Paul and Protevi, John, eds (2003) *Between Deleuze and Derrida*. London: Continuum.

Pefanis, Julian (1991) *Heterology and the Postmodern: Bataille, Baudrillard, and Lyotard*. Durham, NC: Duke University Press.

Protevi, John (2001) *Political Physics: Deleuze, Derrida and the Body Politic*. London: Continuum.

—, (2003) 'Love', in *Between Deleuze and Derrida*, ed. Paul Patton and John Protevi. London: Continuum.

Proust, Marcel (1990) *A la Recherche du temps perdu: Le Temps retrouvé*. Paris: Gallimard.

Rabaté, Jean-Michel (2003) *The Cambridge Companion to Lacan*. Cambridge: Cambridge University Press.

Rancière, Jacques (2001) 'Ten Theses on Politics', trans. Rachel Bowlby, in *Theory and Event*, 5.3, http://muse.jhu.edu/journals/theory_and_event/voo5/5.3ranciere.html, accessed 23 August 2010; 'Dix thèses sur la politique', in *Aux bords du politique* (éd. augmentée) (Paris: Gallimard, 2004).

—, (2009) 'Should Democracy Come? Ethics and Politics in Derrida', in *Derrida and the Time of the Political*, ed. Pheng Cheah and Suzanne Guerlac. Durham, NC: Duke University Press, pp. 274–88.

Richman, Michèle H. (1982) *Reading Georges Bataille: Beyond the Gift*. Baltimore, MD: Johns Hopkins University Press.

Robbins, Lionel (1945) *An Essay on the Nature and Significance of Economic Science* (2nd edn). London: Macmillan.

Roudinesco, Élisabeth (1997) *Jacques Lacan: An Outline of a Life and a History of a System of Thought*, trans. Barbara Bray. Cambridge: Polity; *Jacques Lacan: Ésquisse d'une vie, histoire d'un système de pensée* (Paris: Fayard, 1993).

—, (2003) 'The Mirror Stage: An Obliterated Archive', in *The Cambridge Companion to Lacan*, ed. Jean-Michel Rabaté. Cambridge: Cambridge University Press.

Rousseau, Jean-Jacques (1986) 'Économie ou œconomie', in *Encyclopédie ou dictionnaire raisonné des sciences, des arts et des métiers* (articles choisis), ed. Alain Pons. Paris: Flammarion.

—, (1993) *The Social Contract and Discourses*, trans. G. D. H. Cole. London: Everyman; *Du Contrat social* (Paris: Flammarion, 2001).

Safranski, Rüdiger (1998) *Martin Heidegger: Between Good and Evil*, trans. Ewald Osers. Cambridge, MA: Harvard University Press; *Ein Meister aus Deutschland: Heidegger und seine Zeit* (Munich: Carl Hanser, 1994).

Sahlins, Marshall (1972) *Stone Age Economics*. Chicago, IL: Aldine–Atherton.

Sartre, Jean-Paul (1992) *Notebooks for an Ethics*, trans. David Pellauer. Chicago, IL: Chicago University Press; *Cahiers pour une morale* (Paris: Gallimard, 1983).

Saussure, Ferdinand de (1983) *Course in General Linguistics*, trans. Roy Harris. London: Duckworth; *Cours de linguistique générale*, ed. Charles Bally and Albert Riedlinger (Paris: Payot, 1964).

Schrift, Alan D. (1995) *Nietzsche's French Legacy: A Genealogy of Poststructuralism*. New York: Routledge.

—, (1997) 'Why Gift?', editor's introduction in Schrift, ed., *The Logic of the Gift: Toward an Ethic of Generosity*. New York: Routledge.

—, (2004) 'Is There Such a Thing as "French Philosophy"?, or Why do we Read the French so Badly?', in Julian Bourg, ed., *After the Deluge: New Perspectives on the Intellectual and Cultural History of Postwar France*. Lanham, MD: Lexington.

—, (2006) *Twentieth-Century French Philosophy: Key Themes and Thinkers*. Oxford: Oxford University Press.

Schmidt, Dennis (1999) 'Ruins and Roses: Hegel and Heidegger on Sacrifice, Mourning, and Memory', in Rebecca Comay and John McCumber, eds, *Endings: Questions of Memory in Hegel and Heidegger*. Evanston, IL: Northwestern University Press.

Schumpeter, Joseph A. (1976) *Capitalism, Socialism and Democracy*. London: Routledge.

Sheppard, Darren, Simon Sparks and Colin Thomas, eds (1997) *On Jean-Luc Nancy: The Sense of Philosophy*. London: Routledge.

Smith, Daniel W. (2003) 'Deleuze and Derrida, Immanence and Transcendence: Two Directions in Recent French Thought', in Paul Patton and John Protevi, eds, *Between Deleuze and Derrida*. London: Continuum.

Sprinker, Michael (1999) *Ghostly Demarcations: A Symposium on Jacques Derrida's* Specters of Marx. London: Verso.

Stiegler, Bernard (2004) *Mécréance et discrédit: 1. La Décadence des démocraties industrielles*. Paris: Galilée.

—, (2005) *De la Misère symbolique: 2. La catastrophe du sensible*. Paris: Galilée.

Still, Judith (1997) *Feminine Economies: Thinking Against the Market in the Enlightenment and Late Twentieth Century*. Manchester: Manchester University Press.

Stivale, Charles J. (2000) 'The Folds of Friendship: Derrida, Deleuze, Foucault', *Angelaki*, 5:2, pp. 3–15.

Stoekl, Allan (1995) 'Recognition in *Madame Edward*', Carolyn Bailey Gill, ed., *Bataille: Writing the Sacred*. London: Routledge.

Strathern, Marilyn (1988) *The Gender of the Gift*. Berkeley, CA: University of California Press.

Surya, Michel (2002) *Georges Bataille: An Intellectual Biography*, trans. Krzysztof Fijalkowski and Michael Richardson. London: Verso; *Georges Bataille: La Mort à l'œuvre* (Paris: Gallimard, 1992).

Valentin, Jérémie (2006) 'Gilles Deleuze's Political Posture', in Constantin V. Boundas, ed., *Deleuze and Philosophy*. Edinburgh: Edinburgh University Press, pp. 185–201.

Wall, Thomas Carl (2005) '*Au hasard*', in Andrew Norris, ed., *Politics, Metaphysics, and Death: Essays on Giorgio Agamben's* Homo Sacer. Durham, NC: Duke University Press.

Weber, Max (1992) *The Protestant Ethic and the Spirit of Capitalism*, trans. Talcott Parsons. London: Routledge; 'Die protestantische Ethik und die Geist des Kapitalismus', in *Gesammelte Aufsätze zur Religionssoziologie I* (Tübingen: Mohr, 1934).

Weiner Annette B. (1986) *Inalienable Possessions: The Paradox of Keeping-While-Giving*. Berkeley, CA: University of California Press.

Williams, Caroline (2001) *Contemporary French Philosophy: Modernity and the Persistence of the Subject*. London: Athlone.

Williams, James (2005) *Understanding Poststructuralism*. Chesham: Acumen.

Wolin, Richard (1993) *The Heidegger Controversy: A Critical Reader*. Cambridge, MA: MIT Press.

—, (2004) *The Seduction of Unreason: The Intellectual Romance with Fascism from Nietzsche to Postmodernism*. Princeton, NJ: Princeton University Press.

Wurzer, Wilhelm S. (1997) 'Nancy and the Political Imaginary after Nature', in Darren Sheppard, Simon Sparks and Colin Thomas, eds. *On Jean-Luc Nancy: The Sense of Philosophy*. London: Routledge.

Young, Julian (1997) *Heidegger, Philosophy, Nazism*. Cambridge: Cambridge University Press.

Žižek, Slavoj (1989) *The Sublime Object of Ideology*. London: Verso.

—, (1997) *The Plague of Fantasies*. London: Verso.

—, (1999) *The Ticklish Subject: The Absent Centre of Political Ontology*. London: Verso.

—, (2000) *The Fragile Absolute or, Why is the Christian Legacy Worth Fighting For?* London: Verso.

—, (2001) *Enjoy Your Sympton! Jacques Lacan in Hollywood and Out* (2nd edn). New York: Routledge.

—, (2002) *Welcome to the Desert of the Real*. London: Verso.

—, (2003) *The Puppet and the Dwarf: The Perverse Core of Christianity*. Cambridge, MA: MIT Press.

—, (2004) *Organs without Bodies: On Deleuze and Consequences*. London: Routledge.

—, ed. (2006a) *Lacan: The Silent Partners*. London: Verso.

—, (2006b) *The Parallax View*. Cambridge, MA: MIT Press.

Zupančič, Alenka (2000) *Ethics of the Real: Kant, Lacan*. London: Verso.

—, (2003) *The Shortest Shadow: Nietzsche's Philosophy of the Two*. Cambridge, MA: MIT Press.

—, (2006) 'The "Concrete Universal" and What Comedy Can Tell Us About It', in Slavoj Žižek, ed., *Lacan: The Silent Partners*. London: Verso.

Index